"The Nesser brothers, Ralph Hay, Leo Lyons, Joe Carr—they were the pioneers and this is the land where football set down its roots."

George Halas, Class of 1963

"Don Hutson set records for pass catching only legislation can wipe out."

Dante Lavelli, end, Cleveland Browns

"That's the way with football, the longer you're away from the sport, the greater you become. It thrills me to death to think how great I'll be when I'm a hundred years old."

Mel Hein, Class of 1963

"Nagurski is no mere name. It's an international way of saying football."

Don Miller, one of Notre Dame's Four Horsemen

"This Hall of Fame immortalizes the greatest warriors of the greatest game."

Al Davis, managing general partner, Oakland Raiders presenting Jim Otto, Class of 1980

"It was through football that I learned how to win, and it was through football that I learned how to enjoy the thrill of success. It was also through football that I developed the will to succeed."

Willie Davis, Class of 1981

The Pro Football Hall of Fame Presents
Their Deeds and Dogged Faith

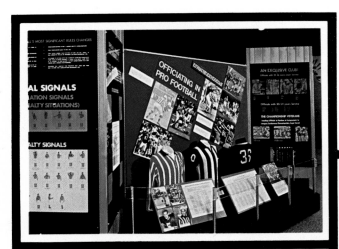

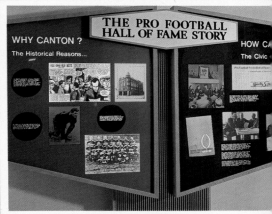

The Pro Football Hall of Fame Presents
Their Deeds and Dogged Faith

by Mike Rathet and Don R. Smith

Rutledge Books
Balsam Press, Inc.
New York

300 Mercer Street, New York, New York 10003.
Produced in association with Rutledge Books.
Designed by Allan Mogel
Edited by Hedy Caplan
ISBN: 0-917439-02-3

Manufactured in Hong Kong

Library of Congress Cataloging in Publication Data

Rathet, Mike.
    The Pro Football Hall of Fame presents Their deeds and
dogged faith.

    1. Pro Football Hall of Fame (U.S.)   2. Football—
United States—History.   I. Smith, Don, 1926–
II. Pro Football Hall of Game (U.S.)   III. Title.
IV. Title: Their deeds and dogged faith.
GV950.R373   1984   796.332′64′074017162   84-11188
ISBN 0-917439-02-3

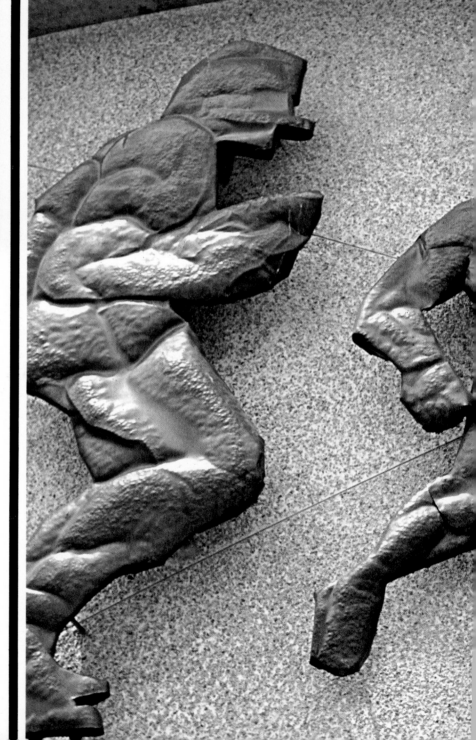

Distributed by
Kampmann & Company
9 East 40 Street
New York, New York 10016

Acknowledgements

The authors wish to express their gratitude to a number of people who made this project an enjoyable experience, particularly Earl Schreiber, Clayton Horn, Pete Elliott, and Joe Horrigan of the Pro Football Hall of Fame. Mr. Horrigan, the Hall's curator-researcher, provided invaluable research assistance.

Thanks also must be tendered John and Fred Sammis and our editors, Deborah Weiss and Hedy Caplan, of Rutledge Books; Jim Campbell of NFL Properties, Inc.; Chuck Such of Canton, Ohio, and the winning photographers of the first 15 Pro Football Hall of Fame photo contests.

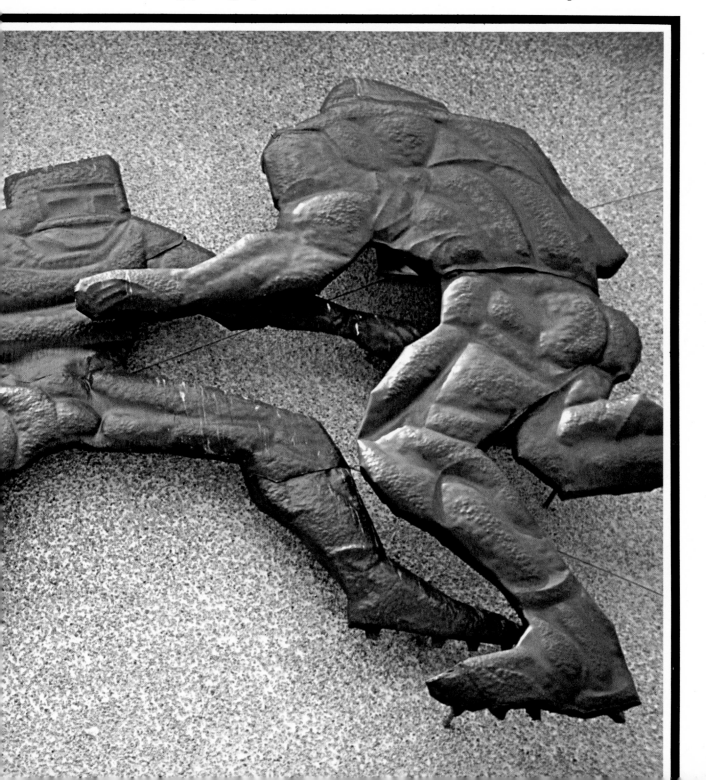

John E. Biever, Milwaukee Journal-Sentinel, "Freeze Framed." Third Place Color Feature, 1978.

Contents

Introduction
Foreword by Pete Rozelle

Introduction

Each year more than two hundred thousand visitors make their ways on pilgrimages to a midwestern town—a town whose pro football history dates back farther than any of the 28 cities that house NFL franchises. They come because here, in Canton, Ohio, stands pro football's Hall of Fame, a shrine built in tribute to the men whose contributions have made the game the most popular sport in history.

In these pages, the authors and editors have attempted to capture the excitement, the highs and lows, the curiosities and the legends of a game that has gained a unique hold on the imaginations of its followers. Once numbering only a few hundred who stood zealously in the mud on the sidelines, football's audience has grown to include the hundreds of thousands who weekly fill the stadiums across the country and the millions who watch on television, but, most importantly, it includes you.

Using the essence of the Hall of Fame itself as a thematic springboard, this book will take you on a tour of this fascinating facility and, with the aid of its contents, on an equally exciting journey through pro football's story.

Inside the Hall, in its rooms and passageways, you will discover artifacts and memorabilia of all kinds—from ice tongs and a desk marred by discarded cigar butts to jerseys and game balls—that have been assembled from fans and players alike. These are vehicles through which you will rediscover many memorable moments of the past and the best players who have ever played the game. These exhibits and displays are here because of your celebration of and enthusiasm for the game as it is played today. In that sense, it is your Hall of Fame.

Welcome.

To Lois, Shari, Ilyse, and Brooks, the members of my Hall of Fame.
Mike Rathet

To Helen, Ron, Rich, and Melissa, my strength and inspiration for many years.
Don R. Smith

Foreword

When I first heard that Mike Rathet and Don Smith were collaborating on a book about the Pro Football Hall of Fame, I was delighted. Each was uniquely qualified to handle with complete professionalism the project he was undertaking.

Now that it has come to fruition, and I have had a chance to see the proofs, I can only say that they achieved their goal, and more.

The Pro Football Hall of Fame is more than a museum, more than a collection of memorabilia and mementoes, more than the home of pro football history. It is an ever-expanding tribute to all those people who gave so much to the game each of us has watched grow to perhaps the most popular sport in America today.

It's about Red Grange and Bronko Nagurski and Jim Thorpe and George Halas and Bert Bell and Sammy Baugh and Mel Hein, yes; but it is also about Walter Payton and Randy White and Terry Bradshaw and Jack Ham and Art Shell and other future Hall of Famers who help create so much enjoyment for millions of football fans each weekend from August to January.

It's about people like William A. Umstattd, who wouldn't let go of the dream of Canton, Ohio, to house the Hall. It's about the other leaders in the Canton/Massillon area who found the dollars to buy the silver shovel with which I turned the first bit of earth back in 1962 and then the many thousands of dollars that caused the first Hall of Fame structure to rise from the earth in 1963. It's about those same leaders and citizens, plus football fans throughout the country and the world, whose interest and support permitted that structure to be expanded twice into the magnificent building it is today.

Mike Rathet has experienced pro football's growth from four aspects—as a talented writer for The Associated Press, as publicity director for the American Football League, as public relations director for the Miami Dolphins (he assisted Don Shula in that 17-0 year in 1972), and now as editor for the fine sports section in the Philadelphia *Daily News*.

Don Smith was one of the early AFLers with the Denver Broncos, and was the first public relations director for the New Orleans Saints before becoming the public relations director for the Pro Football Hall of Fame in 1968. He's helped nurture its growth since that time and now is one of the Hall's vice-presidents. No one knows more about the Hall than he.

This book has been long in coming. Now that it is here I can guarantee you that the pages that follow will take you on an adventure through professional football that you will thoroughly enjoy.

PETE ROZELLE
Commissioner, National Football League

Jim Thorpe, the first big-name American athlete to play pro football, could do everything on the football field—run, pass, kick, and tackle. When the National Football League picked an all-time team in 1969, Thorpe was honored as simply "The Legend."

Chapter 1

Birth of a Hall

The first step in a 50-year evolutionary process that would carry pro football to unparalleled popularity on the American sports scene began with a moment of decision for an obscure businessman named Jack Cusack.

For three years, from 1912 to 1915, Cusack had managed to juggle two jobs. While working for the East Ohio Gas Company, he also managed the Bulldogs, the pro football team in Canton, Ohio. In 1915, however, he was faced with an ultimatum—give up one or the other.

"After seven years in the gas company office," Jack Cusack has written, "I was, at twenty-three, the chief clerk, my principal duty being to take charge of the daily cash receipts and make the bank deposits. I had been told by Ralph Gallagher, the general superintendent [and later president of Standard Oil of New Jersey], that I would have to give up football or resign, and I promptly resigned."

There is little acclaim for Cusack in all the books that have been written about pro football. Rarely is there even a perfunctory mention, but Cusack played an extremely significant role, beginning with the decision to leave East Ohio Gas and devote his energies full-time to building the Bulldogs into the strongest team in the state. That led Cusack to lure Jim Thorpe, the Sac and Fox Indian considered the "world's greatest athlete," into professional football—a move that triggered the sport's slow but continual rise until eventually, in the 1960's, the NFL began to receive the frenzied response and attention it still gets from fans today. Until Thorpe, who was at the peak of his popularity, came aboard, the sport had lacked the magic he gave it as a "big name" attraction.

Cusack's decision to choose football over gas—and what naturally followed—also laid the foundation for Canton, Ohio, as the logical home for the sport's Hall of Fame, a claim that rests on three solid building blocks. Foremost among them is that Thorpe first paraded his abundant talents as a pro football player in Canton with the Bulldogs. Second is the legacy of the Bulldogs, who between 1915 and 1923, won five championships—and were undefeated four times. Third is the fact that the 1920 meeting at which the American Professional Football Association (which later became the National Football League) was formed occurred in the Canton Hupmobile showroom of Ralph Hay, who succeeded Cusack as manager of the Bulldogs.

There are ample reminders of all of that in the Pro Football Hall of Fame—team pictures of the famed Bulldogs and copies of the newspaper article announcing the birth of the new league—but the biggest display honors Thorpe. The exhibit is set against the backdrop of a huge picture of the Canton Bulldogs in action on a dust-choked field typical of the playing conditions of the pre-NFL years. In the forefront of the display, a simulated figure of a football player sits hunched on a bench. The figure represents Thorpe and is draped with a Bulldogs' blanket he once wore. There is dirt in front of the bench—dirt taken from Lakeside Field, where Thorpe played. Also on view nearby is Thorpe's red and gold sweater from Carlisle Institute, the Indian school at which he first gained national attention for his exploits on a football field.

The blanket under which the Thorpe figure huddles was donated to the Hall of Fame by Karl Hay, a relative of Ralph Hay. Thorpe's Carlisle sweater was given to the Hall by Dr. Lorene Livers,

13

whose father was a trainer for the Bulldogs. Dr. Livers wore the sweater from grade school through her years in college, when she decided it might be better suited to serve as a bed for the family dog. The sweater, which is considerably tattered, was at one time decorated with a ribbon sewn on by an Indian woman for good luck. That has disappeared. It is appropriate that Thorpe be accorded his own display area—as well as a statue just inside the doors that open on the Hall. His decision to join the Bulldogs draped the infant sport with a cloak of respectability in an era when it was anything but a stable business and still was recovering from a scandal that had made its heritage suspect.

Cusack was fully aware of pro football's shortcomings in 1915. In addition, he recognized that his Bulldogs needed an injection of talent if they were to beat out the arch-rival Massillon Tigers and he began to shop around for the required help. It wasn't easy to find. "I knew that in order to compete properly with Massillon we had to secure for Canton the best available talent," Cusack wrote in his autobiography, *Pioneer in Pro Football*, "so I contacted every all-American I could locate, either by mail or personally, but found the response somewhat reluctant. The colleges and most sportswriters around the country were opposed to professional football, as were many of the coaches and graduate players, and many of those I contacted refused to play. Some of those who did agree to consider playing jobs insisted on the use of assumed names, particularly the coaches, who wanted to protect their jobs."

Cusack managed to put together a team that was undefeated in five games heading into a two-game season-ending showdown with Massillon when, as he put it in his own words, "I hit the jackpot by signing the famous Jim Thorpe." Thorpe, at the time, was working as an assistant coach at the University of Indiana, after having tested the pro waters in 1913 with the Pine Village, Indiana, team. Cusack sent one of the Bulldogs' ends, Bill Gardner, to Indiana in an attempt to convince Thorpe to join the team. Gardner had been a teammate of Thorpe's at Carlisle—and was persuasive enough to convince Thorpe to head for Canton and a meeting with Cusack. When Cusack offered to pay him $250 a game, Thorpe agreed and Cusack's friends moaned. "Some of my business 'advisors' frankly predicted that I was leading the Bulldogs into bankruptcy by paying him the enormous sum of $250 a game," Cusack wrote.

Even Cusack couldn't have anticipated the response to Thorpe's arrival. The Bulldogs' attendance had been approximately twelve hundred a game before the fabled Indian joined the Canton

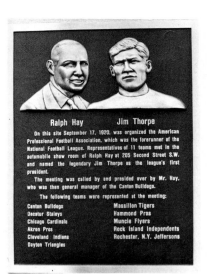

Bottom left: *Jim Thorpe, a Sac and Fox Indian, was called Wa-Tho-Huck by his native tribesmen.*
Top far left: *This plaque was dedicated in Canton, Ohio, in September 1983.* Top center: *Jack Cusack, the man who signed Jim Thorpe to a Canton Bulldogs contract in 1915.* Bottom: *A new display explains how and why a small city like Canton, Ohio, became the Hall of Fame home for a big-city sport like pro football.* Top left: *The most famous posed action photograph of Jim Thorpe.*

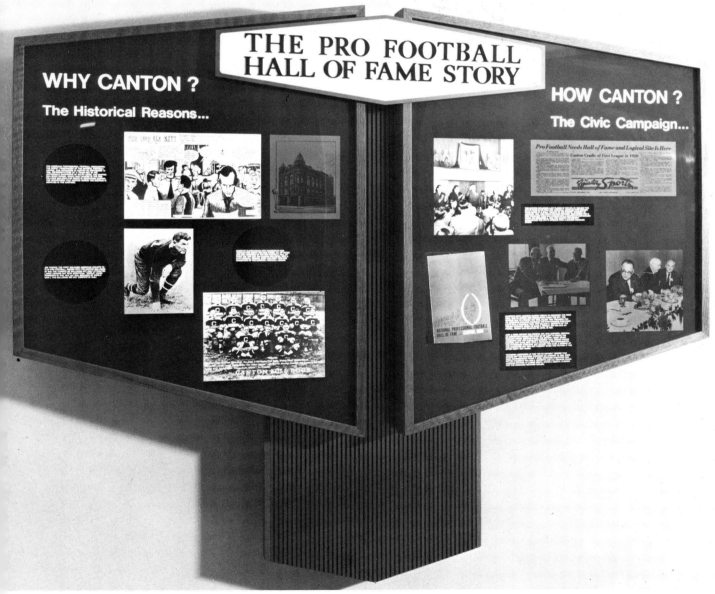

THE PRO FOOTBALL HALL OF FAME STORY

WHY CANTON ?
The Historical Reasons...

HOW CANTON ?
The Civic Campaign...

Top: *This excellent shot of a Canton-Akron game in the early 1920's shows two Hall of Famers, Pete Henry (third from left) and Guy Chamberlin (leaping) in action. Right: Jim Thorpe is one of the most honored athletes in the Pro Football Hall of Fame's display area. One particularly valuable memento is his Carlisle Institute football sweater.*

team, but capacity crowds turned out for the two-game battle that ended the 1915 season—eight thousand in Massillon and ten thousand in Canton. Thorpe was everything Cusack had expected him to be—an exceptional talent and a gate-attraction unparalleled on the American sports scene, a player who continued to be a major factor on the field and at the gate for the next several seasons as the Bulldogs became the premier team in pre-NFL football. But, to fully understand the impact Thorpe had on professional football, it is essential to trace the elements that already had made him a legend.

James Francis Thorpe was born in a one-room cabin near Prague, Oklahoma, on May 28, 1888. His mother was three-fourths Indian and one-fourth French; his father was half-Indian and half-Irish. In the community of the Sac and Fox Indians, Thorpe was named Wa-tho-huk, meaning Bright Path. And Thorpe found himself on a path to success when in 1904 he was recruited to attend the United States Indian Industrial School in Carlisle, Pennsylvania, commonly known as Carlisle Institute. The school operated on a half-school half-work principle and Thorpe, then 16, went to work as a tailor. Two years later, he competed in organized sports for the first time as a guard on the tailors' football team in the Shop League. He was on his way to an athletic career that made his name synonymous with excellence.

Carlisle played a major college schedule, and Thorpe was Carlisle's best at almost everything. He was a slugging first baseman; an unbeaten hurdler, jumper, and sprinter; an exceptional talent in basketball, lacrosse, wrestling, and football. Although he had enormous natural ability for running and kicking the football—there are those who insist even today that there never has been anyone better—he gained his most lasting fame and notoriety for his unprecedented feat of winning the decathlon and pentathlon events at the 1912 Olympics at Stockholm, Sweden, then finding himself stripped of his medals after a controversy over his amateur standing.

Thorpe made the mistake that cost him his medals when, in 1909, instead of returning to Oklahoma after school was out, he joined two Carlisle baseball players—Jesse Young Deer and Joe Libby—who played baseball in North Carolina that summer for the Rocky Mount team. "I got short of money," Thorpe said, explaining his predicament, "so when the manager offered me fifteen dollars a week to play third base, I didn't even think about doing anything wrong, because there were a lot of other college boys playing there." Thorpe also played baseball professionally in 1910, then re-

turned to Carlisle in 1911 at the urging of Glenn "Pop" Warner, the school's football and track coach. Warner wanted Thorpe, who had grown into a strapping young man, 6 feet 1½ inches, and 185 pounds, to lead his football team and begin preparing for the Olympics. Thorpe did both.

He gained all-America honors in 1911 while Carlisle captured national recognition for the first time and capped its season by upsetting mighty Harvard, 18-15. With a touchdown and four field goals, Thorpe was responsible for every one of the Indians' points in that stunning victory. In 1912, en route to the national championship, Thorpe and Carlisle ripped through a tough schedule sprinkled with the country's top college powers. All Thorpe did was score 25 touchdowns and amass 198 points. He scored 28 of Carlisle's 34 points against Pittsburgh and 22 in Carlisle's 27-6 victory over Army. Ten of his touchdowns came on runs of 40 or more yards, including a 120-yarder against Lafayette (the larger end zones in use at the time made a run of that distance possible).

But all the glamour and glory, all the acclaim and applause ended with the season when the Amateur Athletic Union declared Thorpe was no longer an amateur because he had accepted money for playing baseball with Rocky Mount. The International Olympic Committee then demanded that Thorpe return the medals he had won in 1912 and ordered his name stricken from the record books. The American public, in general, sympathized with Thorpe, realizing that he had, at worst, been naive to accept money for playing baseball. They never considered him the rogue the AAU and IOC did. Still, Thorpe was deeply affected, though he seemed able to cope as long as he played professional sports.

Unfortunately, it would be more than 70 years after its original decision and 30 years after Thorpe's death, before the International Olympic Committee finally would vote to restore Thorpe's medals and thus erase an undeserved black mark from his brilliant record. The Hall of Fame, however, has always recognized Thorpe's achievements, and one memento of his days as an Olympian—the coat he wore as a member of the U.S. team—has been on display for years.

Thorpe played major league baseball for seven summers—from 1913 to 1919—with the New York Giants, the Cincinnati Reds, and the Boston Braves. But it was as a football player that he received his greatest rewards. He made from $14,000 to $15,000 a season playing for a number of teams from the time Cusack signed him in 1915 until his last appearance in 1928.

"Those were wonderful days," Thorpe said

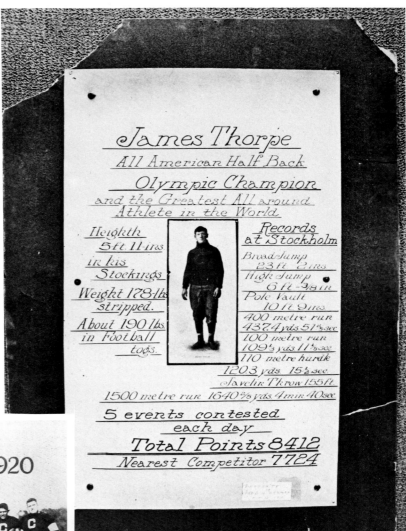

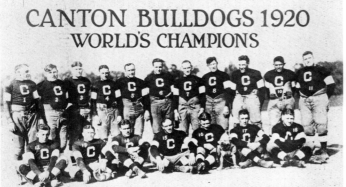

CANTON BULLDOGS 1920
WORLD'S CHAMPIONS

1-GRIGGS, 2-BUCK, 3-O'CONNOR, 4-COCORAN, 5-MARTIN, 6-DADUM, 7-EDWARDS, 8-THORPE, 9-GUYON, 10-CALAC, 11-HENRY, 12-GREEN, 13-WAHLEN, 14-GILROY, 15-SPECK, 16-FEENY, 17-HALEY, 18-HENDREN

Above: The Canton Bulldogs did not have the record to back up their claim as the 1920 league champions. Even Jim Thorpe experienced just average success with the Bulldogs that year. He played only one more season, in 1926, with the Bulldogs. Above right: The records Jim Thorpe set in the decathlon competition in the 1912 Olympics may not be impressive by today's standards but they were record-breakers at that time. Opposite page: With Jim Thorpe as the big attraction, the Canton Bulldogs were a big gate success both at home and on the road. Playing conditions weren't always the best, but rivalries between neighboring cities developed rapidly, and enthusiastic fans flocked to the games.

about his Canton career. "Best team I ever saw. We had boys like Peck of Pitt, the all-American center; Jock Sutherland; Doc Spears; Fats Henry; and the gang from Carlisle—Pete Calac, Joe Guyon, Little Twig, Red Fox, and Long-Time Sleep. We didn't lose a ball game for three or four seasons."

That wasn't quite accurate. The Bulldogs never put together a string of three or four unbeaten seasons, but they lost only one game in the three seasons played after Thorpe joined the team (because of World War I the 1918 season was canceled) and gained general acceptance as the unofficial world champions all three years. They did that by compiling a 9-0-1 record in 1916 (tying Massillon), an 8-1 record in 1917 (losing to Massillon), and a 9-0-1 record in 1919 (tying Hammond). The 1916 team was so strong that it gave up only seven points in ten games, and on occasion thoroughly manhandled the opposition, as in its 77-0 victory over the Buffalo All-Stars. But Cusack and Canton knew

19

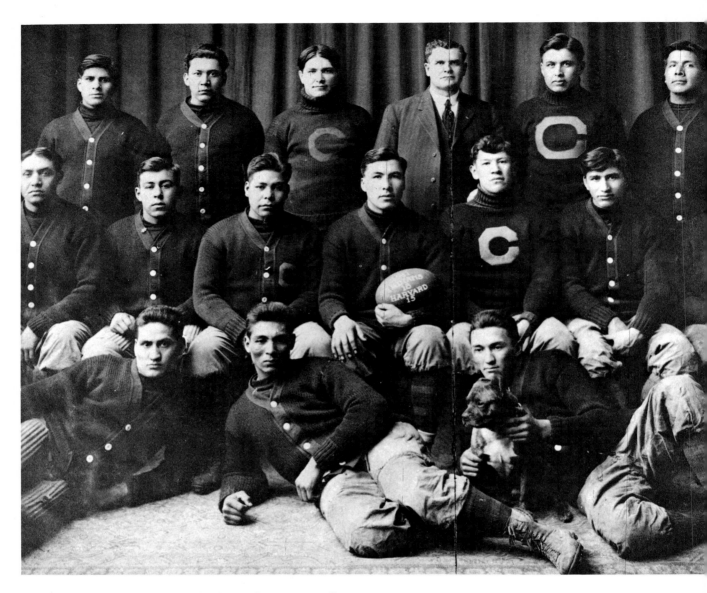

Above: *Jim Thorpe first gained athletic fame as an all-America halfback at Carlisle Indian Institute in 1911, an honor he repeated in 1912. Coach Glenn (Pop) Warner, who later became an all-time great college coach, is pictured third from the right in the back row.*

Opposite top: *Knute Rockne was best known as the Notre Dame head coach in the college ranks, but he did try pro football briefly in the late teens. Here he is pictured in the uniform of the 1919 Massillon Tigers. Opposite bottom: Ralph Hay (left) was the Canton Bulldogs owner in whose garage the American Professional Football Association was formed in 1920. Jim Thorpe, the Bulldogs' star player, was named the new league's president, a post he held only one year.*

what they had when, in 1915, Thorpe put on a Bulldogs' uniform for the first time against Massillon.

Massillon won that first game, 16-0, but, as *The* (Canton) *Repository* reported, "Only the slippery surface of the field kept the Indian [Thorpe], ideal in build and a finished football man, from scoring at least one touchdown, when he slipped on the Massillon eight-yard line. On another occasion, after skirting Massillon's left end, he slipped with almost a clear field ahead of him." In the rematch, the Bulldogs bounced back with a 6-0 victory as Thorpe provided all the scoring with two field goals, one by dropkick, one by placekick.

Thorpe's exploits tend to be exaggerated in many accounts, and it is not always easy to separate fact from fiction. There is no question, however, that he was blessed with exceptional and versatile skills. He could run with speed as well as bruising power. He could pass and catch passes with the best. He could punt great distances, from end zone to end zone on occasion. He could kick field goals either by dropkick or placekick, and his range was beyond midfield. He blocked well and, on defense, he was a bone-jarring tackler whom opponents tried to avoid whenever possible.

If he had a weakness, it was his relaxed approach to the game. Never a dedicated practice player—Thorpe claimed it was just plain foolishness to practice something he already knew he could do supremely well—it was difficult for him to provide meaningful guidance for players when he served as a player-coach. There are also any number of reports of Thorpe's drinking ability. Particularly in the later years of his career, there were those who felt that he was not always in the best condition. And, while he wasn't a lazy player, as his detractors sometimes contended, he seemed to hit his highest levels of performance only when he was angered—particularly when someone cast aspersions on his reputation as the best player on the field.

Knute Rockne, an end for the Massillon Tigers, who later became Notre Dame's most famous football coach, decided he would try to embarrass Thorpe by keying on him. As it turned out, Rockne only aroused Thorpe. The first two times Thorpe tested Rockne's end of the line, the Massillon star nailed the Indian for losses. Thorpe looked at him reproachfully and chided him for his actions. "You shouldn't do that," Thorpe said. "Look at all those people who paid to see Jim run."

"Go ahead and run, if you can," Rockne retorted.

Thorpe swung wide on the next play and let Rockne have every weapon at his disposal—knees, elbows, stiff arm—as he trampled the Tigers' end

21

and raced 60 yards for a touchdown. Then, as he trotted back upfield, Thorpe noticed Rockne, tottering and bleeding, being helped off the field. Thorpe edged up to the staggering end and offered whispered words of congratulations. "Nice work, Rock. You sure let old Jim run."

The Bulldogs became the number one team in pro football as the Thorpe legend grew. Even though Thorpe missed the first two games in 1916 (finishing the baseball season with the Giants), the Bulldogs were undefeated going into the two-game final series with Massillon. The first game in Massillon ended in a 0-0 tie, but Thorpe led Canton to a 24-0 win at home. The situation was almost the same in 1917. Canton hadn't lost going into the Massillon series. Thorpe engineered a 77-yard drive and completed it with a short touchdown plunge as the Bulldogs won the opener, 14-3. A week later, Massillon stung Canton, 6-0, although the Bulldogs claimed the championship on the basis of their overall record.

A manpower shortage created by World War I all but shut down pro football in 1918, but a year later Thorpe returned to Canton for what would be his last outstanding season. He led the team in scoring, touchdowns, extra points, and field goals as the Bulldogs posted a 9-0-1 record and made it three successive championships. Thorpe would remain a gate attraction of unrivaled success—but his ability to perform on the playing field had begun to wane. The 1919 season was Canton's last hurrah with Thorpe as a major factor.

The 1919 Canton team also had a new manager, Ralph Hay, who took over when Cusack left to enter the oil business in Oklahoma. Hay became as much of a force as Cusack had been, rebuilding the Bulldogs into champions after Thorpe's departure. But he is best remembered as the man who provided the meeting place when representatives of 11 teams convened at his Hupmobile agency on September 17, 1920, and agreed to the formation of the American Professional Football Association, which two years later was renamed the National Football League. The formation of the new league did not exactly create headline news around the pro football world. As a matter of fact, *The* (Canton) *Repository* ran only five paragraphs and buried the story on page 3 of its sports section.

Despite public skepticism and nonchalance, the pro football leaders with vision had recognized for some time that a formal organization was absolutely necessary to bring order out of chaos. Before 1920, players jumped from team to team with startling rapidity. The Columbus Panhandles, for example, claimed that Knute Rockne played against them six times in one season—each time with a different team. It was common practice for college players to use assumed names while playing for professional teams. Scheduling was haphazard and, in some cities, so were finances. It was

Right: *Joe Carr became president of the American Professional Football Association in 1921. The league's name was changed to the National Football League in 1922, and Carr served the NFL with distinction until his death in 1939. Opposite top and bottom: The Canton Bulldogs became the first two-time champion of the National Football League with undefeated seasons in 1922 and 1923. Three future Hall of Famers, tackles Pete Henry and Link Lyman, and player-coach Guy Chamberlin, were the leading stars.*

TWO-BITS

—Oscar Hendrian, Harry Robb, Ben Jones, Louis Smythe, Cecil Griggs, Wallace Elliott, Walcott Roberts.

Row—Elmer Carroll, Wilbur Henry, Capt. Robert Osborne, Larry Conover, Roudolph Comstock, Roy Lyman, B. Guy Chamberlin

Row—Norman Speck, Herman Smith (trainer), Joe Williams.

CANTON BULL DOGS
World's Professional Champions

Right: Player-coach Guy Chamberlin led the Bulldogs to two straight titles in 1922 and 1923. Far right: "Mr Football," George Halas of the Chicago Bears, chats with Hall of Fame board member Clayton Horn before the annual HOF football game in 1968. Bottom: Guy Chamberlin and a Bulldogs fan pose for a pregame picture during the Canton championship years.

not at all unusual for visiting teams to insist on receiving payment for appearing before the opening kickoff—experience had taught them that waiting until after the game could mean going home with empty pockets.

The APFA began with an unlikely president—Thorpe. The position was first offered to Hay, but the Bulldogs' manager declined, recommending Thorpe. "Thorpe should be our man," he said. "He's by far the biggest name we have. No one knows me." That was true, but Thorpe, as might have been suspected, proved to be an ineffective leader. With no business or organizational experience, he commanded little respect from the team managers in the league. And, he still was the player-coach of the Bulldogs, a responsibility that occupied most of his time. Simply, Thorpe was nothing more than a figurehead who brought none of the prestige to the APFA that Hay had envisioned. After a year, the APFA was reorganized and Joe Carr of the Columbus Panhandles took over as president, a postion he filled with distinction for the next 18 years.

The Bulldogs and Thorpe were dismal disappointments in 1920. The team finished with a 4-3-1 record, and Thorpe was able to contribute only three field goals the entire season. That was the end of Thorpe's association with the Bulldogs. Without him for the first time since Cusack lured him to Canton in 1915, the 1921 Bulldogs were only able to post a 4-3-3 record. But in 1922 and 1923, Canton returned to center stage, becoming the first two-time champion in NFL history and putting together consecutive undefeated seasons in a final fling with fame. The cornerstones of the Bulldogs' success were player-coach Guy Chamberlin, an end and halfback; wily receiver Bird Carroll; and a sensational pair of tackles—Pete "Fats" Henry and rookie Link Lyman.

The key game of the 1922 season occurred on the last weekend in October, when the Bulldogs met the defending-champion Bears in Chicago in a battle of unbeatens. The Bulldogs built a 7-0 lead when Ed Shaw cracked the last five yards in three carries, then kicked the extra point. The Bears battled back late in the game, scoring the first touchdown of the season against Canton, but lost an opportunity to tie when they missed the extra point. The Bulldogs closed out the season with a 10-0-2 record, scoring 184 points and allowing only 15. And in 1923, they did even better, posting an 11-0-1 record while scoring 246 points and permitting just 19. Henry had an exceptional year, personally winning two games in succession in the middle of the season when he kicked two field goals in a 6-0 victory over the Bears and then provided

the impetus for a 7-3 win over Akron with an 85-yard punt. He wound up as the team's leading scorer with 58 points.

Despite the unparalleled success of 1922 and 1923, Canton did not field a team in the NFL in 1924 and, when the Bulldogs returned a year later, the magic was gone. Canton was 4-4-0 in 1925, an embarrassing 1-9-3 in 1926, and then dropped out in 1927—never to return—when the NFL shrank from 22 teams to 12. The Bulldogs, however, had made their mark in history, having landed at the top of the pre-NFL standings three successive times during Thorpe's Canton career, and in two consecutive seasons without Thorpe. There is little doubt that from 1915 through 1923 Canton was the center of the pro football world. The Bulldogs' accomplishments are above dispute; their 47-1-5 record in their 5 championship seasons has not been matched in the more than half a century since they stepped off the field.

Though Canton won two championships without Thorpe, Thorpe never was able to match his successes without the Bulldogs. In 1922 and 1923, he was player-coach of the Oorang Indians of LaRue, Ohio, a team on which every member was at least part-blooded American Indian. Thorpe played in just five games in 1922 and scored only three touchdowns for a 3-6-0 team. It was even worse the following season; the Indians won only 1 of 11 games and Thorpe managed just 1 field goal in 9 games. Thorpe lingered on the scene, playing sporadically for a number of teams—he even returned to Canton in 1926—until 1928, when he made his final appearance for the Chicago Cardinals in a Thanksgiving Day game against the Bears. Thorpe played only briefly, and The Associated Press wrote his football epitaph by reporting he was "muscle-bound and only a shadow of his former self."

The same description could have been used to underscore his life off the field once he was no longer able to play professional sports. As soon as his playing days were over, he seemed to flounder both financially and emotionally. Thorpe worked for $4 a day digging ditches; he was an extra in Hollywood movies, a guard in an automobile plant, a deckhand on a freighter. He even managed a girls' softball team. Nothing seemed to work, and when the 1932 Olympics were held in Los Angeles, he could not afford the price of a ticket to watch the events he had dominated 20 years earlier. Without a place to hang his hat, he began to publicly cry out for help to have his Olympic medals reinstated.

"In the twilight of my life," Thorpe said, "the one thing I dream of constantly is that the Ameri-

Above: *The Hall's first director, Dick McCann, who served many years in the front office of the Washington Redskins, spent countless hours accumulating artifacts for the historical displays.* Below: *William Umstattd of The Timken Company fronted the effort to bring the Pro Football Hall of Fame to Canton. Here he studies a large brochure about the city that he was to present to the NFL owners, who later gave site approval to Canton.* Opposite page: *The first enshrinement of new members to the Pro Football Hall of Fame was held in nearby Fawcett Stadium in 1963.*

can people will try to get back for me the Olympic trophies I won in 1912. I'd be the happiest man in the world if I could get my medals back."

"Jim," said his wife, Patricia, "wants to be vindicated as an honest athlete before he goes to his happy hunting ground."

That didn't happen, however, and Jim Thorpe died March 28, 1953, in the modest trailer in which he lived with Patricia in Lomita, California, a Los Angeles suburb. But, while he never did get his medals back during his lifetime, he did get one final round of applause from the city of Canton and a number of the players he played with and against while he was a member of the Bulldogs.

Some of Thorpe's teammates remained in Canton long after their playing days were over. Pete Calac stayed on and became a policeman; Joe Little Twig was a member of the city recreation department. But it wasn't until January 30, 1952, that the city paid tribute to Thorpe—with a dinner held in his honor. The men most responsible were hotel owner Frank Onesto and Earl Schreiber, who later became the president of the Hall of Fame's board of trustees.

More than seven hundred people attended the dinner, whose unstated purpose—to provide the down-and-out Thorpe with some money to live on—netted Thorpe a thousand dollars. But there was more—the adulation of teammates like Calac and Art Deibel and Fred Rehor, the reminiscences of such opponents as Wallace "Doc" Elliott and Fred Heyman and Harry Robb, and the appreciation of such newcomers as Marion Motley and Horace Gillom of the Cleveland Browns. According to *The Repository*, "Tears dimmed the eyes but sharpened the memories, as 703 of his admirers rose in unison for a thunderous ovation."

Earl Schreiber believes that the events of that evening stirred emotions among the city's movers and shakers that would be rekindled—and never quenched—when Canton seriously sought to get NFL sanction for the Pro Football Hall of Fame. "The principal thing was to be nice to Thorpe," Schreiber emphasizes. "These people had watched him play and knew of his Canton connection. It brought back memories. And that's what a hall of fame is supposed to do—stop time and bring back memories. It showed the community that with the lineup [of community leaders] we had, something could be done—and that we had something to rally behind."

Seven years later the city actually began a Bring-the-Hall-of-Fame-to-Canton movement. The NFL already had approved Latrobe, Pennsylvania, as the site for the proposed Hall of Fame, giving sanction in 1947 to the city near Pittsburgh on the

basis of an erroneous belief that the first paid professional had played for a Latrobe team. While Latrobe remained the front-runner for years merely for lack of any other contenders, the Pennsylvania city never was able to advance the project beyond the planning stages.

The Timken Roller Bearing Company and the Canton *Repository* took up the banner with efforts to focus the business community's sights on bringing the Hall of Fame to Canton. "No one else had the imagination, financial resources, or physical assets," commented sportswriter Chuck Such. "Paul Brown [at the time coach of the Cleveland Browns] would talk about the needs of pro football, including a Hall of Fame, during the idle hours at

Hiram [the Browns' Ohio training base]. It was just light banter at dinner. Germane Swanson, like myself a *Repository* sportswriter, brought back to Clayton Horn, the paper's top editorial executive, the suggestion that a Hall of Fame project might be something we could get involved in."

Horn had started working for *The Repository* in 1928 as a sportswriter, earning $30 a week. He covered high school sports for six years, then began to step up the executive ladder until, by 1959, he was executive editor of Brush-Moore papers, a group of 12 daily papers across the country, including *The Repository*. Horn, who later became vice-president of the Hall of Fame's board of trustees, had in his years in Canton become totally familiar with the city's role in the early days of professional football and he recognized the strength of Canton's claim to be the site of the Hall of Fame. "Why shouldn't Canton have the Hall of Fame?" Horn recalls asking. "And why shouldn't *The Repository* take the lead?" Obviously, what was needed was a spark to light the flame. Horn called Such into his office and challenged him with these words: "Pro football needs a Hall of Fame, and the logical site is here."

On a quiet Sunday, December 6, 1959, after the football season had ended, the media blitz that would give the campaign exposure opened with a story written by Such that was bannered across the top of all eight columns of the lead page of *The Repository's* sports section. The headline virtually duplicated the words with which Horn had challenged Such. *The Repository* had the ball rolling. Such, meanwhile, felt he had an arsenal of weapons to use—in just one man. "I had the greatest human encyclopedia sitting across from me, sports editor Monte Cross," says Such. "He had walked up and down the sidelines covering Jim Thorpe and had spent fifty-five years on the sports desk of *The Repository*. He was a fountain of information. No town or community could match Canton—it was the cradle of professional football."

In the offices of the Timken Roller Bearing Company, Such's first story was read with more than passing interest by H. H. Timken, Jr., the company's chairman of the board. He phoned Such and offered his support. Timken turned Earl Schreiber, the company's recreation director, loose on the project.

Born in Canton, Schreiber had played high school football and basketball and later joined Timken. He was fully aware of Canton's sports heritage. "You grew up with sports in Canton—that's the way it was," Schreiber says. "It was because of the Bulldogs. They were the major topic of conversation in the city." Schreiber was to be the point man for Timken, just as Such was for *The Repository*. Day in and day out they pursued the vision of the Hall of Fame for Canton. "I spent four years on the Hall," says Such. "[NFL Commissioner] Pete Rozelle publicly said it—he was delighted to see the Hall of Fame get off the ground so he wouldn't have to answer my phone calls. I guess I was quite frequent and persistent."

There were other significant contributors, including Paul Brown, George Halas of the Chicago Bears, Edwin Anderson of the Detroit Lions, Art Rooney of the Pittsburgh Steelers, and several members of the Hall of Fame's original board of trustees—Stu Wilkins, A. A. "Tink" Ulrich, and Bill Belden. There also was William E. Umstattd, chairman of the Timken executive committee, assigned by H. H. Timken, Jr., to appear before the NFL owners' meeting in New York in 1961 to make Canton's formal bid for sanction as the site of the Pro Football Hall of Fame.

Umstattd traveled to New York with Schreiber and an architect's scale model of the proposed Hall of Fame. "I remember," says Schreiber, "we went to the Warwick Hotel, put the scale model on a piano, and not one owner looked at it. Then Mr. Umstattd made his presentation. It was a less-than-ten-minute presentation in which he estimated the cost of the Hall of Fame at two hundred fifty thousand dollars. He said Timken would give an additional one hundred thousand dollars and would see that the town raised the two hundred fifty thousand. At that point the owners sat up and gave us their attention." It wasn't long, however, before Latrobe was insisting its original claim be honored while Green Bay, Detroit, and Los Angeles tried to launch campaigns of their own. It was too late. Timken's $100,000 seemed to have sealed the deal. On April 27, 1961, the NFL sanction for Canton was voted.

What followed may have been the most amazing step in the entire process. On December 7, 1961, Canton launched its drive to raise the $250,000 in pledges Umstattd had promised the NFL. On February 8, 1962, just two months later—the fund drive ended with all the money pledged. It is interesting to note that the pledges came not only from the major businesses in the city but from the average citizen as well. Russell Harmon, Jr., for example, pledged $300 and paid that off in monthly installments of $6.25 (with an occasional extra payment thrown in when things were going well) until he finally finished on December 31, 1969.

Still, on February 8, 1962, when building pledges had reached a total of $378,026, Canton's Hall of Fame remained simply a vision without a single Hall of Famer and without any of the memorabilia required to tell pro football's story in an interesting, informative, and entertaining manner. "When you decide to build a Hall of Fame, it's usually because you have a lot of stuff you want to display," Schreiber points out. "We had the building on the way but nothing to display in it." Finding the right man to begin the collection process and to establish the tone of the Hall became the next step. On April 4, 1962, Dick McCann, a long-time club official with the Washington Redskins, became the Hall's first director. Dedicated and intelligent, abrasively efficient but entertainingly hu-

Above left: *August 11, 1962: Harry Stuhld-reher, one of the Notre Dame Four Horse-men, looks on as NFL Commissioner Pete Rozelle breaks ground for the original Pro Football Hall of Fame. Above right: April 15, 1970: HOF board member A.A. "Tink" Ulrich watches as William E.Umstattd turns ground for the Hall's first expansion. Bottom: November 14, 1977: Board Vice President Clayton Horn breaks ground for the second expansion. Board Chairman Earl Schreiber (left) and NFL Executive Director Don Weiss look on.*

morous, McCann was exactly what the Hall needed at the time—a dynamic worker and an innovative thinker.

McCann proposed the selection process that, with slight refinements, is used today. He also determined the format for the induction ceremonies, held for the first time on September 7, 1963, when the charter class of 17 immortals was enshrined. And he authored the words that greeted them when they stepped forward to be honored. "These," said McCann, "are the milestone men of pro football. Their deeds and dogged faith wrote the history of this great game." That charter class consisted of Sammy Baugh, Bert Bell, Joe Carr, Dutch Clark, Red Grange, George Halas, Mel Hein, Pete Henry, Cal Hubbard, Don Hutson, Curly Lambeau, Tim Mara, George Marshall, John "Blood" McNally, Bronko Nagurski, Ernie Nevers, and Jim Thorpe.

The Hall of Fame has grown in magnitude ever since. A $620,000 expansion in 1971 and a $1.2 million expansion in 1978 have added two buildings to the original pair to display the memorabilia of a sport that will soon date back a hundred years. But the Hall of Fame houses not only the busts and records of more than 120 football immortals and a mountain of memorabilia that has been collected since McCann took over, but some 15,000 photographs, 7,500 game programs, 2,500 books, 500 miles of film, and an art collection—all gathered together to tell the pro football story. And it is a story that is told to more than two hundred thousand people who visit the Hall each year. In fact, more than three million people have passed through its doors in the two decades since the Hall opened in 1963.

But the citizens of Canton—industrial magnates, civic leaders, and private persons alike—have not been satisfied simply to honor pro football's best with enshrinement in the Hall of Fame. They have created a series of activities that center around the annual ceremonies and the preseason game played at nearby Fawcett Stadium. The city of Canton boasts of "Football's Greatest Weekend"—and perhaps it is. At the end of a typical Hall of Fame festival weekend, more than twenty-seven hundred people will have attended a mayor's breakfast, a fashion show, and a civic banquet—all held on Friday. More than two hundred thousand will have viewed the colorful parade through the city streets on Saturday, and between eight and ten thousand will have watched the enshrinement ceremonies on the front steps of the Hall of Fame. Later, more than twenty-three thousand people will have attended the game that marks the opening of the NFL's preseason schedule for the year. In addition, approximately five thousand visitors will have walked through the Hall of Fame for the first time.

The Hall of Fame will continue to grow—by mandate at least three new enshrinees must be added each year—and there is little question that the shrine to pro football's heroes will continue to be sensitive to the needs of the people it honors. That became evident in 1973 when—as a "one-time special"—the surviving members of the charter enshrinee class were invited to Canton for a tenth anniversary reunion. The reunion proved so popular with the aging Hall of Famers that ten-year reunions now have become part of the weekend's traditions. The first twenty-year reunion was staged in 1983, and brought together again all-time greats Mel Hein, John "Blood" McNally, Bronko Nagurski, and Don Hutson.

Opposite: *The 10-year reunion of the charter class of enshrinees in 1973. (Front row left to right): Ernie Nevers, Red Grange, George Halas, and Johnny "Blood" McNally. Back row: Mel Hein, Cal Hubbard. Top: Each enshrinement weekend concludes with the AFC-NFC Hall of Fame game which traditionally opens each NFL preseason. The Philadelphia Eagles and the Miami Dolphins squared off in the 1978 game. Center: A halftime highlight at the AFC-NFC Hall of Fame game, which is televised nationally each year, is the formal introduction of the newest enshrinees. Raymond Berry, the great end of the Baltimore Colts, was a 1973 enshrinee. Bottom right: Frank "Bruiser" Kinard, who excelled as a two-way tackle for the old Brooklyn Dodgers, was elated with his halftime ovation at the Hall of Fame season-opener.*

31

William (Pudge) Heffelfinger was thought to be the first pro football player when he accepted $500 to play for the Allegheny Athletic Association on November 12, 1892.

Chapter 2

Professionals Take the Field

The doors to the Pro Football Hall of Fame open to reveal a 7-foot, 300-pound bronze statue of the fabled Jim Thorpe, a gift to the Hall by Jack Cusack, the manager of the Canton Bulldogs who brought the legendary athlete onto pro football's stage in 1915. The statue shows the Sac and Fox Indian holding a football, his body leaning forward, his legs flexed in a pose that suggests he is evading tacklers as he did 70 years ago, when he became the sport's first legitimate superstar.

When the visitor leaves the Thorpe statue, he winds his way up a gently sloping ramp to the main or upper level, where most of the Hall of Fame's exhibitions are housed. The first display rotunda is a circular area surrounding the cavity created by the 52-foot, football-shaped dome that gives the Hall its unique exterior appearance. Here the history of pro football is traced in roughly chronological fashion starting with the very first game on November 12, 1892, when William "Pudge" Heffelfinger was paid $500 to play for the Allegheny Athletic Association in a game against the Pittsburgh Athletic Club. Pro football's "birth certificate" is a yellowed expense accounting sheet in the Hall's First Game display. The sheet, signed by O. D. Thompson, the manager of the AAA, lists as a game expense: "Game performance bonus to W. Heffelfinger for playing, cash, $500."

Settling on pro football's birth date is, however, a relatively recent development. For years the Hall of Fame's First Game display reflected persistent claims that professional football began in Latrobe, Pennsylvania, about 40 miles east and slightly south of Pittsburgh. There, on September 3, 1895, a 16-year-old quarterback from Indiana College in Pennsylvania—John Brallier—accepted $10 and "cakes" (expenses) to play for Latrobe against neighboring Jeannette. That transaction had, indeed, actually transpired and, with no significant evidence to the contrary, NFL historians accepted the payment to Brallier as the first instance of a player being paid. They were so convinced that Latrobe had witnessed the birth of professional football that the city was given site approval in 1947 as the home of the Hall of Fame. Even when Canton replaced Latrobe as the site of the Hall, the First Game display freely recognized Latrobe as the game's birthplace.

But all of that began to change some 20 years ago when a visitor walked into the offices of the Pittsburgh Steelers and asked to see Dan Rooney, one of the team's chief executives. Rooney's guest was a researcher who presented a 49-page report detailing the origins of direct payments for playing football. The information varied sharply from anything previously written on the beginnings of the sport. The visitor's stay was brief and Rooney, now the Steelers' president, remembers only vaguely that he may have introduced himself as "Nelson Ross." But, while Rooney isn't certain about the identity of the mystery guest and the mystery guest never has stepped forward to identify himself, Rooney was certain about the importance of the research material.

"As soon as I had time to thoroughly read his report, I recognized that here was something of immense historical value," Rooney said. "I immediately shipped it to the National Football League office for safe-keeping." The paper received safe-keeping, but little attention for a number of years.

For a short period of time, it was lost in the shuffle at NFL headquarters. Then, after the Pro Football Hall of Fame was opened in 1963, the report was sent to Canton and assigned to an obscure spot on the shelves. Finally, in 1969, a new staffer, browsing through the archives in a get-acquainted mission, noticed the historic document, and the Hall went to work to change its First Game display. Curiously, the Hall already had on display the Allegheny Expense Accounting sheet from 1892, along with a similar document from 1893 that showed that three players—Wright, Van Cleve, and Rafferty—were paid $50 a game on a season contract basis. However, without the Ross research to fully substantiate the information on the expense accounting sheets, the Hall's first director, Dick McCann, elected to stick with the Brallier and Latrobe first-game theory.

The Ross paper, which is now in the archives of the Hall of Fame, describes the events leading up to the confrontation of the Allegheny Athletic Association (AAA) and the Pittsburgh Athletic Club (PAC) in November, 1892. The AAA team, formed in 1890, and the PAC (in 1891) already were heated rivals when they met for the first of two games in the 1892 season, and wound up in a 6-6 tie. Adding fuel to the fire was the AAA claim that the PAC's

top player and coach, William Kirschner, was a professional because, as a paid instructor for the PAC, his salary went up and his class load down during the football season. With controversy raging, both sides began to explore methods of beefing up their squads.

A practice in vogue at the time both in the East and in the Chicago area—and among many AAU football clubs—was the technique of rewarding stars with expensive trophies, which they could sell, and/or with expense money far in excess of actual expenses. The trophy arrangement ultimately was outlawed by the AAU, but the expense-money policy was allowed to continue. The Chicago Athletic Association team adopted a "double expense money" practice and, as a result, had difficulty finding college or "pure amateur" teams in the area willing to schedule games with them.

One of the Chicago stars was Heffelfinger, who had been an all-America guard at Yale in 1889, 1890, and 1891. In 1892, he took a job as a low-salaried railroad office employee in Omaha, Nebraska, and was granted a leave of absence so that he could play with the Chicago team on a six-game tour of the East. According to a Chicago newspaper report, Heffelfinger would be tendered the "usual expense arrangement" on the tour. Meanwhile, in

Expense Accounting Allegheny Athletic Assoc.
~ Football Club ~

Game of Oct. 29, 1892 ~ AAA vs. Washington, D.C.
balance carried over (account) $432.20
guarantee's gross profit (check) $258.00
team traveling expenses (cash) $221.85
net profit $ 36.15
total balance $468.35

Game of Nov. 12, 1892 ~ AAA vs. Pittsburg A.C.
balance carried over (account) $468.35
game receipts gross profit (cash) $1,683.50
visitors guarantee expense (check) $ 428.00
park rental expense (check) $ 50.00
Donnelly, Malley, Heffelfinger expense (cash) $ 75.00
Schlosser hotel bill for above (check) $ 9.00
game performance bonus to
W. Heffelfinger for playing (cash) $500.00
total expenses $1,062.00
net profit $621.00
total balance $1,089.85

Game of Nov. 19, 1892 ~ AAA vs. W.J. College
balance carried over (account) $1,089.85
game receipts gross profit (cash) $ 746.00
visitors guarantee expense (check) $ 238.00
park rental expense (check) $ 50.00
payment B. Donnelly for playing (cash) $ 250.00
total expenses $ 538.00
net profit $ 208.00
total balance $1,297.00
This above accounting is hereby certified as
correct by the below signed team manager:
O.D. Thompson.

Opposite: *The entrance to the memento-filled Exhibition Rotunda, which tells the pro football story from 1892 to the present. Above: The Allegheny Athletic Expense accounting sheet that pinpoints pro football's first game.*

Pittsburgh, Kirschner had been sidelined with an injury. The PAC manager, George Barbour, realizing the necessity of finding an adequate substitute for his star, decided to scout the Chicago team in its tour-opener against the Cleveland Athletic Association. Chicago won, 29-0, and Heffelfinger had an outstanding game, convincing Barbour that he would make an ideal replacement for Kirschner.

The Pittsburgh *Press*, on October 30, 1892, reported, "A very improbable sort of story is being circulated at present about the PAC offering Heffelfinger and [Knowlton 'Snake'] Ames of the Chicago football team $250 to play with the East End team on Saturday, November 12, against the AAA." Thus alerted, AAA emissaries did a little scouting of their own. In talking with several Chicago players after the final game of their tour, they found that Donnelly, a star end, and another player named Malley would be willing to play for the usual double expense money. They also learned that, while Ames was unwilling to risk his amateur status for any price, Heffelfinger took a more subtle approach—he said he couldn't risk his amateur standing for a mere $250. In effect, pro football had its first "holdout" even before it had its first pro. When the AAA representatives learned that Pudge would play for

$500, they readily agreed to that sum.

For the next week or so, both sides kept quiet about any player maneuverings they might be contemplating. But when the teams took the field on November 12, bedlam broke loose. PAC players quickly noticed that Heffelfinger, Donnelly, and Malley were working out with the AAA team and obviously intended to play. PAC manager Barbour immediately pulled his team off the field. A major factor in the bitter dispute was that followers of both sides had wagered heavily on the game. Once they realized that the AAA team had loaded up with ringers, PAC backers yelled foul. After lengthy de-

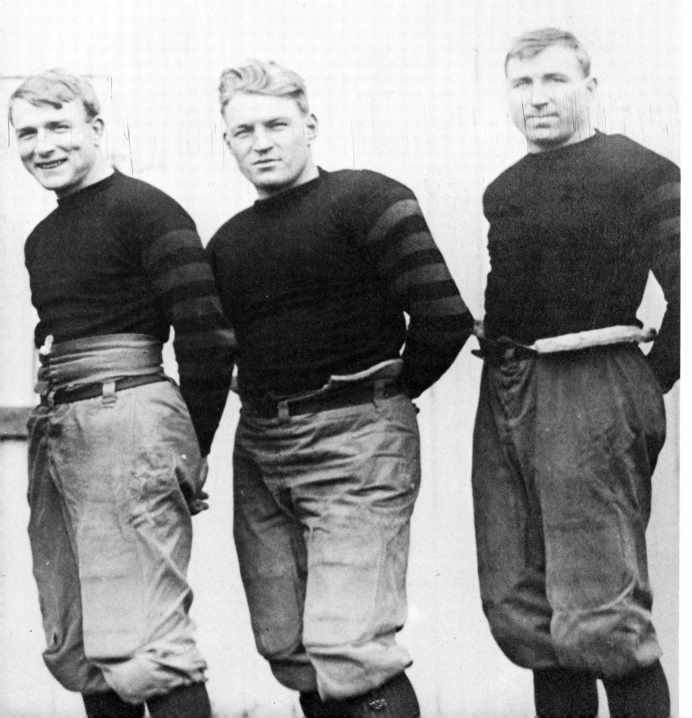

bate, it was agreed that the game would be played as an exhibition—and that all bets would be off.

The bickering had delayed the kickoff so long that in an attempt to beat the autumn darkness soon to descend on Pittsburgh, the teams had to agree to reduce the game's length to two 30-minute halves. Rules of the day called for two 45-minute halves, although no time-outs were allowed and teams could take as long as they cared to put the ball in play after each down.

Midway through the first half, Heffelfinger scored the game's only touchdown when he forced a fumble, recovered it, and raced 25 yards for a score. Touchdowns counted only four points in 1892, so the AAA had a 4-0 victory. Few were happy with the result. AAA fans were angry because they were unable to collect on their bets. PAC followers were furious over the use of the Chicago players and openly charged that Heffelfinger had been paid a straight cash sum as well as his expense money. For his part, the AAA manager, O. D. Thompson, insisted he had acted prudently and had merely done "what the Pittsburghs had tried to do. Only

we were successful where they had failed." It should also be pointed out that the charges of professionalism were not documented until the discovery of the AAA expense accounting sheet which showed, incidentally, that the Allegheny club realized a net profit of $621 for the game, despite the "huge" payment to Heffelfinger. Since winning and maintaining financial solvency were dual objectives, the AAA's first venture into pro football had proved satisfactory.

After the Allegheny-Pittsburgh game, pro football spread quickly in western Pennsylvania. Lawson Fiscus, a famous Princeton player, openly admitted—although no one paid much attention—that he had received double expense money in 1893 and expense money plus $20 a game while playing for the Greensburg, Pennsylvania, town team in 1894. By 1895, both the Latrobe Athletic Club and the Pittsburgh Duquesnes were considered to be professional teams. The McKeesport Olympics and the Jeannette Indians turned pro in 1899, and the Homestead Steelers and the Braddock Carnegies followed in 1900. It is not certain

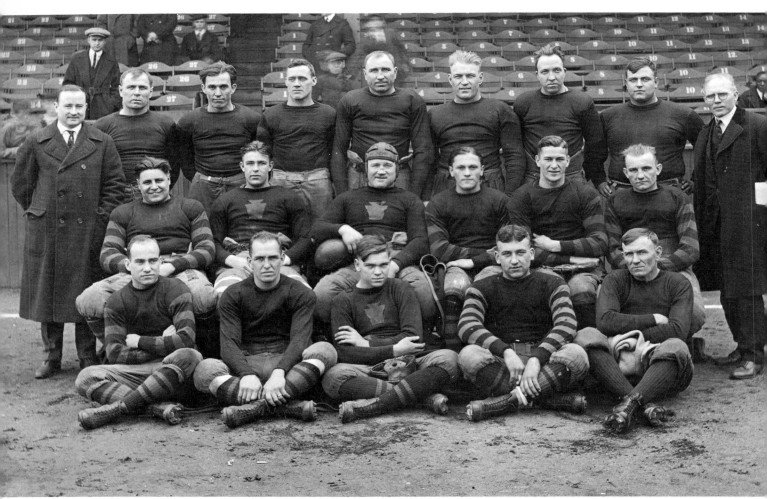

Opposite: *The 1921 Columbus Panhandles with six Nessers and team founder, Joe Carr (third row, right).* Above: *Al Nesser played in the National Football League throughout the 1920s. He was the last active player among the Nessers.*

Above: *Jim Thorpe's Carlisle Institute football sweater, his jacket from the 1912 Olympics, his outstanding marks in the Olympics, and pictures of him in action in several sports are included in one of several displays honoring the exceptional Indian star.*

just how many players were paid on each team, but it is fairly safe to figure that virtually every player on all of those teams was compensated for his services in some way. But pro football did not flourish for long in western Pennsylvania. Some of the earliest teams were disbanding even before the turn of the century. The very first team, the Allegheny Athletic Association, quit after the 1897 season. By 1905, most of western Pennsylvania's first pro teams had vanished.

Once disbanded, most teams were quickly forgotten. There was one notable exception—Connie Mack's Athletics. After the 1902 American League baseball season, the famous manager of the champion Athletics announced his team would also play a pro football schedule in the off-season. While the baseball franchise still exists today as the Oakland Athletics, the football experiment lasted just one year. But the football team was good enough to claim the "world championship" in its only season.

The common impression of those who remember that there actually was a Philadelphia Athletics pro football team is that Mack used his baseball players to fill out his football roster. What he really did was make an all-out effort to assemble the best football talent available. The impression, however, lingers because, for a time, the Athletics' great left-handed pitcher George Edward "Rube" Waddell was a member of the football team. While he showed some promise as a tackle and occasionally played with enthusiasm, Rube found it hard to concentrate on much of anything. He loved to chase fire engines, watch parades, spend hours at a circus, and wander off to fish. As much as anything, Mack may have recruited him for his football team so that he could keep an eye on him during baseball's off-season.

Waddell's pro football career was short-lived. The night before a crucial game in Pittsburgh, Rube wandered off to watch a billiard match between Willie Hoppe and Pedro DeOra. He bet heavily on the loser and, when he approached Mack at the hotel with a plea to cover his losses with a loan, he instead received a severe tongue-lashing and an order to go to bed. As Waddell turned to go, he reached into his pocket, possibly for a handkerchief or a room key, and out fell a loaded revolver. When it hit the floor, it fired, the bullet just missing a shaken Mack. The next morning, Rube was on the train home, his football days ended. In the Philadelphia Athletics' team picture on display at the Hall of Fame, Connie Mack is seated in the middle of his 18-man squad, but Waddell is nowhere to be seen.

Actually, the Philadelphia Nationals (now the Phillies), the other major league baseball team in

Restoration by
Amatucci and Morgans

John Brallier for many years was erroneously considered to be the first pro because he accepted "$10 and cakes" when he played for the Latrobe, Pa., team.

the City of Brotherly Love, prompted Mack's entrance into pro football. The Nationals had organized a football team, and Mack had decided the A's would be natural rivals, even on the football field. Lending major assistance to Mack in building and recruiting his team was Blondy Wallace, a tackle just out of Penn who in a few years would become the central figure in the pro football scandal that almost ruined the sport "out west" in Ohio. The principal opponent for the Athletics and Nationals was the Pittsburgh Professionals, the city's last legitimate pro football team until Art Rooney came along with the Pittsburgh Pirates (now the Steelers) 31 years later. Some historians claim this three-way association was actually the first attempt at an organized football league.

Strangely, it was the Pittsburgh team—not the two teams from Philadelphia with baseball heritages—that included an all-time baseball star on its roster. Christy Mathewson, one of baseball's great pitchers, was a star back for the Professionals. And Mathewson wasn't the only "name" baseball player who tried pro football as a sideline. Charlie Dressen, destined to gain fame and notoriety as a major league baseball manager, was a member of the Decatur Staleys in both 1919 and 1920. He is pictured with the 1920 Staleys in a Hall of Fame display. Several Pro Football Hall of Fame members, on the other hand, played major league baseball, although football was their primary sport—Thorpe, Ernie Nevers, Ace Parker, Red Badgro, Joe Guyon, and Cal Hubbard. Hubbard, an outstanding football tackle, became a long-time baseball umpire and today is the only person enshrined in both the Baseball and Pro Football halls of fame.

The Athletics' record against the Nationals and Professionals was only 3-2-1, but they claimed the world championship in 1902 on the basis of an 11-2-1 overall mark. A three-game series against Pittsburgh was the highlight of the season. Each team won by an 11-0 score, and a third game wound up in a scoreless tie. The tie game on Thanksgiving Day almost was canceled at the last moment because of Mack's concern that the meager crowd wasn't large enough to assure his $3,000 guarantee. A Pittsburgh-Washington and Jefferson college game in Pittsburgh that same day had cut the pro crowd far below expectations. Finally, a restless fan came down on the field to learn what the trouble was. When he was told, the fan proceeded to whip out his checkbook and present Mack with his $3,000 guarantee. Mack, however, had to be convinced that the stranger's check wouldn't bounce. That was accomplished when the fan identified himself as William Corey, the head of Carnegie

Steel, a staunch football fan and owner of the Homestead Steelers football team.

The Athletics were involved in one pro football "first" in 1902. On their way to Pittsburgh for the showdown matches with the Pros, the A's scheduled three tune-up games, including a game against the Kanaweola A.C. in Elmira, New York, that was played at night. The lights were at ground level, bordering the field, and hampered the game somewhat since they shone directly into the players' eyes.

A second pro football "first" occurred at the end of the 1902 season when the manager of Madison Square Garden in New York, looking for a premier attraction for his arena over the New Year's holiday, decided to stage a gridiron "world series." For this first indoor football venture, the manager, Tom O'Rourke, envisioned matching the top four teams in the country: the two Philadelphia teams, the Pittsburgh Pros, and a powerhouse team from Watertown, New York.

The Watertown Red and Blacks, who already claimed the 1902 "world championship" in spite of a mid-season loss to the Athletics, decided they could best defend their laurels by not playing. O'Rourke himself decided that Pittsburgh would not be a good draw, but the two Philadelphia teams did join forces to enter the tournament as one team. O'Rourke, anticipating that this would be the eventual winner, gleefully dubbed the team "New York" so that hometown fans could cheer for a champion.

He also invited the New York Knickerbockers, the Warlow Athletic Club of Long Island, and the Syracuse, New York, Athletic Club. Confident that the "New York" Philadelphians would easily conquer these foes, he then invited the Orange, New Jersey, Athletic Club to play in the championship game on January 1, 1903, against the erstwhile hometown favorites.

Thus O'Rourke was set for his historic attraction, but the cramped quarters of the indoor arena would drastically alter the style and caliber of play. As tournament time neared, *The New York Times* reported:

> The wooden flooring of the big garden was taken up and the gridiron was laid out on the earthen surface, which proved to be too sticky and holding for fast work. The goal lines were seventy yards apart and the width of the playing surface was scarcely more than thirty-five yards.

The miniature field and slow surface tended to favor the heavier teams and to neutralize the punting game, which in 1902 was usually a major factor in any gridiron struggle. With the arena wall inching close to the sidelines, the playing field

Top left: *Earle "Greasy" Neale, who later became a Hall of Fame football coach, and the famous baseball manager, Connie Mack.* Top right: *Tackle Cal Hubbard, who later became a great baseball umpire.* Bottom: *The 1902 Philadelphia Athletic football team led by Connie Mack.*

The site of the Canton-Massillon football game in 1906. Note the marking of the field. Lines were both vertical and horizontal because of certain rules in effect at the time.

proved to be a physical hazard for the players.

Still, the indoor games got under way, and O'Rourke's master plan for a New York-New Jersey title showdown might have worked had it not been for the Syracuse Athletic Club which, on realizing it could not successfully compete with its regular-season squad, quickly loaded up with outstanding "borrowed" talent. After signing a rock-ribbed line headed by Glenn "Pop" Warner, Syracuse turned to the Watertown Red and Blacks for all three of its running backs, one of whom was a rugged fullback named Harry Mason.

With its formidable array, Syracuse upset favored "New York," 5-0, whitewashed the Knickerbockers, 36-0, on New Year's Eve, and then repeated the 36-0 margin against the Orange A.C. on New Year's Day. Mason scored a touchdown in each of the last two games. Just recently, Mason's bib-overall-style uniform, complete with flimsy helmet and hard-rubber nose guard, which he wore in the Madison Square Garden series, was donated to the Pro Football Hall of Fame by Mason's son. It is now prominently displayed.

Pro football may have been born in western Pennsylvania, but it flourished for the first time a hundred miles west of the Pittsburgh area in the Massillon-Akron-Canton triangle of northeastern Ohio. The Massillon Tigers became the state's first pro team in 1903, when they were organized by the city editor of the Massillon *Independent*, Eddie Stewart, who was interested in filling the sports void that existed in the city. The Tigers easily defeated a number of amateur teams, including nearby Canton, in the first of many bitter battles between the two cities, then challenged the defending state amateur champions, undefeated and unscored upon East Akron Athletic Club. Buoyed by

several professionals recruited from the Pittsburgh Athletic Club, Massillon won, 12-0. Once the die was cast in Ohio, professional football spread rapidly. The Canton Bulldogs, Akron Indians, Shelby Blues, Dover Canals, Salem Athletic Club, and Lorain Athletic Club all turned pro in 1904. Toledo joined in 1905, Columbus in 1907, Marion in 1908, and Youngstown in 1912. Curiously, the first two club teams in the state, Dayton and Cleveland, did not turn professional until 1916.

From the beginning, Canton and Massillon, located just seven miles apart in central Stark County, became fearsome rivals. The pro football confrontation between the two was relatively short-lived—Massillon played its last major pro football game in 1919—but the intense competition continues today in one of America's most noted high school rivalries—between the Massillon Washington Tigers and the Canton McKinley Bulldogs.

Once in the pro football picture, Canton set out to produce a team capable of beating Massillon. Just before the 1905 game with the Tigers, the Bulldogs signed Willie Heston, a piston-legged halfback who had led Fielding Yost's mighty University of Michigan team. But, even with Heston and several other outsiders, Canton still lost, 14-4. "Canton sportsmen are out about $20,000 on the game," the Massillon *Independent* reported on November 30, 1905. "Canton devotees of the sport were to be found last night at the leading bars lined three deep trying to drown their sorrows. . . ." The stage was thus set for the tragic, almost fatal, 1906 showdown that triggered a gambling scandal and threatened the existence of the sport.

It began when Blondy Wallace, the same ex-Penn star who had guided Connie Mack into pro football in 1902, was hired to coach the Bulldogs

and play a major role in recruiting top talent. As one historian noted, "Wallace knew where to get the right men, how to condition them, and how to build up an attack and a defense, but he never won anyone's confidence with his integrity and honesty." Clearly, Canton was about to embark on a fanatical effort to overtake its neighboring city. For openers, Wallace lured four stars—linemen Clark Schrontz, Herman Kerckhoff, and Jack Lang, plus quarterback Jack Hayden—away from the Tigers. Then, when the forward pass was legalized for the first time that year, he shipped his entire team to Pennsylvania State College to learn the intricacies of the new rules.

The two-game Massillon-Canton series was scheduled to conclude the 1906 campaign, and the games were eagerly awaited by fans and writers who traveled surprising distances to attend. Grantland Rice, the most famous sportswriter of that age, wrote before the first game:

> There have been a few football games before. Yale has faced Princeton, Harvard has tackled Penn, and Michigan and Chicago have met in one or two steamy affairs. But these were not the Real Product when measured by the football standard set by the warring factions of Stark County, Ohio, now posing in the football limelight.

The series opened in Massillon on a field near the Ohio state asylum. A picture of the setting is exhibited at the Hall of Fame and graphically captures the mood of the day. A near-capacity crowd is on hand. Many fans stand atop a trolley car parked on the tracks nearby, while others perch on a wooden fence surrounding the field. Wooden bleachers line both sidelines, but, oddly, every fan in the park—even those with what should be a good view—is standing. American flags wave from

each goalpost standard in either end zone. The field, too, has curious markings. There are the usual five-yard markers (horizontal lines), but, in addition, there are vertical lines five yards apart that run parallel to the sidelines. These strange field markings can be explained by a new rule, adopted in 1903, that allowed a player receiving the ball from center to run across the scrimmage line provided he was five yards from the point where the ball was snapped. Within a few years, the rule was amended and the vertical lines disappeared. A common belief that the term *gridiron* developed because of this type of field marking is inaccurate. Research shows that the term had been used as early as the mid-1880's.

Canton won the first game, 10-5, but Massillon came back two weeks later in Canton and evened the series with a 13-6 victory. Controversy, which had been growing all season, burst into the open after the second game with the revelation of a gambling scandal. During the 1906 campaign, Canton players, fearing that they might lose their money playing poker or on "some other extravagances," asked Coach Wallace to hold the bulk of their pay in safekeeping. Then, before the first game in Massillon, they asked Wallace to bet their money on a Canton victory. After the game, however, Wallace told his players he had decided instead to bet the money on the second game. After the second game, the Massillon *Independent* accused Wallace of trying to rig the outcome of both games. It printed a written statement by Manager E. J. Stewart of the Tiger football team, and H. A. Croxton, one of the team's major backers. The statement said in part:

> The time has now arrived to make clear some peculiar and unpleasant conditions which have surrounded

the Tigers' coach and management during the entire season. . . . Many Massillon fans were surprised at the discharge of Walter R. East who played right end on the Tiger team. . . . East was the man who attempted to engineer a deal, with Coach Blondy Wallace of the Canton team as an accomplice, and they were backed by a crowd of gamblers who agreed to furnish $50,000 to be used for betting purposes and all expenses incurred and $5,000 in cash to the Tigers' coach and management.

East and Wallace made the mistake of their sporting life when they figured that the Massillon team, coach, and management could be bought. . . . Their scheme was that Canton was to win the first game, Massillon win the second game, and a third game would be played in Cleveland and this game to be played on its merits.

The *Independent* further charged that, failing in his attempt to use East as an accomplice, Wallace turned to a member of the Bulldogs to throw the game in Canton. The implicated Canton player denied the accusation but did leave town on the first train, still dressed in his playing uniform. Canton fans who had lost heavily on the game confronted the players in the Cortland Hotel bar that evening. Angry words were followed by angrier

punches and then a full-scale brawl before police intervened. Blondy Wallace sued the Massillon *Independent* for libel, but the case was thrown out of court. As Jack Cusack reported years later, "The *Independent* apparently had the evidence." Shamed, Canton bowed out of football for several seasons. When Canton did resume big-time pro play in 1912, the nickname Bulldogs was at first shunned in favor of Professionals. In a short time, Cusack took over the team and had it running smoothly and openly. Pro football had survived its first—and worst—scandal.

Thus, with Canton out of the picture and Massillon toning down its program, the pro football focus began to shift to other cities in the Buckeye State. One was Columbus, where the Panhandles were organized by Joe Carr in 1907. Carr, an enterprising young assistant sports editor of the *Ohio State Journal*, already had displayed the flair for sound athletic management and promotion that would make him an outstanding president of the National Football League 15 years later. In 1900, he had organized a baseball team from employees of the Panhandle Division of the Pennsyl-

Opposite page: *In this major display area, the evolution of pro football is traced in colorful form through the first decade of the National Football League.* Above: *The unusual 1926 season of the Duluth Eskimos is remembered in this exhibition featuring Ernie Nevers.* Left: *Flimsy shoulder pads and face-covering helmets were standard equipment in the early days. Also on display is a large Columbus Panhandles blanket.*

Two pieces of equipment worn in the early days of football: the leather face covering of the helmet (above) made it hard for players to see and breathe, while the hard-rubber nose guard (below) proved to be more of a hazard than a help.

vania Railway, then headquartered in Columbus. He made a similar attempt to put together a football team in 1904, but there was little response, and it folded after only two games. In 1907, however, the Panhandles' football team created enough interest to remain in business. For 20 seasons, until 1926, the Panhandles were not a particularly successful football team. Yet they were, next to the Canton Bulldogs of the Jim Thorpe era, probably the best-known team of the pre-NFL years. The team's lasting fame and much of its success on the field came about because of the Nesser family, which provided the nucleus of playing talent through the Panhandles' first decade and, to a lesser degree, several years after that.

Six Nesser brothers—John, Phil, Ted, Fred, Frank, and Alfred—were long-term Panhandles. For a game or two in 1921, a seventh Nesser brother—Raymond, the youngest of the clan—also wore the maroon-and-gold Columbus uniform. Legend tells us that the mother of the Nesser brothers busied herself patching uniforms between games while Papa Nesser served as the team's water boy. If all of this is true, it would mean that nine Nessers simultaneously contributed to the team. Like most members of the Panhandles, the Nessers worked in the yards and shops of the railroad as boilermakers or blacksmiths. "We toiled for five hours, then we ate lunch and practiced on full stomachs before going back to work," Al said. "There was an athletic field right outside the gates."

The Panhandles did have one advantage that helped them stay afloat financially during years when other teams were folding. Because most of the players were employed by the railroad, they could ride anywhere free. And, by playing mostly on the road, the Panhandles paid no stadium rentals. On longer trips, they did have to find overnight quarters, but that was not always a problem, either. "We preferred the yearly trek to Toledo," said Lee Shoots, a longtime halfback for the Panhandles. "We would leave Columbus on Saturday night and stay over at a small town called Carrothers. We ate at a saloon and boardinghouse there and, in the back of the house, there was a barn with the upstairs furnished somewhat. The Nesser boys preferred this barn to the house and, after a card-playing session, off to bed they would go. The snoring coming from the barn was a fright from midnight on." None of that would have bothered the Nessers, however. Later, they admitted that the years they had spent in the boiler factory had impaired their hearing.

The Panhandles, and particularly the Nessers,

became known for their rough, and talented, play. None certainly ever was accused of using finesse. Accounts of Panhandles games commonly included reports of rival players being forced out of action with broken bones and assorted injuries. The Nessers could also take it. They shunned the use of padding or helmets and, as Carr once remarked, "There aren't three good ribs amongst the lot of those Nessers." Knute Rockne, the famed Notre Dame product who was a talented player in Ohio, expressed the feeling of the opposition. "Getting tackled by the Nessers," he said, "is like falling off a train—while it is going over a trestle."

The Nesser clan had its beginning in the German city of Trier, located in the far western part of the country a few miles from Luxembourg. It was there that father, Theodore, and mother, Katherine, began raising their brood, until Papa Nesser grew tired of life in Germany and decided to migrate to the United States. He arrived in Columbus in the early 1880's and immediately took a job with the Panhandle Division. His wife and five children soon followed him to America. Seven more Nessers, including five boys, would be born in Ohio, until finally there were eight boys and four girls. Having been toughened by the rough-and-ready existence of an immigrant family, the Nesser boys spent their days on the Columbus sandlots learning the new American game of football. Pro football provided a natural outlet for their skills.

Ted, the first brother born in America, was also the first to become a pro. He played with the Massillon Tigers' state championship team in 1904, 1905, and 1906, while brother John played with the Tigers in 1905. Once the Panhandles were formed, the Nessers quickly vowed their allegiance to the Columbus club. Phil, Fred, Frank, and Al also signed. Curiously, the biggest Nesser of them all, Pete, at 350 pounds, did not play football, and no amount of urging by his family could get him to change his mind. John, born on April 25, 1875, in Trier, was the oldest and, at 185 pounds, also the smallest. A quarterback, he was reputed to be an exceptional blocker and tackler. Ted, the player-coach, could play any position—on the 1906 Massillon roster he was listed as having played tackle, end, guard, halfback, and fullback. He was best at halfback, however. At 225 pounds, he continually punished enemy tacklers with his bruising runs. Frank, at 250 pounds, was the largest Nesser to play football. He played fullback, but was also a sensational passer who had a reputation for being able to throw 50 or 60 yards with exceptional accuracy. In addition, he was a kicking specialist who once was credited with a 63-yard field goal by placekick. Old-timers remember his punts consistently trav-

eling 70 yards. Supporting the three Nessers in the backfield were three more who played on the line. Phil (236 pounds) was a tackle and Fred (235 pounds) often played tackle, as well. But Fred, at 6 feet 5 inches, was the tallest of the clan and sometimes lined up at end or in the backfield. The sixth of the regular Nessers was 190-pound Al, an outstanding end and guard.

Several of the Nessers were active, and even excelled, in other sports. Al, Raymond, and Fred took up professional boxing, and Fred at one time was considered to be a prime contender for Jess Willard's heavyweight crown. John was a hammer thrower of national repute, while Phil also wrestled and competed in track and field as a pole vaulter. Frank spent ten years as a first baseman in organized baseball, including a brief tenure with the Columbus Senators in the American Association. But all were most at home on the football field. "They were the roughest, toughest pack of outlaws ever to put on a football suit," said Suey Welch, who quarterbacked against them when he played with the Akron Pros. "There isn't a doubt in anyone's mind who played against them that they would have been all-American."

No Nesser ever won all-American acclaim simply because no Nesser ever attended college. Frank was offered a chance to go to Notre Dame to play football, but decided instead to get married. In 1909, Ted left Columbus for Texas, where he had received an offer to play for A&M Coach Charley Moran, an old friend. Moran thought he might be needed when A&M played its most bitter rival, the University of Texas. Although Ted, the oldest of the Nessers, actually wore a freshman beanie cap the week he was on campus, he did not get to play, sitting on the bench and watching as A&M beat Texas, 7-6. Afterward, he and Moran went duck hunting and then Ted headed home. He was $200 richer because he had been paid expenses, and as an employee of the railroad, he rode home free. Would Moran have used him if Texas A&M were losing? The question remains unanswered.

In the 1913 season, Frank defected from Columbus to play in Akron. For the Akron-Columbus game that season, Frank was matched at tackle against brother Ted, still with the Panhandles. Legend has it that fans largely ignored all aspects of the game except the titanic struggle taking place between the two brothers on the line. Akron won the game; the personal struggle was declared a draw.

The 1909 Dayton-Columbus game provided a perfect example of how the Nessers could dominate a football game. Both Fred and Frank scored touchdowns. Phil raced from his tackle position, took the ball around end, and sped 40 yards for a third touchdown. John blocked and tackled as well as any player, while Ted provided the inspiration his role as team leader demanded. Columbus won 16-0. (Touchdowns by this time counted five points each. It wasn't until 1912 that they took on their present-day six-point value.)

While the Nessers left their mark in pro football history, they didn't get rich doing it. Fred, who played 14 years with the Panhandles, reported his top single-season salary was $950. Brother Al remembered at least one better year. "When I first started," he said, "the players split five or six hundred dollars at season's end. But in 1915, one of our most successful years, the first-stringers collected fifteen hundred dollars apiece. I felt like a millionaire."

By the time the Panhandles joined the new American Professional Football Association (the forerunner of the NFL) in 1920, the Nessers already had begun to disperse. In 1917, Frank moved on to play for Detroit, and Al for Akron. Four Nessers—John (age 46), Phil (41), Ted (37), and Fred (35)—retired after the 1921 season. That year, incidentally, Ted's son Charles played briefly with the Panhandles, thus giving that team a rare father-son combination. Frank hung on through 1926, Columbus' final NFL season. He was 37 when he quit. Until George Blanda came along a half century later, John Nesser bore the distinction of being history's oldest pro football player.

Al Nesser enjoyed a considerable amount of success during the NFL's first decade, initially with the Akron Pros and then with the New York Giants. He was an all-NFL end at Akron in 1922 and an all-league guard with the 1927 champion Giants. He retired at age 38 after spending the 1931 season with the Cleveland Indians. Al was the only Nesser to outlast the Panhandles, the team his family had made famous. With most of the Nessers retired, the team even changed its name to Tigers after the 1922 season. And when the NFL cut its membership roster from 22 teams to 12 before the 1927 season, Columbus dropped out of major league pro football. The team's 20-year record was a bleak 72-91-13. Only in 1914, 1915, and 1916, when the Panhandles were serious contenders for the coveted Ohio state championship, did the team experience any significant success. Nevertheless, the Nesser clan was so unique that the Panhandles are spotlighted in the Hall of Fame display.

The 1920's are known as the Roaring Twenties, but for the National Football League that ten-year period might be better labeled the Tempestuous Twenties. Ironically, the lack of stability that had prompted the formation of a league continued. When the 11 team representatives gathered in Canton in 1920, the reasons for calling the meeting were clear cut. Pro football was in a disastrous state of confusion. Teams were loosely organized with many players shifting allegiances weekly. Competitive bidding for talented players occurred without controls of any kind. Blatant raids of opposition rosters were commonplace. Most business arrangements were slipshod, and no regulations existed that could govern how teams operated against one another. Yet, despite the birth of an organized league, immediate improvement was virtually imperceptible. A membership fee, established at $100 to give the organization an air of respectability, was ignored by every charter member. APFA teams played independent clubs as well as fellow members and, particularly in the first year or so, even tried to include non-league games in the official standings.

Akron, Buffalo, and Canton all claimed the first APFA championship. Considering its won-lost record, Canton had no basis for such a claim, but Akron and Buffalo, with considerably better records, did. A hastily arranged series of play-off games failed to decide the issue, but did create an interesting by-product—one of the additional games pitted the Canton Bulldogs against the Buffalo All-Americans in New York City. Billed as "the first real game played between representative teams in New York," the game in the Polo Grounds attracted 15,000 spectators. Buffalo won, 7-3, when one of Jim Thorpe's punts was blocked in the end zone for the decisive touchdown. The inaugural season also produced the first recorded player transaction when Akron sold Bob Nash, a tackle and end, to Buffalo for $300 and 5 percent of the gate receipts. League reorganization in 1921 brought in Joe Carr as president, and while again the results were not immediate, the hard-working, talented, and experienced sports executive from Columbus was destined to successfully lead the fight to bring order and respectability to the NFL in the nearly two decades he served until his death in 1939. His first order of business was to award the 1920 APFA championship to Akron.

The pre-NFL years of pro football are recaptured in the first major display in the exhibition rotunda . The bib-overall style uniform in the display was worn in the first indoor football game in Madison Square Garden in 1902.

The National Football League championship trophy pictured above was awarded to the Cleveland Bulldogs in 1924.

ERNIE NEVERS' ESKIMOS

FROM DULUTH

1926·'27

Chapter 3

Indians, Eskimos, and Maroons

The Hall of Fame displays numerous articles from the NFL's early years that clearly demonstrate the meager beginnings of pro football, even the organized variety. For example, there is the Detroit Tigers' 1921 season-ticket book cut in the shape of a tiger's head. It sold for $5, plus 50c war tax, and was good for seven games plus a championship game if held in Detroit. Then there is the 1922 VIP pass signed by Joe Carr. (It simply is a 1921 APFA pass with the old year crossed out and the new year substituted in ink. No attempt was made to include the new name—National Football League—on the pass.) Also on display are tiny gold footballs from both the 1922 and 1923 seasons that went to members of the champion Canton Bulldogs. Similar awards have long been given to high school athletes. The 1924 NFL championship trophy presented to the Cleveland Bulldogs stands only about 15 inches high and is a silver-plate reproduction of the balloon-shaped football used in the 1920's.

During that first decade, at one time or another, no fewer than 36 cities were on the NFL membership roster. There was only one flaw: The franchises were basically based in small cities. There were Kenosha and Racine in Wisconsin; Hammond and Evansville in Indiana; Rock Island in Illinois; but cities with such small populations could not support major league teams. Even the birthplace city, Canton, Ohio, did not last long.

When the 1930 season opened, just 10 of the 36 teams remained in business. Of these, four franchises remain in the NFL today: the Green Bay Packers, the New York Giants, the Chicago Bears, and the Cardinals, who played in Chicago until 1960, when they moved to St. Louis.

Even winning championships wasn't enough to insure a pro football team's existence. The Canton Bulldogs won consecutive championships in 1922 and 1923, but failed to take the field in 1924, although it tried again in 1925 and for a final season in 1926. Many stars from the Canton team migrated to Cleveland, which won the 1924 title. Two seasons later, that franchise was out of business. The Frankford Yellowjackets, with an eye-opening 14-1-1 record, grabbed the 1926 NFL championship, but dropped out of the NFL after the 1931 season. That same year, the 1928 champions, the Providence Steam Roller, rolled to a halt.

There was one notable exception among the small-city teams—the Green Bay Packers, who not only survived the tough early years, but became a leading league power and the NFL's first three-time champions, winning titles in 1929, 1930, and 1931.

In 1926, as the NFL battled the challenge of the newly formed American Football League, league membership numbered 22 teams, with several new teams forming to keep the AFL out of as many of the available stadiums as possible. This first AFL-NFL war was short-lived, and, by 1927, the National Football League had cut all the way back to 12 teams, including the New York Yankees, the only survivor from the AFL. Casualties in the big membership reduction included the Canton Bulldogs, the Akron Indians, and the Columbus Panhandles (Tigers), three teams that had been a major portion of the nucleus of the league when it was organized

The Duluth Eskimos of 1926 and 1927 were one of early pro football's most interesting teams largely because they played most of their games on the road. Ernie Nevers was the team's do-everything superstar.

just seven years earlier.

While the smaller cities did not play a significant role in the league's evolution, they did produce a handful of outstanding teams and left behind some of the most interesting and unusual chapters in the unabridged book of NFL history. Many of the stories fall in the novelty classification, but because of their unique nature, they have remained the favorites of football buffs long after the era in which they occurred faded into obscurity.

The unusual saga of the Oorang Indians, who played in the NFL in 1922 and 1923, is typical. The Oorang Indians existed solely because of one man's love for a special breed of dog and his desire to publicize and sell the animals all around the country. The man was Walter Lingo, owner and operator of the Oorang Kennels in the tiny town of LaRue, in central Ohio. In his house organ, *Oorang Comments*, he explained the rare breed:

> About 60 years ago, the common man of Great Britain found it necessary to create a dog different from any in existence. The bird dog became lost in the bush when at stand, the hounds were too noisy, and the retrievers lacked stamina. Therefore these folks secretly experimented by a series of crossbreeding old types, including the otter hounds, the old English sheep dog, the black and tan terrier, and the bulldog. From this melting pot resulted the Airedale, so named because he was first produced by the people along the dale of the Aire river between England and Scotland. The new dog combined the good qualities of his ancestors without their faults. It was a super dog.

Lingo had little, if any, knowledge of football, but next to Airedales, Indians were his greatest interest. He believed his Airedales might learn something from Indians that they could not possibly acquire from the best white hunters. The most famous Indian in the world in 1922 was Jim Thorpe who, legend tells us, had once endeared himself to Lingo by telling an entertaining dog story. In 1921, Lingo invited Thorpe and Pete Calac, also a player of Indian descent, to LaRue for some hunting and unwittingly set in motion his entry into the NFL. During the visit, Lingo decided it would be wise to purchase an NFL franchise for $100, the going rate. (A prize Airedale that year was selling for $150.) The team would be made up entirely of full- or part-blooded Indians. Thorpe would run the team. And the primary goal of the entire project would be to publicize the fabulous Airedales.

Since LaRue had no football field, the team designated Marion, a city of 30,000 about 15 miles from LaRue, as its home base. Marion had just been put "on the map" as the home of the new American president, Warren G. Harding. Finding a field, however, was only a minor problem compared with the job of putting together an all-Indian team.

Many who tried out hadn't played in several years, and some were older than the 34-year-old Thorpe. Of the squad that was finally assembled, 15 Oorang players had performed at Carlisle, the Indian industrial school, many in Thorpe's time. The roster included such names as Big Bear, Bobalash, Dick Deer Slayer, Xavier Downwind, Eagle Feather, Long-Time Sleep, Joe Little Twig, Ted Lone Wolf, Red Fang, David Running Deer, War Eagle, and White Cloud. Many of them can be seen in the team picture that hangs in the Hall of Fame. Besides Thorpe, the starting backfield included Calac and Joe Guyon, both high-quality players with NFL experience. Nine players came from Guyon's Chippewa tribe, but the Mission, Pomo, Mohican, Mohawk, Wyandotte, Cherokee, Seneca, Sac and Fox, and Winnebago tribes also provided players for the unusual roster.

Unfortunately, the Indians never took the matter of winning football games too seriously. The players found it difficult to concentrate on the game when Lingo directed all of his attention to flamboyant pregame and halftime shows. Featured were exhibitions of Airedales at work training and even treeing a live bear. In addition, fancy tomahawk work, knife and lariat throwing, and Indian dances were a part of each show. It also was suspected that, as player-coach, Thorpe was far from a strong disciplinarian.

Most Oorang stories reflect on the team's off-the-field activities rather than on-the-field accomplishments. A favorite tale relates how, one night in Chicago, the team rebelled when a bartender wanted to close up before the players were finished drinking. They tossed him into a telephone booth, turned it upside down, and then drank until dawn. Another time they left a St. Louis bar too late to catch the last trolley back to their quarters. Using more muscles than they usually did on the football field, they found a trolley heading in the opposite direction, lifted the vehicle off its tracks, and turned it around to face the direction in which they wanted to travel.

The Indians played only one game at home (a winning effort against the Columbus Panhandles), but drew good crowds when they took their novelty show on the road to such stops as Chicago, Minneapolis, Milwaukee, Buffalo, Indianapolis, and several Ohio cities. The 1922 team won three and lost six in NFL play, including a 62-0 loss to Akron, a 36-0 thrashing by Dayton, and a 33-6 defeat by the Chicago Bears. In retrospect, however, those were virtual high points. In 1923, the Indians won only one game, a 12-0 victory over the Louisville Brecks in their final game. In ten losses, they were shut out six times, and the margins ran as high as

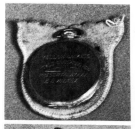

Above: This unusual team picture of the 1924 Cleveland Bulldogs NFL championship eleven was put together years after the team played its last game. Left: Unusual mementoes from the first decade of the NFL. (Clockwise from top right) A gold football awarded to Canton's championship team members, a 1922 NFL season pass, a Detroit Tigers 1921 season ticket book, and a 1925 Frankford Yellowjackets championship watch.

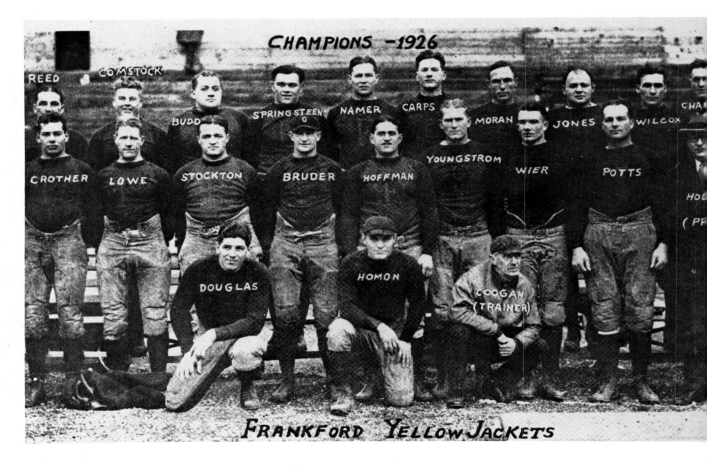

CHAMPIONS —1926

REED · COMSTOCK · BUDD · SPRINGSTEEN O · NAMER · CARPS · MORAN · JONES · WILCOX · CHA

CROTHER · LOWE · STOCKTON · BRUDER · HOFFMAN · YOUNGSTROM · WIER · POTTS · HO (PH

DOUGLAS · HOMON · COOGAN (TRAINER)

FRANKFORD YELLOW JACKETS

57-0 against Buffalo and 41-0 against Canton. Thorpe's total production consisted of one field goal in the nine games he played.

There were, however, a few fleeting moments of glory. Thorpe had a 75-yard punt at Milwaukee and Guyon returned an interception 96 yards against the Chicago Bears. But a member of the Bears, player-coach-owner George Halas, contributed by far the most memorable moment when he scooped up a Thorpe fumble and returned it 98 yards for a touchdown. The play was an NFL record that stood until 1972.

Fan response to the Indians waned in 1923. Crowds everywhere were smaller than a year earlier. Even Thorpe's magic name could no longer lure the fans. Clearly, the novelty of the Oorang Indians had run its course, and Lingo gave up the franchise. Through it all, however, Lingo achieved his goal of providing a showcase for his Airedale dogs. But pro football also was a winner. The Oorang Indians provided color and mystique during a period when anything that attracted attention to the new league was badly needed—and certainly welcomed.

Two years later, another small city—Pottsville,

a coal-mining town in northeastern Pennsylvania—burst onto the NFL scene and wound up in a controversy that lasted more than 50 years. It all began harmlessly when the Pottsville Maroons put together a talented group of athletes who stormed to a 10-2 record, including a 21-7 win over the Chicago Cardinals in what was billed as an NFL championship game. In celebration of their league title, the Maroons scheduled an exhibition against the Notre Dame All-Stars, a team that included the famous Four Horsemen—Jim Crowley, Elmer Layden, Don Miller, and Harry Stuhldreher—and other former Irish stars. When the Maroons won, 9-7, joy reigned in Pottsville . . . for a few hours.

The game had been played in Philadelphia's Shibe Park, the home territory of the Frankford Yellowjackets. And, according to the Pottsville version of what occurred, Frankford protested the Maroons' invasion of its territorial rights even though the Yellowjackets' season was over. Then, NFL President Joe Carr was supposed to have upheld the protest and ordered the Maroons to forfeit their championship. Pottsville also claimed that Carr then ordered the Cardinals to play two more games, so that their final 11-2-1 record would be

Opposite: *The 1926 Frankford Yellowjackets, champions of the National Football League.* Left: *Ernie Nevers, the fabled leader of the Duluth Eskimos who played 1714 of a possible 1740 minutes in 1926.* Below: *The Oorang Indians of 1922 and 1923. Jim Thorpe (middle, back row) was the player-coach.*

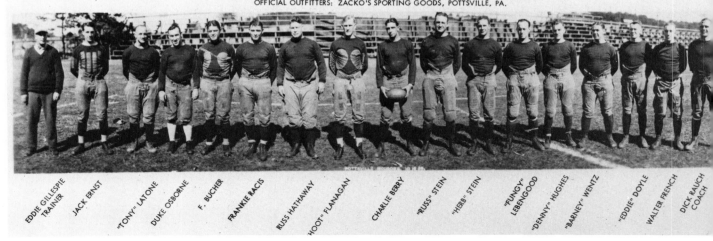

OFFICIAL PHOTO
POTTSVILLE MAROON FOOTBALL TEAM - 1925
NATIONAL LEAGUE CHAMPIONS - 1925. DEFEATED THE CHICAGO CARDINALS, AT CHICAGO DECEMBER 6, 1925 - 21 to 7.
WORLD CHAMPIONS - 1925. DEFEATED THE "FOUR HORSEMEN AND SEVEN MULES" OF NOTRE DAME, AT SHIBE PARK, PHILADELPHIA, PA.
DECEMBER 12, 1925 - 9 to 7. THE FIRST "ALL STAR" GAME PLAYED IN THIS COUNTRY.
OFFICIAL OUTFITTERS: ZACKO'S SPORTING GOODS, POTTSVILLE, PA.

EDDIE GILLESPIE TRAINER — JACK ERNST — "TONY" LATONE — DUKE OSBORNE — F. BUCHER — FRANKIE RACIS — RUSS HATHAWAY — "HOOT" FLANAGAN — CHARLIE BERRY — "RUSS" STEIN — "HERB" STEIN — "FUNGY" LEBENGOOD — "DENNY" HUGHES — "BARNEY" WENTZ — "EDDIE" DOYLE — WALTER FRENCH — DICK RAUCH COACH

Top: *The 1925 Pottsville Maroons team that compiled an excellent record and for many years claimed that it had actually won the NFL championship. The title was subsequently withdrawn by executive action of the league commissioner Joe Carr. Latest information uncovered after lengthy research proves that the Pottsville team actually never won a championship and that the league had acted correctly in awarding the 1925 championship to the Chicago Cardinals. Above and right: Jim Thorpe was the most famous Indian athlete to play pro football, but he has to share some distinction with another outstanding Indian running back, Joe Guyon. Like Thorpe, Guyon is a member of the Pro Football Hall of Fame.*

superior to Pottsville's 10-2 mark in the permanent standings.

Pottsville dropped out of the NFL after the 1928 season, but the controversy continued to rage. As late as 1962, a delegation of Pottsville supporters petitioned at an NFL owners' meeting for official recognition of their 1925 championship claim. The motion was turned down, but, undaunted, the Maroons' fans fashioned a championship trophy that consisted of a seemingly silver-colored, life-sized football made from a piece of solid anthracite coal. That unique trophy was offered and accepted eagerly at the Hall of Fame, whose first director, Dick McCann, solidly endorsed the Pottsville case of the "stolen championship." For almost 20 years, the Hall accepted the Pottsville version of what had occurred. But in 1981, new studies were completed that revealed evidence that should bring a permanent end to the controversy. Working in close harmony with the Hall of Fame's research department, the Professional Football Researchers Association accumulated information that underscored the fact that Pottsville never actually had a championship to lose in the first place.

The 1925 season had not been a successful year attendance-wise in the NFL, but Red Grange's arrival in Chicago on Thanksgiving Day for the Bears-Cardinals clash had immediately changed the outlook for the entire league. More than thirty-six thousand people—at the time the largest crowd ever to see a pro football game—turned out on a cold day to watch Grange in action. Fans continued to turn out in record numbers as Grange and the Bears took their show on the road. Chris O'Brien, the Cardinals' owner, had an outstanding team, but had not done well at the gate. With the Bears and Grange out of town early in December, he sensed that a game with the Pottsville Maroons— billed as "the NFL championship showdown"— would draw a large crowd. The matchup was logical, and the publicity in advance of the game was excellent, except for one small detail—the regular season had not ended. That meant that the game against the Maroons was nothing more than a game to decide the league leadership that particular week.

A year earlier, the NFL had experienced a similar situation when the Chicago Bears had challenged and defeated the league-leading Cleveland Bulldogs. That game had been played in early December, but in 1924, league rules stated that the regular season would end no later than November 30. Carr, upholding the league rules, voided the Bears-Bulldogs game and awarded the championship to Cleveland. In 1925, partially to avoid a similar problem, the NFL's regular season was extended to December 20. Chicago and Pottsville met on December 6. Believing that he had a chance to schedule the Bears and Grange again on December 20, particularly if the Cardinals had the best record in the league, O'Brien hastily scheduled two additional games, one with Milwaukee on December 10 and the other with Hammond on December 12. The Pottsville contention that Carr ordered the Cardinals to play these games after he voided the Pottsville championship cannot in any way be substantiated. Actually, the Pottsville-Notre Dame game was played the same day the Cardinals played Hammond. The two games O'Brien added had nothing to do with the Pottsville situation; the decision was based solely on his desire to schedule another game in which Grange would appear. When Grange was injured the following week, O'Brien did not even try to line up another game with the Bears.

Much of the Pottsville enthusiasm following the game against the Cardinals can be attributed to the comparatively low regard in which many NFL teams held Pottsville throughout most of the season. The Maroons played most of their home games on Sunday after their opponents had played Frankford the day before, fostering the suspicion that Pottsville was beating tired teams. But once the Maroons knocked off the Cardinals, they earned instant respect throughout the league. In this state of euphoria, Pottsville's manager, Dr. J. G. Striegel, scheduled the Notre Dame game. He clearly violated NFL rules in doing that. Protecting a home territory was one of the main reasons teams sought to join the NFL, and Shibe Park definitely was within Frankford's territorial limits. In fact, the Yellowjackets had an NFL game with Cleveland scheduled across town in Philadelphia the same day the Maroons played the Notre Dame All-Stars. Frankford did protest although there was no need to do so. As soon as Carr heard about the situation, he notified the Pottsville management that he would step in and act if they persisted with their plans. Newspaper accounts of the day prove conclusively that, in advance of the game, Carr spelled out the penalties he was considering.

The day the game was played, Carr wired Striegel to inform him that the Maroons had been fined $500, had been suspended from all rights—including the right to compete for the championship— and had had their franchise forfeited. The Providence team, scheduled to play Pottsville the next day, was ordered to find another opponent.

Without question, O'Brien's billing of the December 6 game between the Cardinals and Maroons as a championship game did much to confuse the issue. So, too, did his hasty scheduling of the two extra games the following week. The fact that the Maroons played again in the NFL in 1926 also made it easy to forget that the Pottsville franchise had been revoked following the Notre Dame game. By 1926, the NFL was locked in a serious conflict with the upstart AFL and one team, the Rock Island Independents, already had bolted the NFL for the new league. Pottsville may have been in the NFL doghouse, but it did have an excellent team. Carr recognized the folly of letting the Maroons defect to the AFL, so he supported the team's readmittance. The Maroons' exile had lasted just two days short of seven months. However, none of this stopped the Maroons from wearing jackets— one of which is on display at the Hall of Fame— with the words *World Champions 1925* emblazoned on the back.

The National Football League that Pottsville reentered in 1926 was, just like the league the Maroons had left late in 1925, still preoccupied with improving attendance in any way possible. But 1926 brought an additional problem—competition from the American Football League that was being formed around Red Grange, the box-office sensation who had so buoyed NFL hopes late in the 1925 campaign. The NFL desperately needed a superstar to create excitement of its own. On the West Coast, a 6-foot 1-inch, 205-pound fullback named Ernie Nevers was winning acclaim as an 11-letter man at Stanford. He excelled in basketball, but gained national attention for his sensational play in the 1925 Rose Bowl game against Notre Dame. Playing on what amounted to two broken ankles, Nevers still rushed for 114 yards and was named the game's Most Valuable Player, even though Notre Dame won 27-10. After the game, the Stanford coach, Glenn "Pop" Warner, who had also coached Jim Thorpe at Carlisle, compared the two: "Nevers can do everything Thorpe can and he always tries harder. Ernie gives sixty minutes of himself every game." The Willow River, Minnesota, native was in tremendous demand when he finished at Stanford. He signed both pro basketball and pro baseball contracts and immediately started pitching for the St. Louis Browns. A year later, he was destined to throw 2 home run pitches to Babe Ruth during his historic 60-home run season.

The knowledge that Nevers was a prime signing target of the NFL was not at all surprising, particularly in view of Grange's move to the AFL. But the fact that the man destined to sign him was the owner of one of the league's financially destitute franchises was startling. Nevers' pursuer was 23-year old Oluf "Ole" Haugsrud, who had joined with his partner, Dewey Scanlon, in buying the

NFL's Duluth franchise for one dollar several months earlier. Haugsrud had served the Duluth Kelleys' team in a business capacity since its inception in 1922. When financial losses mounted and the original owners wanted out, Haugsrud handled the team's business matters and Scanlon became the coach. To help reduce the club's debts, Haugsrud sold several of the team's better players. In spite of this, Haugsrud set out to sign Nevers. The two had been friends since boyhood, and Nevers agreed to play with Duluth providing Haugsrud would match the offer being extended by C. C. "Cash and Carry" Pyle of the rival AFL. With George Halas of the Chicago Bears and Tim Mara of the New York Giants offering their endorsement, Haugsrud agreed. Nevers was to get $15,000 and a 25 percent share of the gate.

When other Duluth players heard of Nevers' signing, they enthusiastically appreciated what he could do for the team and refused to quibble over their own salaries. They asked Haugsrud if he thought a scale of $50 if they lost, $60 for a tie, and $75 for a win would be fair. He readily agreed, and that was that. Eventually, Duluth came out $4,000 ahead for the year, but there were times during the long season when the club fell behind in its salary payments. Even then, the players patiently waited until Haugsrud had the necessary funds.

For the Duluth team to get its money back on the Nevers investment, it became necessary literally to put the show "on the road." The NFL readily endorsed the plan because it would give more fans around the league a chance to see Nevers in action. Haugsrud lined up an ambitious 29-game schedule, 13 of them regular-season NFL games and the remainder exhibitions. The schedule was arranged so that Duluth played all the teams in one geographic area before moving on to a different part of the country. Even with that, the Duluth players were faced with the most extensive away-from-home schedule in organized sports history. They played a home game against the NFL's other road team, the Kansas City Cowboys, in September and then left on a 17,000-mile journey that would take them from the Atlantic to the Pacific and would not end until January. During one stretch, they played five games in eight days.

When a local clothier provided the squad with big white mackinaws with an igloo on the back and the lettering ERNIE NEVERS ESKIMOS, Haugsrud instantly adopted that tag as the new team nickname. Those great coats, along with the team's equipment trunk and Nevers' complete uniform, are now on display in one of the Hall of Fame's major exhibitions.

Left: Ernie Nevers played only five years but still was elected to the Pro Football Hall of Fame. Because he played almost every minute of every game, many of his strongest supporters claimed he had actually played 10 years of pro football. Above: Red Grange and his agent C. C. ("Cash and Carry") Pyle, became a famous pair in 1925 when Grange, with Pyle's guidance, signed a lucrative contract to play pro football with the Chicago Bears.

Ole Haugsrud and Dewey Scanlon became National Football League owners in 1926 when they purchased the Duluth Eskimos for $1.00. The contract sealing the deal is pictured at right.

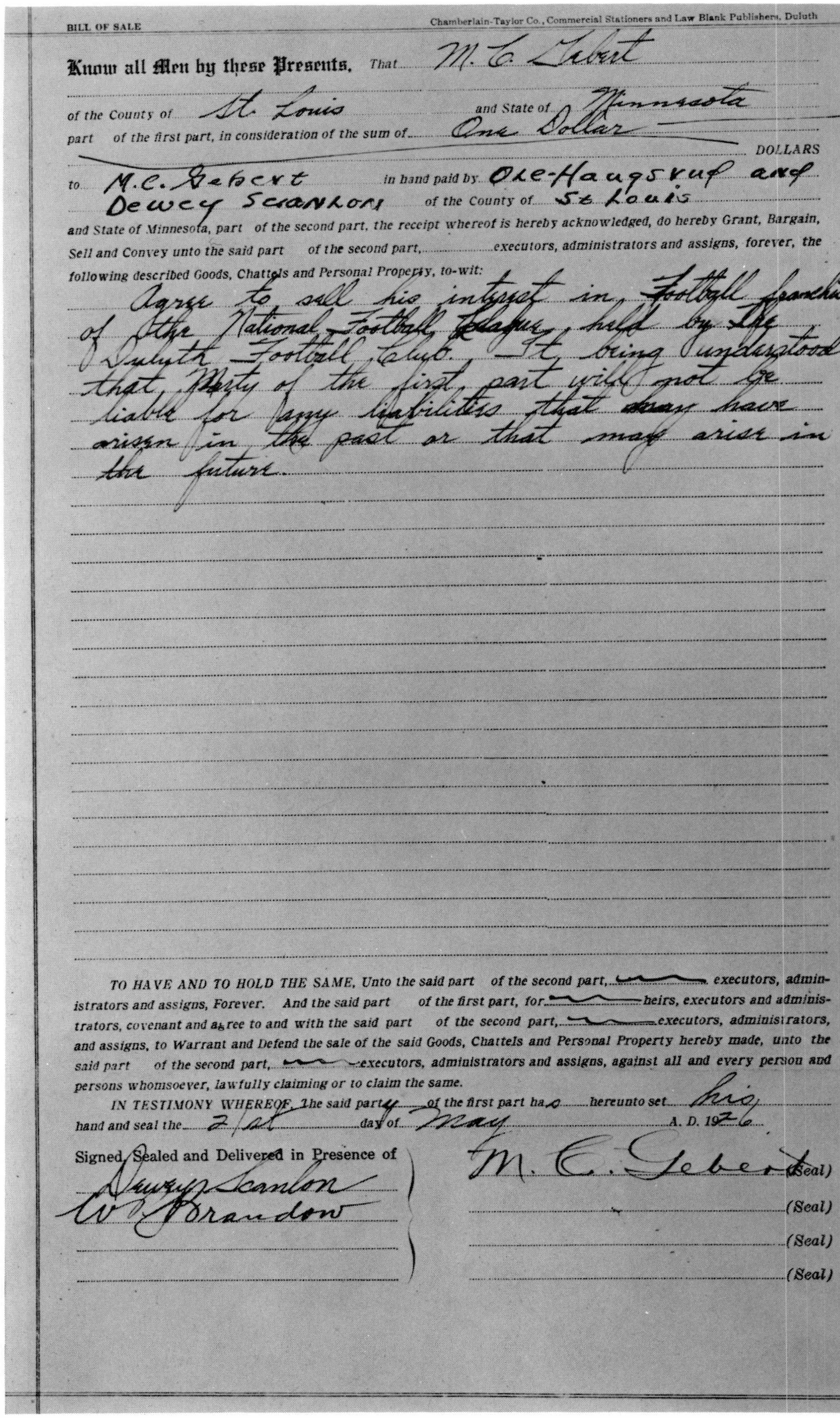

BILL OF SALE   Chamberlain-Taylor Co., Commercial Stationers and Law Blank Publishers, Duluth

Know all Men by these Presents, That _M. C. Gebert_

of the County of _St. Louis_ and State of _Minnesota_
part of the first part, in consideration of the sum of _One Dollar_
_____ DOLLARS

to _M. C. Gebert_ in hand paid by _Ole Haugsrud and Dewey Scanlon_ of the County of _St. Louis_

and State of Minnesota, part of the second part, the receipt whereof is hereby acknowledged, do hereby Grant, Bargain,
Sell and Convey unto the said part of the second part,_____ executors, administrators and assigns, forever, the
following described Goods, Chattels and Personal Property, to-wit:

Agree to sell his interest in Football franchise of the National Football League, held by the Duluth Football Club. It being understood that Party of the first part will not be liable for any liabilities that may have arisen in the past or that may arise in the future.

TO HAVE AND TO HOLD THE SAME, Unto the said part of the second part,_____ executors, administrators and assigns, Forever. And the said part of the first part, for_____ heirs, executors and administrators, covenant and agree to and with the said part of the second part,_____ executors, administrators,
and assigns, to Warrant and Defend the sale of the said Goods, Chattels and Personal Property hereby made, unto the
said part of the second part,_____ executors, administrators and assigns, against all and every person and
persons whomsoever, lawfully claiming or to claim the same.

IN TESTIMONY WHEREOF, the said part of the first part ha_s_ hereunto set _his_
hand and seal the _21st_ day of _May_ A. D. 19_2 6_.

Signed, Sealed and Delivered in Presence of

Dewey Scanlon
W. Brandow

M. C. Gebert (Seal)
_____ (Seal)
_____ (Seal)
_____ (Seal)

62

While the Oorang Indians may not have been overzealous in their football pursuits, the Eskimos certainly were. Overall, they won 19 games, lost 7, and tied 3. In league play, they finished with a 6-5-2 record and in eighth place in the 22-team NFL. Through most of the season, the Eskimos survived with only a 13-man squad. Sometimes, to avoid embarrassment, Haugsrud and Scanlon would also suit up and work out with the squad. That tactic backfired on Haugsrud once when, with the Eskimos safely ahead of St. Louis by a 52-0 score, Nevers called him in from the bench to try a dropkick. Haugsrud had been practicing the dropkick in pregame workouts, and so he assumed that Nevers merely intended to give him the thrill of trying one in game action. But when it was time for the snap from center, the Duluth line opened up and let a horde of St. Louis players swarm over Haugsrud and smash him to the ground. Haugsrud understood the joke, but got the last laugh. When, after the game the Eskimos came to him for their checks, he feigned a broken hand. "Sorry, boys," he explained. "But that dropkick play of yours backfired. Now I can't sign the checks."

The 1928 Providence Steam Roller (top) was the last team not currently in the NFL to win the league championship. Their home games were played at a bicycle-racing rink (above). Particularly at the corners of the field, the fans were literally seated on top of the action.

A big back by 1926 standards, Nevers did everything for the Eskimos. He did most of the ball carrying and passing and all of the placekicking and punting. He returned punts and kickoffs, called signals, played defense, and eventually became the player-coach. Of a possible 1,740 minutes in the season. Nevers played all but 26. In one game against Milwaukee, when doctors ordered him not to play, the frustrated Nevers inserted himself into the lineup just before halftime. He promptly threw a 62-yard bomb to end Joe Rooney and then kicked the extra point that gave Duluth a 7-6 victory.

If Nevers had a weakness, it was his refusal to alter his game plan even when opposition defenses were stacked heavily against him. Those who played with him admitted that this stubbornness may have cost him touchdowns on several occasions. Still there were times when Nevers prevailed in spite of the stacked opposition. Playing against the New York Giants in 1926, he carried 9 straight times and ended a personal 55-yard march by scoring a touchdown against one of the league's top defensive teams.

Nevers was with Duluth again in 1927, but was forced to sit out the entire 1928 campaign with a broken transverse process. When he was ready to return to action in 1929, the Duluth team had been sold, and he wound up playing as the field captain of the Chicago Cardinals. The talent-thin Cardinals struggled through a 6-6-1 season, but Nevers achieved lasting personal recognition when he scored 40 points in the Cardinals' Thanksgiving Day triumph over the crosstown-rival Bears. His outstanding feat still stands as an NFL single-game scoring record. Since he had scored all 19 of his team's points in a shutout of the Dayton Triangles a week earlier, his 2-game total of 59 consecutive points is one of sport's most remarkable achievements.

Nevers retired following the 1931 season, after only five active years in the NFL, the shortest tenure of any Hall of Fame member. Yet longevity never was an issue when the Hall's board of selectors named him to the charter class in 1963. Some say he really played ten years of pro football in five seasons. There is no question that his experience with the Duluth Eskimos was one of history's truly magnificent iron-man feats. For providing the NFL with a true superstar when it needed one the most, Nevers realized financial rewards far beyond his fondest expectations. But, as he reported later, he did make one major mistake. "I forgot," he said, "to ask how long the season would be."

The NFL of the twenties had run the gamut of out-of-the-ordinary and never-to-be-repeated circumstances. In the Oorang Indians, the league had witnessed history's only advertising gimmick compile a 4-16 won-lost record over a two-year span. The Pottsville Maroons became the only team ever to scream "foul" over a stolen championship that never existed in the first place. And the Duluth Eskimos became the first team to find more followers on the road than at home, simply because they never played at home. It was left to the Providence Steam Roller to add two more firsts to the list.

Providence was the first team to omit the traditional "s" at the end of its nickname and the only team ever to call a bicycle-racing stadium home. No one is certain why the Providence team, which was organized as an independent in 1916 and first joined the NFL in 1925, was called the Steam Roller rather than the Steam Rollers. A Providence sports editor told Hall of Fame researchers in the 1970's, "We thoroughly checked our files and could never find a reason for the name. When the reporter was referring to the team as a unit, he would write 'the Providence Steam Roller.' But when he spoke of team members in a group, he would refer to them as 'Steam Rollers.' "

On the other hand, how the Steam Roller acquired its home playing field is well documented. One of the team's co-owners, sports promoter Pete Laudati, built the Cyclodrome in 1925, about the same time the Steam Roller joined the NFL. The Cyclodrome, pictured in the Hall of Fame, seated 10,000 and was designed specifically for bicycle racing. The wooden track was banked steeply around the ends but was comparatively flat on the straightaways. If you overlooked several obvious inadequacies, a football field could just be squeezed inside the track. One problem, however, was that one end zone was limited to five yards in depth because the banked track cut across it. On the sidelines along the racing straightaways, the stands were so close that players being tackled often were bounced into the seats.

The dressing-room situation was particularly bothersome. The home quarters consisted of two showers in a room designed to accomodate a handful of bicycle racers. The visitors had absolutely no dressing rooms and were forced to suit up at their hotel or on the train before coming to the Cyclodrome. Yet from a spectator's viewpoint, all seats were close to the action and priced right at $2, $1.50, and $1.

On the field, the 1928 Steam Roller had few inadequacies. The squad was led by player-coach Jimmy Conzelman, one of the NFL's most colorful and talented performers in the early years. A 6-foot, 180-pound quarterback, Conzelman had seen service for the Decatur Staleys, Rock Island

DO YOU REMEMBER?

Above left: *Red Grange (in action at Illinois) shocked the sports world by turning pro immediately after his final game with the Illini in 1925. The historic signing (left) took place with Chicago Bears co-owners Edward Sternaman and George Halas, and Grange's agent, C.C. Pyle in attendance.*

ST...AMAN   GEORGE HALAS   HAROLD RED GRANGE   C.C. PYLE

...D" SIGNS HIS FIRST PRO CONTRACT, NOVEMBER 1925.

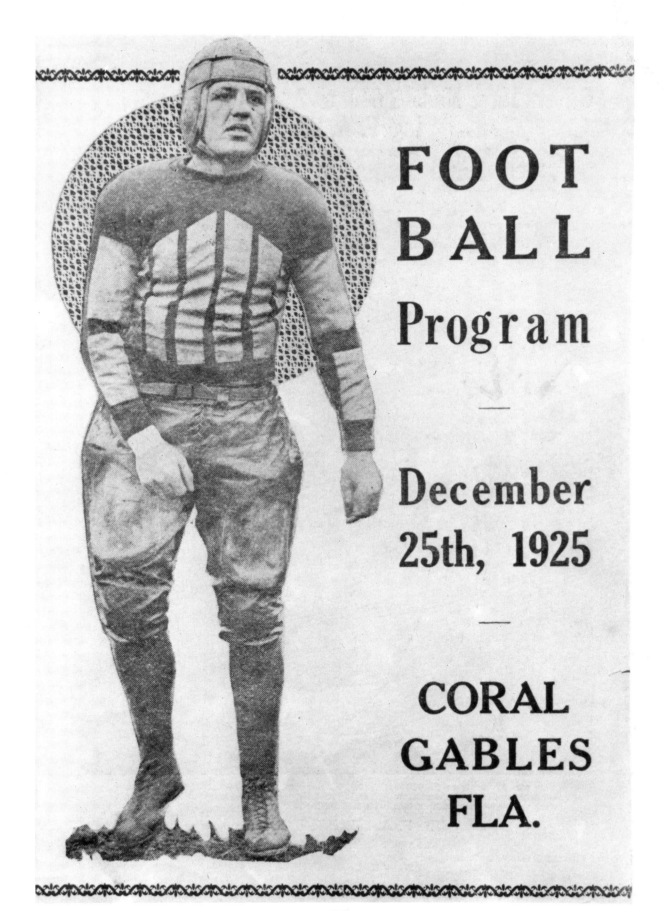

FOOT BALL Program

December 25th, 1925

CORAL GABLES FLA.

Independents, Milwaukee Badgers, and Detroit Panthers before joining the Steam Roller in 1927. There he was paid $292 a game for his dual responsibilities, which included recruiting a collection of some of the most talented players of the late 1920's. The number-one Steam Roller star was fullback George "Wildcat" Wilson, who appropriately also topped the team salary scale at $375 a game. The entire 1928 squad first met at the Cyclodrome on September 17, then played a practice game on September 23 in preparation for the league opener against the New York Yankees on September 30.

Most of the 1928 home games drew capacity crowds of approximately 10,500. A 30-piece band, possibly the first team band in the NFL, sat in the stands and played during the games. Providence won the opener against the Yankees, 20-7, and then lost the second week to the Frankford Yellowjackets, 10-6, a defeat that turned out to be the Steam Roller's only loss. When the team traveled to New York for a rematch with the Yankees, many fans followed the team to Yankee Stadium on the Fall River Line boat, waving Steam Roller pennants similar to the one that hangs in the Hall of Fame. Hundreds more stayed in Providence and paid 50 cents to get into either the Arcadia Ballroom or the Empire Theater to listen to play-by-play reports relayed to Providence by Western Union. The Steam Roller beat the Yankees that day, but lost Conzelman with a knee injury so severe he never played again.

The Steam Roller continued to win each week and was locked in a tight struggle with the Yellowjackets as the season progressed into mid-November. On the showdown weekend—Saturday, November 17, and Sunday, November 18—the Yellowjackets and Steam Roller were scheduled for home-and-home duels. While playing two games on one weekend for a pair of league leaders would be a scheduling impossibility today, it was not particularly rare for teams of that era to play two games on a single weekend. It was unusual, however, for such a match up to occur between the NFL's top two contenders.

The teams met first on Saturday in Frankford, a Philadelphia suburb, and battled to a 6-6 tie. Both squads then boarded a midnight sleeper train to Providence for the Sunday contest, in which Providence squeezed out a 6-0 victory. That was all the edge the Steam Roller needed. They won their next two games against the 1927 champion New York Giants and the Pottsville Maroons, then headed into the final game against the Green Bay Packers, needing a victory or a tie to earn the NFL crown. The Steam Roller got a 7-7 tie and, with it,

Above: *Red Grange was a dynamic whirling dervish as a ball-carrier, and he could do everything there was to do on a football field—and do it well.* Opposite: *Shortly after the 1925 National Football League season was completed, Grange and the Bears took off on an extensive barnstorming tour that attracted huge crowds coast to coast. For the first time, the play-for-pay game was definitely in the public eye.*

the 1928 championship. Thus Providence became the last of the small-city teams, except for Green Bay, to win an NFL title. Putting it in another perspective, the Steam Roller was the last team not currently in the NFL to win a championship.

Unlike what is true of today's champions, there were no large bonus checks awaiting the Steam Roller players after their final game. All they received monetarily were their final game checks. But a happy city did stage a victory banquet and every Steam Roller received a gold watch. Then there was the unveiling of the championship pennant, a relic that hangs on public view at the Hall of Fame. A variety of speakers appeared before the microphone, but Rhode Island Attorney General Charles P. Sisson contributed some particularly farsighted comments. "I've seen the Roller play and talked with other men who have seen them in action and I want to say in all seriousness that, in my opinion, professional football as played by the Steam Roller is really better football than we see on our college gridirons. . . . I think the day is coming when pro football, if it follows the example set by the Roller, will take its place with baseball as the great national professional sport." While Sisson's bold prophecy did not hold true for the Steam Roller—the team dropped out of the NFL after the 1931 season—his remarks nevertheless were a remarkable projection of pro football and its future.

The Oorang, Pottsville, Duluth, and Providence accounts accurately capture the Tempestuous Twenties atmosphere that surrounded the infant NFL. But, while their stories are entertaining, they had little bearing on the eventual success of pro football. Two things—actually two people—provided pro football with the impetus it needed in 1925, combining to make that season possibly the most important in the league's long history. First, Tim Mara paid $500 for an NFL franchise in New York City, giving the league a badly needed berth in the nation's largest city and, with it, the national publicity it had craved for so long. Then Harold "Red" Grange came along toward the end of the season and gave the sport an unmatched drawing card. Both were commodities the young and struggling league desperately needed. Even though they played widely divergent roles in the growth of pro football, Mara and Grange stood on some common ground. Both were critical to the ultimate success of the NFL. Both arrived the same year. And, while Mara was already well off financially when he bought the Giants, Grange, fresh out of college when he joined the Chicago Bears, quickly became a wealthy man.

At first, their paths were closely intertwined.

In early December, Grange's appearance in New York attracted more than 70,000 fans to the Polo Grounds and convinced Mara that pro football did have a future in the nation's largest city. It also helped Mara erase a large operating deficit and finish his first NFL season in the black. Just a few months later, however, Mara and Grange were antagonists in pro football's first interleague war.

Grange and his agent, C. C. Pyle, organized the rival American Football League after they were refused an NFL franchise in New York. The new league sparked a costly battle in which Mara and his New York Giants were destined to suffer. Mara had arrived on the NFL scene about seven months ahead of Grange. In April 1925, Joe Carr tried to persuade Billy Gibson, a fight manager, to purchase a New York franchise. Gibson wasn't interested, but he recommended his friend, Mara. When Mara learned the asking price for a franchise would be only $500, he quickly agreed. "Hell, a New York franchise in anything should be worth five hundred dollars," he snapped. "I'll take it."

A friend of Carr's, Dr. Harry March, was at the meeting between Carr and Mara, and when Mara, who knew nothing about football, found that March did, he immediately hired him as the club secretary. March quickly went to work. He hired a "name" coach, Bob Folwell, from the US Naval Academy, and introduced him to the press at a festive cocktail party, undoubtedly the first such press introduction in NFL history. A formal invitation to that party can be seen at the Hall of Fame.

March and Folwell lined up several genuine all-America choices for the new team and even enlisted the aging and over-the-hill Jim Thorpe on a half-game basis. March figured the fabulous Indian star would be a good drawing card for new fans in New York. He was wrong. Big-time college football—Yale, Harvard, Princeton, Columbia, and all the rest—was flourishing in New York in the mid-1920's and it captured all the headlines the Giants had expected. Even though the Giants finished with an 8-4 record, fourth best in a 20-team league, attendance was so poor that, with one game left in the regular season, Mara's losses had reached the $40,000 level.

Mara, however, was not about to surrender and decided that what the Giants needed was a superstar—Red Grange. He headed west to contact the Galloping Ghost, who was nearing the end of his University of Illinois career. But Mara found that George Halas of the Chicago Bears had beaten him to the punch. Halas came into the picture after Pyle, a brash, imaginative promoter and a theater owner in Champaign, Illinois, asked Grange about playing pro football when his college career

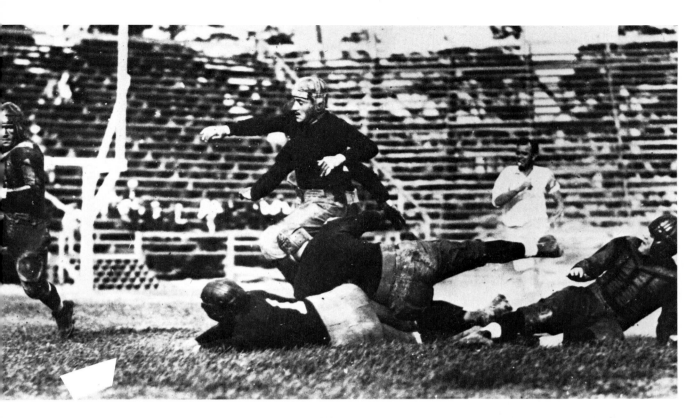

Top: Red Grange breaks into the open for big yardage during one of the 17 games he and the Chicago Bears played on their tour following the 1925 season. Above: The starting lineup of the 1925 New York Giants. Note that Jim Thorpe, who played only briefly for the Giants, is in the starting backfield (second from left). He had been signed as a box office draw for the new franchise.

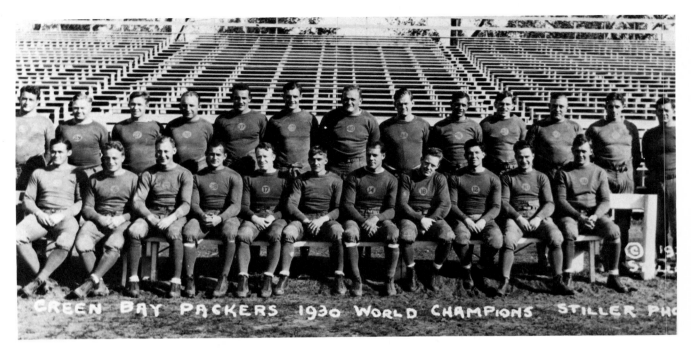

GREEN BAY PACKERS 1930 WORLD CHAMPIONS STILLER PH[...]

ended. Grange, who had worked his way through college by carrying ice during the summers in his hometown of Wheaton, Illinois, expressed interest in playing for pay, and Pyle contacted Halas. The ice tongs that Grange used on his summer job are now exhibited at the Hall of Fame as a memento of his arrival on the NFL stage.

With several weeks still remaining in the college season, rumors began surfacing, indicating Grange was prepared to sign a pro football contract—or had already done so. Since the college set felt the professionals were sordid fellows, protests came quickly. "He is a living legend now," wrote Irving Vaughan in the Chicago *News*. "Why go and sully it?" "I'd be glad to see Grange do anything else except play professional football," said Fielding Yost, Michigan's athletic director. Even Grange's own coach, Bob Zuppke, reacted adversely. "I want to tell you to keep away from the professionals," Zup told him. "Football just isn't a game to be played for money."

"You get paid for coaching, Zup," Grange countered. "Why should it be so wrong for me to get paid for playing?"

In his last college game against Ohio State, Grange rushed for 192 yards, threw for a touchdown, and intercepted a pass to preserve a 14-9 victory for the Illini. In the locker room after the game, he announced his intention to sign a contract with the Bears.

Ten days later, on Thanksgiving Day, he was in the Bears' lineup against the Cardinals, the eventual league champions. The record crowd of 36,000 booed lustily as the Cardinals' star, Paddy Driscoll,

continually punted away from the fleet-footed Grange and the game ended in a scoreless tie. Questioned about his tactics after the game, Driscoll's answer was matter-of-fact. "If it came down to a matter of Grange or Driscoll looking bad, I decided it wasn't going to be Driscoll," he said. "Punting to Grange is like grooving a pitch to Babe Ruth."

Driscoll pondered the situation further when he talked with his wife after the game. "It's really too bad they booed Grange," he said. "That kid never really had a chance today."

"They were booing all right," his wife countered, "but they weren't booing Grange. They were booing you for being afraid to punt to him."

An unprecedented barnstorming tour in which the Bears played 7 games in 11 days followed. Everywhere large crowds turned out to see Grange. Besides the obvious financial advantages, the tour helped dispel many of the prejudices that existed against pro football. Countless new fans were attracted to the sport. Recognizing that he had control of the hottest property in football, Pyle, who had become known as "Cash and Carry" Pyle because of his tough negotiating, notified the Bears that Grange would play for them again in 1926 only if he received a five-figure salary and one-third ownership of the team. The Bears' co-owners, Halas and Dutch Sternaman, balked. Undaunted, Pyle then petitioned for a second NFL franchise in New York. He even signed a lease for Yankee Stadium, in close proximity to the Giants' home at the Polo Grounds. Mara rejected the "second team in New York" petition, but did agree to go

Opposite: *Tim Mara bought the New York Giants franchise and gave the NFL a team it desperately needed in the nation's largest city.* Above: *In 1930, the talent-laden Green Bay Packers won their second of three straight NFL titles.*

along with a team in Brooklyn. But Pyle was adamant: "Either we get an NFL team in Yankee Stadium or we start a new league."

Mara and the other NFL owners weren't convinced Pyle and Grange would follow through on their threat. "I don't think Pyle will be foolish enough to try it," the Giants' owner said, "but I have already offered to bet Grange a hundred thousand dollars that if we have a go at each other, neither of us will make a nickel." Pyle, however, was convinced he could build an entire league around one flagship team and a superstar—the New York Yankees and Grange.

The Giants were a principal target and suffered a number of losses. Their head coach, Folwell, left to join the AFL's Philadelphia Quakers, as did their star tackle, Century Milstead. To keep more players from jumping, Mara upped the salaries of all his players by $50 a game. He also signed many players to full-season contracts and then sat back to lose the money he knew he would. The only question was how much. Besides luring a number of NFL players into his new league, "Cash and Carry" even hired a commissioner—politician and former Princeton athlete Bill Edwards—to administer his nine-team league. Edwards' salary was set at $25,000, compared to the $2,500 Carr was earning as NFL president.

The Giants were staggered by a poor start on the field and atrocious weather. But the same bad weather also hurt the Yankees and the other AFL teams on the East Coast. Mara lost heavily, but the AFL teams lost even more. One by one, they began to fold.

With victory now assured, Mara challenged the Yankees to meet his Giants on the playing field. Pyle, who had once relished such a game, refused to play. Mara then turned his challenge to the AFL champion Quakers, and they accepted. In the first interleague postseason showdown, the seventh-place Giants of the NFL handled the AFL's best with ease, 31-0. The war was over. As a peace concession, the Yankees were granted an NFL franchise for 1927, but no other AFL team survived. However, Grange was severely injured midway through the 1927 season and never regained his full effectiveness. By his own admission, he was only a mediocre runner after that, but he did develop into one of the league's better defensive backs. Grange sat out the entire 1928 season and then returned to the Bears in 1929. He remained in Chicago until he retired in 1934. The Giants, meanwhile, developed into one of the NFL's premier franchises. The 1927 team won the first of its many division and league championships captured over the years. In an 11-1-1 season, the New Yorkers allowed only 20 points, a record that still stands.

Mara, who was born on the Lower East Side of New York in 1887, had known hard times when he was a youngster, and so his sympathies were easily aroused by those in distress. After the stock market crash of 1929 that provoked the Great Depression, those in distress outnumbered those who weren't. One day the debonair mayor of the city, Jimmy Walker, phoned Mara and asked, "Tim, would you be willing to schedule a charity game and turn over the receipts to the unemployment relief fund?"

"You name the team and we'll play them," Mara unhesitatingly responded.

It was decided that the best possible draw in New York would be a team of former Notre Dame stars including the legendary Four Horsemen. The well-conditioned, finely tuned Giants easily downed the Notre Dame stars, 21-0, but the New York City Unemployment Fund was the big winner. After the game, Mara turned over a check for $115,153 to Mayor Walker. That check is one of several mementoes from pro football's first big charity game on display at the Hall. "Cash and Carry" Pyle, even though he threatened the NFL in forming the rival AFL, nevertheless also is remembered in the Hall of Fame. As always he is linked with Grange—in a picture of the two together.

As the National Football League finished its first decade and turned into the 1930's, the Green Bay Packers emerged as a dominant team by winning successive championships in 1929, 1930,

71

and 1931. Except for the same Packers more than thirty years later in 1965, 1966, and 1967, that feat has never been equaled. And in spite of a strange set of circumstances that brought about a bizarre finish to an already unusual season, the Packers easily could have won—and almost did win—a fourth consecutive title in 1932. As it turned out, the Chicago Bears and Portsmouth Spartans met in the NFL's first officially recognized championship game. The events surrounding that game, played indoors on a midget-sized field, led to sweeping rules changes that almost immediately transformed pro football into a far more pleasing spectator sport.

When the 1932 campaign started, no one would have believed the NFL was on the verge of a major evolutionary breakthrough. In many ways, the 1932 season was a drab one—even the eventual champion Bears failed to score a single point in their first four games. But an exciting three-way struggle for first place did develop among the Packers, the Bears, and the Spartans, who were playing only their third season in the league. Featuring a T-formation offense instituted by Ralph Jones, the Bears had finished third behind the Packers each of the previous two years. The Spartans, led by their all-time great quarterback Earl "Dutch" Clark, had lost out to the Packers by a single game

in 1931. Green Bay's record during its three-year string of championships was 34-5-2. Led by a number of stars who are now enshrined in the Hall of Fame—Arnie Herber, Johnny "Blood" McNally, Clarke Hinkle, Cal Hubbard, and Mike Michalske— the Packers ran up a 10-1-1 record their first 12 games in 1932. Portsmouth, a team from the southern Ohio river town, had only one blemish on its record—a 15-10 loss to the Packers, although the Spartans did tie four games. The Bears opened the season with three consecutive scoreless ties, then lost to the Packers, 2-0. It was hard for Chicago fans to imagine there would be much to cheer about in 1932. The Bears, however, did not lose again, although they were tied three more times.

The Packers, with wins over the Bears and the Spartans early in the year, led until the final two games. But they couldn't hold on. First Portsmouth derailed the Packers with a 19-0 upset, and then the Bears belted their arch rivals, 9-0. That left the Packers with a 10-3-1 mark (.769), while both the Bears (6-1-6) and the Spartans (6-1-4) wound up with .857 percentages. Had ties counted half wins and half losses as they do today, the Packers would have clinched a fourth consecutive title. However, Chicago and Portsmouth officials agreed to a postseason showdown that would determine the league championship. The championship game first was

Opposite top and bottom: *Fan enthusiasm, always a trademark of the Green Bay Packers, is what has enabled the Packers to survive as the representative of the only small city in the big-city NFL.* Above: *When the stands at Hagemeister Park in the early 1920s proved to be inadequate for the thousands of partisans, a new City Stadium was built nearby to accomodate even larger crowds.*

scheduled for Wrigley Field in Chicago, but, when the weather bureau promised more of the snow and bitter cold temperatures that had plagued the Windy City for more than a week, the game was moved indoors to Chicago Stadium.

The change of sites proved to be a tremendous break for the capacity crowd of 11,198 that turned out for the unique event. Besides the obvious temperature improvement, the indoor site enabled Chicago fans to see pro play close at hand for the first time. The impact of every vicious block and crackling tackle provided proof for anyone who doubted whether the pros did play for keeps. "It was the difference between sitting ringside at a heavyweight fight or in the last row of the upper deck," one sportswriter noted. "All the awful sounds of human beings smashing other human beings were right there and very real."

Field conditions were quite another thing. The field was only 80 yards long and 145 feet wide (standard width is 160 feet) and the sideline was cramped tight against the stands. The stadium's cement floor had to be covered with a mixture of dirt and sod that had been used for a Salvation Army circus that had just concluded its stay in the stadium. ("The stadium was a little too aromatic," a writer reported, "what with the horses and elephants that had traipsed around there a few days before the game.") Rather than try to continually shift the ball to maintain the ordinary scrimmage line to goal line distances of a regulation field, it was mutually agreed just to settle for an 80-yard field. Another special ground rule called for the ball to be moved ten yards inbounds after out-of-bounds plays.

Portsmouth was forced to play the game without Clark, its leading scorer and outstanding field general. He already had returned to his job as head basketball coach at Colorado School of Mines and could not obtain permission to take time off to play in the game. Because of Clark's absence, the Bears were heavily favored. Yet midway into the fourth quarter, the teams were still scoreless. Finally, the Bears' Dick Nesbitt intercepted a pass thrown by Ace Gutowsky and returned to the Portsmouth seven-yard line. On first down, Bronko Nagurski, already a legend in his third NFL season, ramrodded through center for six yards. Two more Nagurski smashes, however, were stopped cold, and it was fourth-and-one. In that situation the Spartans' defenders massed at the goal line to stop the expected fourth plunge by Nagurski. "I lined up as usual, four yards back," Nagurski explained after the game. "Red [Grange] went in motion. The ball came to me. I took a step or two forward as though to begin the plunge everyone expected. The

defenders converged . . . there was no way I could get through. I stopped. I moved back a couple of steps. Grange had gone around and was in the end zone, all by himself. I threw him a short pass."

"Actually, I was on my back," Grange said. "Someone had knocked me down. But I got the ball and hung on to it."

Portsmouth's coach, Potsy Clark, vehemently protested that Bronko hadn't been five yards behind the line of scrimmage when he passed, as the rules demanded. But the touchdown was allowed, and the Bears, adding a safety late in the game, won 9-0. It was the Bears' first championship since 1921, when they were known as the Staleys.

But this game's special significance went far beyond who played or who won or even that it was played indoors. Setting this game apart from all others is the fact it spawned fresh new thinking about pro football as a spectator sport. In the close and unfamiliar confines of Chicago Stadium, the unexciting brand of play in the NFL fostered by conservative rules was brought into clear focus. In 1932, Halas was president of the NFL rules committee and joined forces with George Preston Marshall, the owner of the new Boston franchise, who was deeply interested in improving the spectator appeal of pro football. The two quickly went to work and, finding many of their answers in the ground rules used in the indoor championship game, proposed three major new rules. All three were accepted at the February 1933 owners' meeting. The new rules provided (1) that the goalposts be moved from the back of the end zone to the goal line; (2) that the ball always be placed at least 15 yards inbounds at the start of every scrimmage play; and (3) that the forward pass be legalized if thrown anywhere behind the line of scrimmage. "We hoped the new rules would open up the game," Halas said years later. "I believe the record will show that we were right."

The records show just that. Field goal scoring increased dramatically in 1933, and tie games dropped from 20 in 1932 to half that many in 1933 and none at all in 1934. Total offense accumulations increased for virtually every team, and the number of shutouts was reduced substantially in the very next season. Later, there would be the specialists of the passing game—the Don Hutsons, the Sammy Baughs, the Sid Luckmans—and the carefully designed offenses that would open up the game even more.

All these progressions that helped to make pro football so appealing to the masses emanated from the framework established by the three landmark rules alterations enacted after the 1932 championship game. Finally, a fourth dramatic approach

was adopted in July 1933. Marshall had grasped the box-office appeal of matching two top teams for the championship even under bizarre conditions. So he pushed through a plan for dividing the NFL into two equal divisions, with the champions of each division meeting for the overall title. Again the anticipated results were immediate. Beginning with the first game between the New York Giants and the Chicago Bears in 1933, the NFL championship game soon evolved into an American sports classic.

Above left: An invitation to a meet-the-coach luncheon, a check to the New York Unemployment fund for $115,153., and a ticket to the Notre Dame exhibition game are early-day Giants souvenirs on display at the Hall. Above right: Bronko Nagurski (right) was feared by every NFL opponent for his battering-ram smashes through the line. He was equally effective as a blocker, as he is shown here escorting Joe Sternaman in a practice session.

*Sammy Baugh came out of Texas Christian University in
1937 to set the pro world on fire with his pinpoint passing
that would forever change the offensive concept of the game.*

Chapter 4

To Speed the Evolution

In the Pro Football Hall of Fame, the niches that make up the Enshrinement Galleries honoring the sport's immortals are situated in no particular order—not by alphabetical arrangement, not by year of enshrinement, not by team. The unique random placement was instituted by design: all members are considered equally deserving. But there has to be a beginning to everything, and the first niche the visitor sees belongs to George Stanley Halas, who served pro football for 64 seasons until his death in 1983.

For many years, George Halas was the sole surviving member of the small band of owners who met in Ralph Hay's automobile showroom in Canton in 1920 and formed the organization that became the National Football League. No executive of the Hall of Fame will admit, even unofficially, that Halas was considered pro football's number-one citizen, but it is obvious that his niche placement did not occur by accident.

Born February 2, 1895, Halas spent his college days at the University of Illinois, where he lettered in football, basketball, and baseball and found his life's direction in Coach Bob Zuppke's farewell remarks to the 1917 Illini football squad. "Good-bye makes no sense whatsoever," Zuppke said. "Just when all of you begin to know something about football after three years, I lose you. Football is the only sport that ends a man's career just when it should be beginning." Halas not only decided that there should be football after college for him but, because of the many avenues his career would take, did more than perhaps any other person to provide postgraduate opportunities for all who had the desire and the ability to continue. Halas was an outstanding end who, as a member of the Great Lakes Navy team that defeated a Marine team, was named Player of the Game in the 1919 Rose Bowl. After leaving the Navy, he went to work for the A. E. Staley Starch Company of Decatur, Illinois, which, in the fall of 1919, decided to sponsor a football team. Halas was asked to organize the team. A year later, the Decatur Staleys became a charter member of the new league.

In 1921, Halas himself purchased the Staleys for $5,000 and moved the team to Chicago, where he renamed it the Bears the following season. For the remainder of the 1920's, Halas continued to play and serve the team in every way imaginable—as a general manager, business manager, ticket manager, publicity director, equipment man, trainer, and coach. Anything that needed to be done, Halas tried to do, all the time keeping up with the fast-changing flow of events at the league level of professional football. His 1920-1929 tenure as the Bears' coach was the first of four ten-year periods in which he guided the Bears on the field. And when his coaching career ended after the 1967 season, he had more victories—326—than any other coach in history, college or professional.

Halas replaced himself as coach with Ralph Jones in 1930, and Jones quickly implemented the Bears' T-formation attack with such ideas as the man-in-motion, widening the spacing in the backfield, and splitting the ends. His successful tenure ended with the 1932 championship game that was played indoors. While the team had won its first title since 1921 and Halas was looking forward to the more pleasing brand of football that was expected to result from the major rules changes enacted in the 1932-1933 off-season, the situation was far from bright as the 1933 campaign approached. The team had lost $18,000 in 1932, and as a result, Halas' partner, Ed "Dutch" Sternaman, wanted out. Halas puchased Sternaman's half ownership for $38,000, most of which he had to borrow, then he himself replaced Jones as the head coach. He admitted frankly that his selection of a new coach from a field of 27 applicants was dictated to a large degree by finances. "I came cheap," he recalled years later. "I would coach for nothing."

While Halas and George Preston Marshall of the Boston Redskins both had a great deal of confidence that the decision made after the 1932 season to split the NFL into divisions would eventually reap large dividends for the league, they hardly could have envisioned the NFL championship series becoming the instant success that it did. The Bears and the New York Giants, representing the league's two largest cities, met in both the 1933 and 1934 championship games, and the two spectacular struggles were scriptwriter perfect for the purpose of widening the fan appeal of pro football.

The 1933 divisional races were never close, but they did produce just what Marshall, the master showman, had envisioned—a final championship battle between the league's two top teams. Chicago, with a 10-2-1 record, had the best percentage, with the Giants, at 11-3-0, close behind. In the regular season, the Bears had beaten the Giants, 14-10, then lost to the Giants, 3-0, two weeks later. It was the ideal buildup for the championship game that took place in Chicago's Wrigley Field on December 17 before 26,000 fans, the largest crowd to see the Bears in Chicago since Red Grange's debut eight years earlier.

Coaches of play-off teams today often are criticized for their failure to "open up" in important games, but Halas and Giants' Coach Steve Owen could never have been accused of that in 1933. Each team scored on two touchdown passes, the lead changed hands six times, and the outcome wasn't decided until the final moments, when an outstanding defensive play by an all-time great offensive back—Grange—preserved a 23-21 victory for the Bears. Neither team was afraid to dig into its arsenal of trick plays in an all-out effort to gain the championship. The day's most unusual play came early and, while it did not produce a touchdown for the Giants, it did set the stage for the excitement that followed. Mel Hein, the Giants' Hall of Fame center, remembers it this way:

> We had certain plays where there was only one man on my left. So on this one, we had the left end take a step back just before the snap, thus making me an eligible receiver. Our quarterback, Harry Newman, came right up behind me to receive a snap like in a T-formation. This wasn't normal for the Giants, but we did do it from time to time. When I handed the ball to Harry, he handed it right back and then faded back and fell. This was part of the plan since nobody could see that he didn't have the ball. I started strolling down the field but, after about five steps, things looked pretty much open and I started to run. This alerted the Bears and the Chicago safety, Keith Molesworth, caught me and knocked me down. I got about thirty yards, but not the touchdown we wanted.

The Bears jumped out in front, 6-0, on a pair of field goals by Jack Manders, but the Giants took a 7-6 lead before halftime with a 29-yard pass from Newman to Morris "Red" Badgro. Badgro, who in 1981 became the oldest person ever elected to the Hall of Fame, thus gained the distinction of scoring the first touchdown in the NFL championship series. Manders put the Bears back into a 9-7 lead in the third quarter, but the Giants countered with a one-yard plunge by Max Krause. The Bears then scored on an eight-yard touchdown pass from Bronko Nagurski to Bill Karr. Nagurski, the most-feared line smasher in pro football, faked a plunge before lobbing the football to Karr—the exact same maneuver he had used in the 1932 indoor championship game, which prompted the NFL to make the controversial action legal in 1933. New York rebounded with an improvised play that the *Chicago Tribune*'s noted sportswriter Wilfred Smith insisted "had never been attempted before in football." It all started on Chicago's eight-yard line when Giants' halfback Ken Strong took the ball on a reverse to the left and found himself cornered. In desperation, Strong threw the ball back to a surprised Newman, who regained his senses long enough to move away from the pursuing Bears and look for a possible receiver. The receiver turned out to be Strong, who had drifted into a corner of the end zone. Newman's pass put the Giants ahead, 21-16.

Once again, it was Nagurski who had the answer. Just as he had done earlier, he faked a plunge, jumped up, and tossed to Bill Hewitt, who lateraled to Karr, who in turn streaked 14 yards for the winning touchdown. A picture of this play, captured just as Hewitt is releasing the ball to Karr, is on display at the Hall of Fame. Still, it was not over. Newman went back to his aerial game with a long toss to Badgro, alone behind the Bears' secondary. Only Grange had a chance to catch him, but Hein was trailing Badgro and ready to take a lateral if the famed redhead caught up to the play. Grange also sensed this and, when he did reach the Giants' ballcarrier, he grabbed him around the chest, binding both arms and thus negating the opportunity for a lateral. "Red Grange saved the

Above: Sammy Baugh started his career as a single-wing tailback, so he often ran with, as well as passed, the ball. He was also an excellent safety on defense. But it was because of his passing ability that he became a pro football immortal. Left: On display at the Hall is a life-size replica of his passing hand.

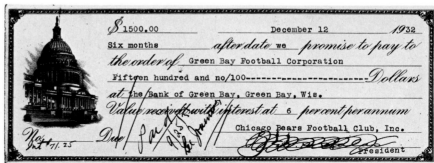

$1500.00   December 12   1932

Six months *after date* we *promise to pay to the order of* Green Bay Football Corporation

Fifteen hundred and no/100----------------------*Dollars*

at the Bank of Green Bay, Green Bay, Wis.

Value received with interest at 6 *percent per annum*

Chicago Bears Football Club, Inc.

President

Opposite: *Chicago end Bill Hewitt laterals to Bill Karr to give the Bears a winning touchdown in the first NFL title game in 1933. Above: Just a year earlier, however, the financially-pressed Bears had to give the Packers a $1500 promissory note for a game guarantee they couldn't pay.*

Above: Superstar end Don Hutson
(left) and ace passer Cecil Isbell
watch intently as long-time Packers
coach Curly Lambeau diagrams a
new play. Right: The Packers
provided pro football with its first
great pass-catch combination when
Don Hutson (left) teamed up with
Arnie Herber in the mid-1930s.

game," Tim Mara, the Giants' owner and Grange's old adversary, said flatly. The rewards, by today's standards, were miniscule; the Bears took home $210.34 checks while the losing Giants picked up $140.22 each. But the rewards couldn't be measured in dollars and cents, rather in the increased fan interest the NFL's leaders were seeking.

The 1934 season also ended with a history-making championship game between the Giants and Bears. But long before the old rivals met on December 9 at New York's Polo Grounds, a number of events and additional rules changes had occurred that would continue to speed the evolution of pro football into the modern era. On August 31, the first College All-Star Game was played before an amazing crowd of 79,432 in Chicago's Soldier Field. The game was the brainchild of Arch Ward, the *Chicago Tribune* sports editor who had been assigned the task of lining up special sports events as part of the city's Century of Progress Exposition.

Earlier that year, Ward had arranged baseball's first All-Star Game. While the football version originally was designed to be a one-time affair, it became the longest continuing series played exclusively for charity in pro football's history. Chicago Tribune Charities received more than $13 million in the 42-year history of the event, which was last played in 1976.

Besides the money it generated for a worthy cause, the College All-Star games provided pro football with a much-needed showcase to prove to the nation's fans that the caliber of play in the pro ranks was at least equal to the best the colleges had to offer. The 1934 game was a scoreless tie, the only one in the series. After ten years, the NFL champions clung to a slim 5-4-1 advantage. But, at the end, the pro champions held a 31-10-1 lead. The College All-Stars won only 2 of the last 20 games played.

The Hall of Fame takes considerable note of the significant role the College All-Star Game played in pro football's acceptance, particularly in the 1930's and 1940's. In addition to a picture of a packed All-Star Game crowd at Soldier Field, the Hall displays the All-Star Game uniform worn by Dan Fortmann in 1936. Fortmann later played with distinction as a guard with the Chicago Bears and today is enshrined in the Hall of Fame. Arch Ward is also honored as one of the Hall's two Pioneer Award winners. The award, given in memory of the Los Angeles Rams' late owner Dan Reeves, honors those people whose innovative off-the-field contributions have improved the sport. The other winner was Fred Gehrke, a halfback for the Rams who in 1949 painted golden rams' horns on his team's helmets,

thus starting the trend to use brightly colored team symbols on the headgear of every team in the NFL.

Other innovations introduced in 1934 added to the offensive scope of the game. First came a new football, one that took a full inch off the ball's girth. The use of a kicking tee also was legalized. Thus, forward passing became more commonplace, as did field goals by placekicking. The once-popular art of dropkicking, however, quickly became extinct. (The NFL's last dropkick occurred during the Bears' 37-9 win over the Giants in the 1941 championship game, when Chicago's Ray McLean, as a lark, dropkicked the final conversion.) In addition, during the 1933-1934 off-season, G. A. "Dick" Richards purchased the Portsmouth Spartans and moved the team to Detroit, where he adopted the nickname Lions. Thus, with the exception of Green Bay, the "small-city" look of the early NFL had completely disappeared. It would not return.

In the Eastern Division, the Giants had to struggle to gain another title. And, in the West, there was a stirring two-way race between two overpowering teams—the Bears and the Lions, who opened with seven straight shutouts and ten victories in succession. The Bears were 10-0 and the Lions 10-1 when the teams squared off on Thanksgiving Day in Detroit. It was the first NFL game broadcast nationally, with Graham McNamee at the mike for NBC Radio. The Bears won, 19-16, and followed up a few days later with a 10-7 win that eliminated the Lions.

Chicago wound up with a perfect 13-0-0 regular season, the first in NFL history. One of the reasons for the Bears' improvement over 1933 was the presence of a rookie halfback, Beattie Feathers, who teamed with Nagurski to give the Bears an unmatched one-two backfield punch. Feathers became history's first 1,000-yard rusher during the season with 1,004 yards in just 101 carries. Until Steve Van Buren, playing for the Philadelphia Eagles 13 seasons later, no other NFL back cracked the 1,000-yard barrier. Feathers' 9.94 yard-per-carry mark still stands as an NFL record. Unfortunately, he suffered a shoulder separation in the tenth game and never again played with the same effectiveness he displayed early in the 1934 season.

The temperature stood at 6 degrees with the wind blowing 20 miles per hour, but a surprisingly large crowd of 35,059 turned out at the Polo Grounds for the 1934 championship game. Although Feathers and the veteran Red Grange were out of the game, the Bears still were prohibitive favorites. The Giants also were missing several players due to injuries, including quarterback Harry Newman, who had played so well in the 1933

game. As Giants' Coach Steve Owen surveyed the sheet of ice that had formed on the field, team captain Ray Flaherty suggested, "Coach, why not wear basketball shoes? Once when I was at Gonzaga (a college in Spokane, Washington), we played on a day like this, but we used sneakers and had good traction." Owen was willing to try anything, but since it was Sunday, all the sporting goods stores in New York were closed. Suddenly, Owen found the solution. There in the Giants' locker room was Abe Cohen, a die-hard fan who ran a campus tailor shop at Manhattan College, where he also supervised the athletic storeroom. Owen sent Cohen racing off to the college to round up as many pairs of basketball shoes as he could find.

Meanwhile, the game began, and both teams found the going rough. But the favored Bears, with Nagurski powering the attack, led at halftime, 10-3. Few in the frozen throng had reason to expect any significant turnaround in the second half. But waiting in the locker room as the Giants trooped

in were Cohen and 19 pairs of sneakers. Owen ordered every player who could find a pair that fit to wear them in the second half, and nine of the Giants did. Pictures in the Hall not only record Nagurski's effective ground gaining in the first half, but also one of the Giants putting on his sneakers to start the second half. When the Giants came on the field for the third quarter, Walter Kiesling of the Bears nudged Coach Halas and said, "Look, they're wearing sneakers." Halas, however, didn't seem particularly alarmed. "Good," he replied. "Step on their toes."

No immediate improvement in the Giants' plight was apparent—in fact, the Bears built their lead to 13-3 before the Giants, now becoming adjusted to the sneakers and getting better traction, suddenly began to gain yardage almost with impunity. Ed Danowski fired to Ike Frankian for one touchdown, and Ken Strong came right back three plays later with a 42-yard dash past the immobile Bears, putting New York into a 17-13 lead. But the Giants weren't through. Strong scored again and then it was Danowski, completing a 27-point fourth-quarter outburst. The Giants had ruined the Bears' perfect season, 30-13.

Five of the game's heavy-duty performers—Nagurski and Bill Hewitt of the Bears and Strong, Mel Hein, and Ray Flaherty of the Giants—plus both coaches, Halas and Owen, were destined to become members of the Hall of Fame. But the game's biggest hero may very well have been the little 5-foot, 140-pound fan who never played a minute of pro football in his life. His emergency errand made the Giants' big upset possible. As Kiesling put it after the game, "Halas told us to step on their toes. Hell, we couldn't even get close enough to recognize them." What was more significant, however, was that there actually were no losers—pro football again was the big winner. In just two years, two never-to-be-forgotten games had been produced in the NFL championship series.

In the NFL's season-ending showdown of 1935, the Detroit Lions breezed past the New York Giants by a 26-7 margin. Obviously not a nail-biter as its two predecessors had been, the 1935 championship was significant simply because the Lions played the game, not because they won it. This one intrusion by Detroit marked the only break in the first 12 years of NFL championship play in the monopoly maintained by the Giants and Redskins in the Eastern Division and the Bears and Packers in the Western. Except for the Lions in 1935, no other NFL club even played in the title game. To beat the Giants, the Lions unleashed a vicious running attack revolving around a quartet of outstanding backs—Ace Gutowsky, Glenn Presnell, Ernie Cad-

op: *Ace running back Glenn Presnell races through a big* ole *in the New York Giants' line during the 1935 NFL* hampionship game, which the Lions won. Above: *The* aturing Years *section of the Hall's exhibition rotunda* hronicles the growth of pro football from the late 1920's into e mid 1950's.

JOHNSON GEPFORD MAC WHERTER LANUM KOEHLER VEACH STERNAMAN DRESSEN

YOUNG SHANK MAY HIGH ADKINS CLARK FEITCHINGER LO-T PEARCE

TRAFTON JONES INGWERSEN HALAS BLACKLOCK PETTY MINTU

1920 STALEY TEAM

del, and Earl "Dutch" Clark. Clark's twisting 40-yard dash for the second touchdown was the big play of the day and, for those who followed the Lions in the mid-1930's, that was to be expected. The Detroit team had a large array of talent, but just one superstar—Dutch Clark. In 1963, Clark became a charter member of the Hall, where his entire Lions' blue-and-silver uniform, including his number 7 jersey, is on permanent display.

Clark played pro football for only seven years—he was all-NFL six of those seasons. When he was at the controls, his teams won. When he wasn't, they slipped in the standings. It was that simple. In the two years after Clark joined them in 1931, the Portsmouth Spartans enjoyed a sizzling 17-5-4 record and came very close to championships two consecutive years. When he sat out the 1933 season, Portsmouth sagged to a 6-5 record. When Clark rejoined the team after it had moved to Detroit in 1934, he guided the Lions to a 39-18-2 winning record in the next five years. During that

time, the Lions won the 1935 championship and were strong challengers to the supremacy of the Bears and Packers every year in the West. In the five years following his retirement after the 1938 campaign, Detroit's mark fell precipitously to 18-33-3.

Clark was listed as the team quarterback because he called the plays. But the 6-foot, 180-pounder actually was the tailback and one of the last truly great triple threats in pro football. He was a legendary runner, a good passer, a superb field general, a top punter, and the final practitioner of a now-vanished art—the dropkick. Clark had the uncanny knack of being in the right place at exactly the right time, and his teammates insisted that, on a 40-yard scamper, he might cover 100 yards following his interference back and forth across the field. There is a story, perhaps apocryphal, about the Lions' tackle who flattened a Chicago Bears' defender and then made no attempt to move off the fallen athlete. "I hate to hold you

Above: *George Halas began his 64-year NFL career with the Decatur Staleys in 1920. The team moved to Chicago in 1921 and changed its name to the Bears in 1922. Right: Halas filled every conceivable role for the Bears—owner, coach, general manager, as well as player.*

down," the Lions' blocker explained, "but you wait—Dutch'll be back this way in a minute." The Bears' peerless fullback-linebacker Bronko Nagurski put it another way: "He looked like the easiest man in the world to tackle. But the first time I tried grabbing him, I was holding nothing but air." "He's like a rabbit in a brush heap," Lions' Coach Potsy Clark (no relation to Dutch) used to say. "No back ever followed interference better than Dutch. But when he gets into the secondary, he has no plan, just instinct."

Yet there were many aspects of the Dutch Clark story that just didn't fit the ordinary pattern for an all-time great, beginning with the fact that Clark is the only football all-American ever to be produced by Colorado College. Despite gaining such stature, Clark did not play pro football for almost three years, until he joined the Spartans in 1931. Then, because he held the basketball coaching job at the Colorado School of Mines, he had to miss the 1932 indoor championship game and then remained in college coaching throughout the 1933 pro season. The most startling situation, however, concerned Dutch Clark's physical condition—he played with the handicap of severely limited vision in one eye. This became public knowledge during the 1936 College All-Star Game when the field lights at Soldier Field rendered him ineffective. At halftime, his Lions' teammates even feared he had gone, or was going, blind. While the determined Clark returned to lead a last-minute scoring drive and then dropkicked the tying conversion even though the goalposts were only distant blurs to his eyes, his secret was out. "I wasn't blind in my left eye, but I was about half-blind," he admitted. "I didn't wear glasses because I didn't want to depend on them. That would have hurt me in football."

The one characteristic Clark did lack was "color," the indefinable element that makes an athlete a public favorite. It was almost as though Clark came so close to perfection on the football field that his lack of human fallibility made him boring for the fans, as well as for historians. When Clark was cast into the role of player-coach in 1937, the Detroit owner hired a nationally known publicist to glamorize his image. But Clark, humble as always, would have nothing to do with it. "You can't make me into the number-one man in football," he insisted, "because Bronko Nagurski's better and Clarke Hinkle might be, too." It was the same modest attitude he displayed at the peak of his playing days, when he hesitated to call his own signals because his teammates might think he was trying to hog the spotlight. That, however, never would have occurred to any Detroit player. As George Christensen, an all-NFL tackle with the Lions, said, "I figure Dutch does everything with a football twice as good as any other player I have ever seen."

Dutch Clark was one of the brightest stars in the NFL's galaxy during the 1930's, along with Bronko Nagurski, Cliff Battles, Ken Strong, and Clarke Hinkle. However, the brand of football they were playing was not very different—just much better—than a decade earlier. But positive changes were taking place. The new championship series became an immediate smash hit. The three major rules changes enacted after the 1932 season—moving the goalposts to the goal line, creating hashmarks 15 yards inbounds, and legalizing the forward pass anywhere behind the scrimmage line—were creating steady offensive growth. The league's overall point production was slowly rising. The once-worrisome number of tied games no longer was a problem. Except for an unexplained increase in 1934, the number of shutouts also was decreasing sharply. But the NFL still was not experiencing the game-after-game offensive show that the league's owners had envisioned when they so drastically altered the game's ground rules several years earlier. That, however, was about to change.

Two players—Don Hutson, an end, in 1935, and quarterback Sammy Baugh, in 1937—burst onto the scene with specialized talents so rare they provided the impetus for transforming pro football into everything the NFL's most optimistic leaders could have envisioned. Hutson played with the Green Bay Packers for 11 years and became universally recognized as the finest passcatcher in history. Baugh threw bulls-eyes for 16 seasons with the Washington Redskins and established standards of forward passing excellence by which all other passers since have been compared.

When Hutson and Baugh began their pro careers, the forward pass was used with caution and, except in desperate situations, rarely inside the offensive team's 30-yard line. By the time they retired, the pass was an everywhere-on-the-field weapon being used almost as frequently as the more conservative infantry-attack approach. Pro football would remain a rugged confrontation among rugged men, but it would evolve more and more into a test of finesse in which the object was as much to outguess and outsmart the opponent as to overpower him.

Today, almost five decades after his first NFL game, Hutson still ranks as the "yardstick" player of the pass-receiving profession. He wound up with 99 touchdown receptions, far more than any other player. When he retired after the 1945 season, his achievements filled a page in the *NFL Record Manual*. He still holds five records outright and is tied for two others. Along with his career touchdown total, his five consecutive pass-receiving titles and eight seasons in all as a pass-catching champion rank as the most significant. In addition, Hutson, with 105 total touchdowns, joins Jim Brown and Lenny Moore as the only players who have ever surpassed the 100 mark. (Going into the 1984 season, Franco Harris had scored an even 100 touchdowns.) Hutson also once ran up a string of 95 successive games in which he caught at least one pass. That record lasted until the final game of the 1969 American Football League season, when San Diego's Lance Alworth stretched his streak to 96. Hutson was on hand to congratulate the Chargers' star and to autograph the official score sheet. A picture of that historic meeting of two great receivers is included in the Hall of Fame's collection. Hutson's statistical accomplishments, when compared to those men who played when the trend of the game was the same, show clearly just how much "a man ahead of his time" he actually was. In 1942, his NFL-leading total of 74 receptions was a staggering 50 catches ahead of his closest rival. When he retired, he had 488 lifetime receptions. Jim Benton was second at the time with 190.

It was Hutson's good fortune when he joined the NFL to be able to play with the one team that already had a genuine appreciation of the forward pass. Still, had it not been for NFL President Joe Carr's unique handling of a contract dispute, Hutson might have joined the Brooklyn Dodgers, a team that used the forward pass only sparingly.

Both Curly Lambeau of the Packers and Shipwreck Kelly of the Dodgers first spotted Hutson when he was a member of the University of Alabama's 1935 Rose Bowl championship team. Lambeau told Hutson he had a job in Green Bay after graduation if he wanted it. Kelly made a similar promise in the dressing room after the game. "We have a passing team," Lambeau emphasized in a barrage of telephone calls to Hutson. "Brooklyn relies on power. We have Arnie Herber, the greatest passer in football. Our attack is built around passing. You belong in Green Bay."

The Alabama end tried to contact Kelly to see what he had to offer, but when he couldn't reach the Brooklyn official, he signed with the Packers. When he heard the news, Kelly flew to Alabama and convinced Hutson he should also sign with the Dodgers. When the two contracts, each properly signed, reached the NFL office, Carr decided the only fair method of settling the issue would be to award Hutson to whichever team had mailed its contract first. The Green Bay contract had been postmarked at 8:30 A.M., while the Brooklyn docu-

Opposite: George Halas led his Bears to 326 victories—more than any other coach in history—during his 40-year career as the Chicago Bears leader. His teams won six NFL championships.

ment was marked at 8:47 A.M., the same day. Thus by a matter of 17 minutes, Hutson became a Packer. "Going with Green Bay was one of the best things that ever happened to me," Hutson insisted years later. "If I had gone to Brooklyn, I might never have played."

There were many who doubted that a skinny 6-foot 1-inch, 180-pounder such as Hutson could stand the physical pounding he would take in the NFL. But it wasn't long before his mere presence on the field changed the defensive concepts used by all coaches. Such measures as double coverage and triple teaming were unheard of before Hutson came on the scene. Still, there were those who had to see to believe, and Dr. John Bain "Jock" Sutherland, coach of the Dodgers, was such a person.

"How will we set our defenses against Hutson?" an assistant coach for the Dodgers asked Sutherland as the team prepared for the Packers.

"We will cover him the same as anyone else—one man," he replied.

"But every other team in the league covers Hutson with at least two men, sometimes three or four," the assistant countered.

"Utter nonsense!" Sutherland snorted. "No man can be that good."

But Hutson certainly was. With his multispeed movements, Hutson caught six passes, two of them for touchdowns, and the Dodgers went down to defeat.

Hutson scored a touchdown on an 83-yard bomb on his first play in his first pro game, giving the Packers a 7-0 victory over the Bears. But he may have made even more of an impression in the second Packers-Bears game that season. Chicago was leading, 14-3, with three minutes to play when Herber and Hutson went to work. The pair connected for 2 touchdowns, the first on a 60-yard toss by Herber and the second on some brilliant end-zone maneuvering by Hutson. Bears' Coach George Halas couldn't believe what had happened. "I just concede Hutson two touchdowns a game," Halas said in later seasons, "and then I hope we can score more."

Hutson continually faced special defenses throughout his career. Once, Dutch Clark, the Cleveland Rams' coach at the time, planned the usual multi-man defense against Hutson and then added still another player—lightning-quick Dante Magnani—to the scheme. "Your only job today is to cover Hutson," Clark told Magnani, the fastest man on the Rams' squad. "You are under no circumstances to let him get between you and the goal." Once the Packers were past midfield, Hutson struck. From his left end position, he sped diagonally toward the right goalpost. Magnani, as or-

Right: *Center Mel Hein, as he did for 15 years, bulwarked the New York line.*

dered, stuck close to him. At breakneck speed, the slender Alabaman reached the goalpost, hooked the upright with his left arm, and let his momentum spin him around the post. That separated him from Magnani. Then, just as he completed his spin to face the field, Hutson reached out his right arm and grabbed the pass that Cecil Isbell had floated downfield.

Three excellent forward passers, starting with Dixie Howell at Alabama, contributed significantly to Hutson's long tenure as a superstar. Arnie Herber already was on his way to becoming a Hall of Famer and had won three NFL individual passing titles in the first five years such records were kept, when Hutson joined the Packers in 1935. On display at the Hall of Fame are a number of pictures of

this great pass-catch combination in pro football. Also on display is Herber's Green Bay Packers' great coat. When Herber started to age, Isbell joined the Packers from Purdue and the aerial circus, with Hutson as the star, continued unabated. For all his great talents, Hutson might never have been as successful if he hadn't had teammates who could consistently get the ball to him.

Making Hutson's pass-receiving accomplishments even more extraordinary is the fact he was a solid two-way player who performed as a 60-minute man throughout much of his career. Although he wasn't large enough to be a successful defensive end, he excelled as a safety. In his final four seasons—after such statistics were kept—he intercepted 23 passes and once returned one 85 yards

Above: *The Giants and Bears met for the second straight year in the 1934 championship game. Bronko Nagurski (taking pitch from Carl Brumbaugh) provided the Bears with an early lead, but the Giants rebounded for an upset victory.*

for a touchdown. He also was a placekicking specialist late in his career, adding almost 200 points to his lifetime total by kicking. During his career, he once ran for a touchdown on an end-around and once passed off the same formation for a touchdown. But the visitors to the Hall of Fame who view Hutson's famous number 14 jersey remember him primarily as the best pass catcher of his—and maybe any—era.

While Baugh's impact on pro football as a forward passer equalled Hutson's contributions as a pass receiver, the slim Texan entered the pro ranks under significantly different circumstances than the Alabaman had experienced two years earlier. Hutson joined the NFL as a free agent with comparatively little fanfare outside of Green Bay. A year later in 1936, the league adopted the college player selection process—commonly known as the draft which was designed to, and did, promote competitive balance throughout the NFL.

After the 1936 season, the Redskins' flamboyant owner, George Preston Marshall, had decided to move his team from Boston to Washington, D.C., because of poor attendance. Marshall understood the necessity in a new city of building fan interest around a sensational performer, and he believed that the two-time all-American from Texas Christian was the player to do it. The Redskins made Baugh their first-round pick in the 1937 draft, and Marshall quickly signed him to a $5,000 contract. Then he brought him to the capital, where he dressed Baugh in cowboy regalia and, under the glare of newsreel lights, introduced his discovery to the big-city media. While he was uncomfortable in the spotlight, Baugh went along with all the master showman planned. Before he ever threw a pass in the pro ranks, Baugh had been the most photographed and publicized player to date.

Once it was time to play football, Baugh lived up to all his advance notices. At 6 feet 2 inches,

180 pounds, Baugh was considered by some to be too small and too frail to play pro football. But he survived intact for 16 seasons. With the durability of a Texas range rider, he accepted hardship stoically. When opposing tacklers got too rough, he always seemed to find a way to defend himself. Once, early in his career, an overzealous enemy tackle broke through the Redskins' pass blocking and knocked him down. That was proper enough, but the tackle then slugged Baugh.

"Cut that out," Baugh protested.

On the next play, it happened again and the bully also kneed Baugh. The Redskins were enraged. "Want me to pop him for you, Sammy?" asked Turk Edwards, the Redskins' tackle and captain.

"I'll take care of him myself," Baugh responded angrily. "Don't try to block him on the next play. Let him come through."

The tackle surged through for the kill, but Baugh just stood there, his arm cocked to throw. He waited until his tormentor was almost on top of him, then he threw. The ball traveled like a bullet, striking the tackle right between the eyes and knocking him cold.

In the College All-Star Game, Baugh's touchdown pass to Gaynell Tinsley was the only score in a 6-0 upset of the NFL champion Packers. In the season-opener against the Giants—the first NFL game ever played in Washington—Baugh completed 11 of 16 passes in leading the Redskins to a 13-3 victory. At the end of the season, Baugh had another big day as the Redskins swamped the Giants, 49-14, for the Eastern Division crown. More than ten thousand fans who had followed the Redskins to New York nearly stampeded him in their postgame exuberance. Baugh then stepped front and center in the championship game against the Chicago Bears in Wrigley Field, putting on the most spectacular show ever seen in an NFL title game up to that point in history. He threw 3 touchdown passes, all from long range, and wound up gaining 335 yards on 18 completions. Two of his scoring tosses were to Wayne Millner on 55- and 78-yard plays. The most important, however, was a 35-yard hookup with Ed Justice that provided Washington with a 28-21 victory. But it was only the beginning of the impact Baugh had on the sport. In his first ten seasons, the Redskins prospered with five divisional crowns and the NFL championship in 1937 and 1942. After Baugh retired, they didn't win another title until 1972.

Baugh was a six-time individual passing champion who had clogged the record book with his name by the time he retired in 1952. Several of his marks still stand, but his most spectacular record, the 70.33 completion percentage he established in 1945, finally was broken by Cincinnati's Ken Anderson in 1982. This record came in Baugh's second season as a T-formation quarterback after he had spent his first eight years in the NFL as a triple-threat and single-wing tailback. Though not everything came easily for him when the Redskins switched to the T in 1944—he never did, for instance, become a really slick ball handler—Baugh did successfully bridge the gap from tailback to quarterback. As proof of this, three of his six passing titles came after his transformation to a T-quarterback.

With a dry sense of humor, Baugh became almost as famous for his quips as he was for his obvious passing ability. And he scoffed at the T-formation when he first was introduced to it. "Why this is the easiest position in football," he said of the T-quarterback's role. "All you do is hand off and pass. This is like playing with top hat and tails. If the Redskins had been doing this when I started in the NFL, I could have lasted until I was forty years old."

Baugh first learned to throw a football as a young boy in Sweetwater, Texas. He suspended an old tire from a tree and set the tire to swing like a pendulum. Then he'd step back 10 to 15 paces and try to throw a football through the moving object. In high school, he was average in basketball, better than average in football, and outstanding in baseball. He first attended Texas Christian on a baseball scholarship and already had signed to play in the St. Louis Cardinals' organization when Marshall appeared with his lucrative pro football contract.

Dutch Meyer was the baseball coach and assistant football coach who recruited Baugh for TCU. A year later, Meyer was promoted to head football coach and he immediately decided Baugh's future was in football, a fact that obviously had escaped his predecessor. Even in the air-crazy Southwest Conference, Baugh was an instant sensation. In three seasons with the Horned Frogs, he threw for 3,439 yards and 39 touchdowns.

Ray Flaherty, coach of the Redskins, was just

Hailing from tiny Colorado College, where he was the only all-America the school ever had, Dutch Clark joined the Portsmouth Spartans in 1931 and immediately became a triple-threat superstar in the pros. He was all-NFL six of the seven years he played.

Top: 488 career catches, Green Bay Packers end Don Hutson was a man "ahead of his time" when it came to bringing more excitement to the passing game. Above: It took seven Giants to bring down Bronko Nagurski, the Bears fullback, in the 1934 NFL championship game.

95

These four superstars added much to the National Football League scene in the 1930s. Sammy Baugh (opposite) became a threat to go all the way on any play because of his exceptional passing skills. Ken Strong (top) was a multi-talented star for the New York Giants and became one of the game's first kicking specialists. Don Hutson (left) was to receiving what Baugh was to passing, and Dutch Clark (right) was literally a coach on the field, one of the smartest players ever when it came to gridiron tactics.

96

97

as enthused as Marshall about his team's new passing sensation. "We were a good ball club last year," he said earnestly, "but the one thing that stopped us from being great was that we didn't have a forward passer. Now we have one, the best in the world."

In all probability, an incident that occurred in training camp while Flaherty was explaining a play sold him on his new star. "The end takes ten steps straight ahead and flares out to the right," the Redskins' coach said as he diagrammed a play on the blackboard. "When he reaches here, Sam, I want you to hit him in the eye with the ball."

"Which eye?" Baugh drawled.

The most famous Baugh remark came in the dressing room after the 73-0 beating administered by the Chicago Bears in the 1940 NFL championship game. A Redskins' end had dropped a touchdown pass that would have tied the score in the first period, and after the game reporters pressed Baugh to comment on whether the outcome would have been different if the pass had been caught. Baugh dryly replied, "Yeah, it would have been seventy-three-seven."

Somewhat obscured in history is the fact that, just two years later, Baugh and the Redskins avenged their loss to the Bears with a 14-6 win in the 1942 championship game that ended Chicago's perfect season.

Baugh had total confidence in his passing ability and, because of this, was willing to gamble with the forward pass anywhere on the field. But his decision to throw out of his own end zone in the 1945 championship game not only led to an unusual play that cost his team a victory but it prompted another significant rule change as well. "Everyone expected Sam to punt," recalled Wayne Millner, the intended receiver, "because we were backed up to the goal line. There was no one within a mile of me when Sam threw the ball. But the wind shifted just as he threw and blew the football into the goalpost. That cost us a safety instead of the touchdown we almost surely would have had." The two points proved the difference as the Bob Waterfield-led Cleveland Rams, in their last game as representatives of the Ohio city, edged the Redskins 15-14. Before another season started, the Rams had moved to Los Angeles and the rules makers had altered the regulations so that, in the future, a pass hitting the goalpost would merely be ruled an incompletion.

As the Redskins fell from power after the 1945 season, Baugh's outstanding performances became more infrequent. Washington fans, however, never will forget his special day in 1947. Baugh was presented with a new station wagon and nu-

merous other gifts and then went to work on the Chicago Cardinals, who were destined to win the Western Conference. He hit on 11 of 13 in the first half for a 17-7 Washington lead—but he was just warming up. In the third quarter, he threw three touchdown passes and then added a final one late in the game as Washington won, 45-21. For the day, Baugh had 25 completions for 355 yards and 6 touchdowns. Baugh considered this his greatest performance. "I guess," he said, "it was because it was my day I did pretty good."

Casual pro football observers are often so enraptured by Baugh's marvelous accomplishments as a passer that they lose sight of his exceptional all-around talents. Although statistically he was a man ahead of his time as a passer—he wound up with 21,886 yards and 186 touchdowns throwing the football—he also may have been the best punter in NFL history. He led the league four consecutive years, from 1940 to 1943, and holds the all-time records for career average (45.10 yards) and season average (51.40 yards in 1940). He also was an outstanding safety who was a two-way performer during the early years of his career. In a five-year period, from the time the league began keeping interception records until Baugh became an offensive specialist, he swiped 28 opposition passes.

Baugh is remembered in a number of displays at the Hall of Fame. In the rotunda, a plaster replica of his passing hand shows, surprisingly, that Baugh did not have the massive paw one might expect of a premier passer. In the Enshrinee Mementoes Room, his bronzed kicking shoes commemorate another of his talents. Publicity pictures from Marshall's big promotional buildup before the Redskins' first season in Washington also are exhibited. In the Pro Football Adventure Room, Baugh's name appears again on a lighted question-and-answer game board at which visitors try to pair the name of a Hall of Fame member with a spectacular achievement. For most fans, the most difficult match up is the one that links Sammy Baugh to the notation: "He intercepted four passes in one game." Almost everyone remembers Baugh as a great passer and many also know that he was a superb punter, but few suspect that the great passer and punter was also a pass-stealing defensive back. In 1943, he became the NFL's first individual triple-crown statistical winner, leading the league in passing, punting, and interceptions.

Except for Sammy Baugh, only one other player accomplished the distinction of leading the league in three categories. Bill Dudley, of the 1946 Pittsburgh Steelers, won titles in the rushing, punt return, and interception departments. Dud-

Above: While Sammy Baugh was history's first great passer and also the finest punter ever, he was also a fine safety and played that position during the first half of his career. He intercepted 28 passes, including a league-leading 11 in 1943. His four steals in one game against Detroit that year set a league record which has since been tied. Left: Don Hutson was also a fine defensive back early in his career. The former Alabama star also became a placekicker of note and wound up his career with 823 points scored. He is one of only three players to score more than 100 touchdowns in his career.

ley, like Baugh a Hall of Fame member, did not have the lasting impact on the sport that his passing colleague did. Nevertheless, several facets of the Baugh and Dudley careers were remarkably similar. Both were products of the one-platoon era and both were accustomed to spending 50 to 60 minutes on the field every game, particularly in their early years. Standouts on offense and defense, both finally confined their playing time to the offensive unit after two-platoon football took hold. In their triple-crown seasons, the two were brilliant far beyond the bounds of three statistical championships. In 1943, Baugh led the Redskins to their third Eastern Division title in 4 years, completing 133 passes for 1,754 yards and 23 touchdowns—and accounting for almost 70 percent of his team's scoring punch. Whenever the Redskins' offense stalled, Baugh's booming punts put them out of danger. His 50 punts averaged 45.9 yards. On defense, his 11 steals brought him the NFL interception championship. His four interceptions in a single game, against Detroit, established a league record that has been tied but never broken.

For Dudley, 1946 marked his first full NFL season since 1942 when, as a rookie, he won the rushing championship. Army service interrupted his career until late in the 1945 campaign, when he returned for some late-season heroics with the Steelers. Originally considered too small to play with the pros, the 5-foot 10-inch, 176-pounder possessed fiery determination and rare versatility. Playing halfback for the Steelers, he ran, passed, caught passes, returned kicks, played defense, and kicked extra points and field goals. He handled the ball more than any other player in 1946. The fact that he played for a .500 team made his triple crown even more remarkable. With 604 yards rushing, he accounted for almost half of Pittsburgh's entire team total. On his 27 punt returns, he compiled an eye-opening 14.2-yard average per attempt. With ten interceptions, he was three in front of the NFL's second-place finisher. But Dudley did far more than rush, return punts, and intercept passes. He passed 90 times, completing 32 for 452 yards and 2 touchdowns. His 60 punts averaged 40 yards. He returned 14 kickoffs for a 20-yard average and scored 48 points on 5 touchdowns, 12 extra points, and 2 field goals.

For his outstanding efforts, Dudley won the coveted Joe Carr Trophy, an official award given by the NFL to the league's Most Valuable Player.

That trophy occupies an exhibition spot in the Triple-Crown Winners display. It is an award that, for all his brilliance, Baugh never won; Dudley was the last player to win it. The NFL, which first instituted the award in 1938, voted to discontinue it before the 1947 season.

The 1946 campaign was Dudley's last in Pittsburgh. Differences with Steelers' Coach Jock Sutherland prompted Dudley's trade to Detroit for the 1947 season. Three years later, he was sent off to Washington, where he became Baugh's teammate. By 1950, both Dudley and Baugh were beyond the triple-crown stage, although they still were highly effective in spot situations. Baugh retired after the 1952 season, while Dudley sat out Baugh's final year and then came back for a wrap-up shot himself in 1953. Their departures signaled the end of the do-everything player in pro football. The two-platoon approach of the modern game almost guarantees that they were the last of the triple-crown winners.

Right and below: *The Washington Redskins in the period from 1937 to 1952 were blessed not only with a superb forward passer but history's finest punter as well. Sammy Baugh led the NFL in punting four straight years from 1940 to 1943 and, in the process, established many all-time records. His 45.10-yard career average is the best ever, and his 51.4 yard mark in 1940 is the top single-season kicking performance. His bronzed kicking shoes are featured in one Hall of Fame display. Opposite page: Appreciative Washington fans crowded around Sammy after every game and, in 1947, they held a special day in his honor. Baugh responded with six touchdown passes against the Chicago Cardinals.*

The Browns dominated the National Football League in the 1950-56 period, just as they had in the All-America Football Conference. Hall of Fame end Dante Lavelli was one of many exceptional Browns stars.

Chapter 5

"Once A Fire Has Started"

The credit accorded Don Hutson and Sammy Baugh for transforming pro football into a more diversified offensive game is well founded. Baugh, however, must share part of the accolades as history's game-changing passer with Sid Luckman, the chief offensive weapon of the Chicago Bears from 1939 through 1950, who became the premier T-formation quarterback of his era. Because of Luckman and one exceptional performance by his Bears' teammates in the 1940 NFL championship game, pro football took a giant step closer to becoming a universally explosive action sport. The Luckman-led Bears slaughtered the Washington Redskins, 73-0, in what may be history's most significant single game. It was truly a landmark event for, immediately afterward, several NFL teams began to convert to the T-formation attack, which today is the universal offensive formation in football. "The game marked the turning point in pro football," said George Halas, who coached the Bears that day. "The widespread use of all of today's offensive concepts evolved from this game."

While the magnitude of the Bears' victory had a profound effect on pro football, every team didn't immediately embrace the T-formation. The Redskins stuck with their double-wing and short-punt alignments until 1944. The Detroit Lions kept their short-punt offense until after World War II. The New York Giants' Steve Owen stayed with his pet A-formation until 1953. (An ink stamp that Owen used as an aid in diagramming his A-formation plays is displayed in the Hall of Fame.) The Pittsburgh Steelers, steeped in the single-wing tradition of Jock Sutherland, held out against the T revolution until the 1950's. But many teams, both

in the college ranks and among the pros, did make immediate plans to convert to the new attack. Coach Earl "Red" Blaik at Army and later Frank Leahy at Notre Dame both asked Luckman to help them install the new offense at their colleges. Greasy Neale of the Philadelphia Eagles obtained newsreel film of the Bears' game and spent most of the 1940–1941 off-season studying them. Before the end of the decade, there were only a handful of teams not using the T-formation.

The basic T-formation was not new. Amos Alonzo Stagg had used it in college football a half century earlier. Then Ralph Jones, who coached the Bears from 1930 to 1932, began an evolutionary process by introducing such ideas as the man-in-motion, widening the spacing in the backfield, and splitting the ends. According to Halas, Jones deserves the bulk of the credit for laying the foundation for the Bears' T explosion during the 1940's. Clark Shaughnessy, who had great success using the T at Stanford in 1940, also helped Halas refine his new attack whenever he could find the time.

Halas, who had not won an NFL championship since 1933, slowly began putting together his juggernaut late in the decade. By 1938, he was searching for the perfect passer to quarterback his T-formation. He found him at Columbia University, where the Brooklyn-born Luckman was finishing out a successful, though not spectacular, career as a tailback in Coach Lou Little's famed single-wing offense. Halas scouted Luckman just once in a 13-12 loss to Syracuse on a muddy, rain-soaked field. Luckman was hardly exceptional that day, but Halas saw enough. "It was more of a hunch than anything else," Halas recalled years later. "Maybe it was a question of size. Sid was at least three inches taller than Davey O'Brien, the top college quarterback in 1938. That advantage in height means an awful lot when you are under the center."

The Pittsburgh Steelers had the number-one choice in the 1939 draft, but they traded their negotiating rights to the first pick to the Bears. Halas instructed the Steelers to select Luckman. Although Luckman had not intended to play pro football—many of the top college stars of the day did not—he quickly changed his mind when Halas offered him a deal worth $10,000 for his rookie season. What the Bears' coach had in mind for Luckman was a season at left halfback, the man-in-motion position of the T attack, while he learned the intricacies of the new system.

"I was completely shocked by what I saw," said Luckman, commenting on his introduction to the T. "I didn't realize how it could work when you had no blocking in front of the ballcarrier. Then when I saw it in operation, I knew right then it was the most wonderful thing that could have happened to me, because I wasn't fast enough to be a good ballcarrier."

By late season 1939, Luckman was prepared to start operating as a T-quarterback. And, in a game against Green Bay in which he led the Bears to a 30-7 victory, he displayed some of the magical finesse that would typify the rest of his career.

Luckman became a starter in 1940, but contrary to popular belief, the Bears gave little indication of their offensive explosiveness until the championship game. They lost three regular-season games, but did manage to slip past two-time champion Green Bay for the Western Division title. Luckman threw just 105 passes in 11 games.

One of the regular-season losses, a 7-3 defeat by Washington three weeks before the final game, played a major role in firing up the Bears for their championship showdown with the Redskins. With 40 seconds left in the regular-season contest, the Bears completed a long pass to the Washington 1-yard line before being penalized back to the 6 for delay of the game. Two passes fell into the end zone incomplete, but, on the second pass to Bill Osmanski, the Bears protested bitterly—without success—that the Redskins' Frank Filchock had interfered. George Preston Marshall, the Redskins' owner, foolishly got into the act. "The Bears are cry babies," he taunted. "They're strictly a first-half ball club. They give up." Day after day for the next three weeks, Halas reminded his squad of Marshall's cutting remarks. "When we took the train from Chicago," Luckman recalled, "there wasn't anybody talking or joking or playing cards. Everybody had his playbook out. Everybody was study-ing and you could feel there was tremendous determination and desire."

In the Hall of Fame, the atmosphere of the day is captured in a panoramic photo of Griffith Stadium, crammed with a capacity crowd of 36,034 for the December 8 showdown. The Redskins were slight favorites, and legitimately so. They had a more experienced offensive leader in Baugh, they had a better league record, and they had beaten the Bears in Washington. In advance of the game, Halas had conjectured that "any team good enough to get to the play-off is good enough to win it." But Marshall, adding further motivation for the Bears, boasted loudly, "We have whipped them before and we will whip them again."

In the locker room, Halas pinned clippings of Marshall's taunts on the wall. "That's what the people in Washington are saying about you, gentlemen," he told his squad. "I know you are the greatest football team ever. Now go out and show the world."

"We almost broke down the door getting out to the field," said fullback Bill Osmanski.

In addition to the emotional preparation, Halas had built his game plan on the theory that Washington would stay in the same 5-3-3 defense that it had used so effectively against the Bears three weeks earlier. To find out if he was strategically on target, Halas ordered Luckman to call three specific plays to start the game. "I want to call these plays," he told his quarterback, "because they will show us if they are in their same defense. If they are, you will then attack as we have been planning in practice." On first down after the kickoff, Luckman called a fake reverse with a man-in-motion and handed off to George McAfee, who dove for seven yards. More important to Halas, he saw the Redskins had not altered their defense. "I knew then we could collect enough points to win," he said later. "Our adjusted plays could go time and again through the weaknesses we had detected in the Washington defense."

On second down, Halas' choice was an off-tackle play with Osmanski getting the ball. McAfee went in motion to the right and Osmanski, racing hard to the left, took the pitchout, straight-armed a linebacker, and swung to the outside and into the clear. A sensational block by end George Wilson at the Washington 35 wiped out a couple of Redskins as Osmanski raced 68 yards untouched. A photo of the start of this run is on display at the Hall of Fame. Jack Manders converted and, with just 55 seconds played, Chicago led, 7-0. The Bears scored twice more in the first period and held a 28-0 lead at halftime. In the locker room, Halas once again reminded his charges of Marshall's taunts

Above: Bill Dudley, playing for the Pittsburgh Steelers in 1946, was one of only two players ever to earn three individual statistical titles. Left: Sid Luckman, quarterback of the Chicago Bears, was the first great T-formation passer. Below: Red Grange bolted from the NFL to play with the New York Yankees in the first American Football League in 1926.

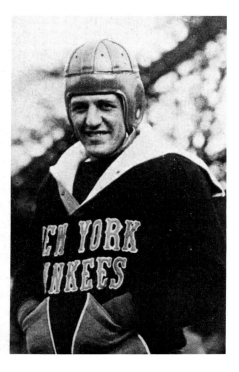

The All America Football Conference is remembered in one historical exhibition.

Top left: *The statistical records of pro football's stars are changed weekly during each football season.* Above: *This football was signed by each member of the 1946 champion Bears.*

that "the Bears were a first-half team."

Any fears of a letdown were unfounded. Chicago scored 26 points in the third period and 19 more in the fourth en route to the biggest score in NFL history. By game's end, the Bears were throwing and running for their extra points because all the available game balls had been kicked into the stands after previous touchdowns. Even though this was the showcase game for the T attack directed by Luckman, he threw only 6 passes, completing 4 for 102 yards and 1 touchdown. He also ran one yard for the Bears' second touchdown. Accolades for the Bears' stunning performance came from everywhere.

"No team on earth could have beaten the Bears today," Giants' backfield star Tuffy Leemans said. "I've never seen a hotter club. Once a fire has started, there's no way to put it out." Or, as Halas said after the game, "We were the hottest club in the world today. It's one of those things that will never happen again."

It is easy to understand why such a performance spurred the widespread shift to the T, but it should also be noted that not everyone enjoyed the success with the T that the Bears did. A major reason for the Bears' success was that Halas had assembled a cast of talented players at every position. By 1941, the Bears had been labeled the "Monsters of the Midway"—and they were. They won NFL championships in 1941, 1943, and 1946, and reached the 1942 title game after an unbeaten regular season. Another major reason for the Bears' success was the leadership Luckman provided throughout the decade, including the war years. Besides their five title-game appearances, the Bears finished second in their division six other times during his tenure. No one will ever know what might have happened if World War II had not intervened.

Luckman enjoyed many exceptional games during his 12-year career, but possibly his two most outstanding performances occurred in 1943. On November 14 in the Polo Grounds, hundreds of his Brooklyn fans turned out to honor him with gifts and speeches. And his mother was in the stands to watch him for only the third time. The Bears' quarterback responded with a seven-touchdown passing barrage that since that day has been equaled but never bettered. The Bears racked up 682 yards total offense in stunning the Giants, 56-7. In the NFL championship game against Washington that same year, Luckman threw 5 touchdown passes on strikes of 31, 36, 66, 29, and 16 yards. Altogether, he had 15 completions in 27 attempts for 276 yards as the Bears won, 41-21.

Honors came frequently. He was all-NFL in 1941, 1942, 1943, 1944, and 1947. In 1943, he won the Joe Carr Trophy as the NFL's Most Valuable Player. In 1965, he was elected to the Hall of Fame, where his number 42 Bears' jersey is now displayed. Of the modern quarterbacks, only Baugh preceded him in winning his sport's highest honor.

An insight into Luckman's effectiveness may be gained by viewing the Top Twenty display at the Hall of Fame, which spotlights the leading individual lifetime records in passing, rushing, receiving, and scoring. Even though Luckman played well before pass patterns had become so sophisticated that pass defenses were severely tested every time an aerial was thrown, he still ranks in the top 20 among the all-time leaders. He is the only passer who played primarily before 1950 able to crack the elite ranks. When he retired after the 1950 season, many observers called him the finest T-formation quarterback in history. At the time, that accolade meant only that Luckman was the best of a comparatively small number of quarterbacks who had played that position. However, with more than thirty years of football elapsed since his final pass, Luckman still ranks high among the all-time leaders, making those lavish pronouncements all the more meaningful today. In the Hall there is one other reminder of Luckman's successes—a 1946 NFL championship game ball signed by every member of the winning Bears. Luckman scored the winning touchdown in that one, a 24-14 victory over the New York Giants. The football is displayed in the Maturing Years section of the exhibition rotunda—an area rich with memorabilia of the era, including the prized possessions of two other Hall of Famers: Displayed side by side are the helmet that belonged to Tony Canadeo of the Green Bay Packers and the bronzed punting shoes of Clarence "Ace" Parker, the Brooklyn Dodgers' triple-threat tailback. (Canadeo joined the Packers in 1941 and became one of the most versatile players in the National Football League. In 1949, he became only the third back to rush for more than 1,000 yards in one season. Parker, the Dodgers' number-one draft pick in 1937, shunned a baseball career with the Philadelphia Athletics to become the 1940 winner of the Joe Carr Trophy.) But the rarest of the items in the section may be the green-and-white number 51 jersey worn by end Lamar Davis of the Baltimore Colts in 1947. So far as is known, this is the only jersey remaining from Baltimore's initial season in the All-America Football Conference, a league that competed against the established National Football League for four seasons, from 1946 through 1949.

The AAFC was the fourth pro league to challenge the NFL in its first 30 years. All three previous rivals bore the name American Football League, and all three AFLs, plus the AAFC, wound up the same way—out of business. The Hall of Fame presents capsule histories of the four rival leagues in the Pro Football Adventure Room that is housed in the shrine's fourth building. The first AFL was organized in 1926 by C. C. Pyle, the manager of the fabled Red Grange. Pyle planned to build an entire league around his one superstar, but the venture, costly to both sides, failed miserably after just one season. Only one team, Pyle's New York Yankees, survived and was granted an NFL franchise, but even it disappeared in just two years. AFL No. 2, founded in 1936, did not pose the immediate financial threat to the NFL that AFL No. 1 had, but the league did manage to lure some fairly big names away from the NFL, including Ken Strong and Morris "Red" Badgro, both of whom had played with the New York Giants and are members of the Hall of Fame. When AFL No. 2 called it quits after the 1937 season, the NFL made no concessions. None were needed. Three years later, AFL No. 3 came along, also for just two years. That league could boast of only a handful of top-grade players—Tom Harmon from Michigan and John Kimbrough from Texas A&M were the biggest names—and it didn't return for the 1942 season.

The All-America Football Conference, however, was quite a different matter. From start to finish, it produced quality football made possible by the acquisition of many of the outstanding players available at the time. In head-to-head signing competition with the NFL, AAFC teams lured more than 100 former NFL stars coming out of the US Armed Forces to its ranks and signed 40 of the 66 members of the 1946 College All-Star team. Many of its better players would later excel in the NFL as well. In fact, several Hall of Fame members began their illustrious careers on AAFC fields. The AAFC also placed the first permanent franchise on the West Coast—both the Los Angeles Dons and the San Francisco 49ers were in business before Dan Reeves moved the NFL's Cleveland Rams to Los Angeles prior to the 1946 season. While NFL teams still were riding trains, AAFC clubs were making charter arrangements with airlines. The AAFC also boldly moved into major stadiums such as Municipal Stadium in Cleveland, Memorial Coliseum in Los Angeles, and Yankee Stadium in New York. In its four years of existence, the AAFC's per-game attendance was a shade better than the NFL's—28,319 to 27,602.

The moving force behind the organization of the rival league was Arch Ward, the *Chicago Tribune* sports editor who had earlier founded the baseball All-Star Game series and football's College All-Star Game. Although Ward had been considered for the NFL commissioner's post in 1940, he had expressed no interest in the job. However, he was dedicated to the growth of the sport and he dreamed of the day when champions of two leagues would play a "world series of pro football." When the NFL showed no inclination to expand, Ward decided to form his own league. Two days before D day, on June 4, 1944, six men met secretly in a St. Louis hotel room and laid the foundation for the AAFC. Representatives from Buffalo, Chicago, Los Angeles, New York, and San Francisco met with Ward, who also held the proxy of Arthur B. "Mickey" McBride, the future owner of the Cleveland Browns. Within three months, franchises had been granted to those cities and, before the league began play in 1946, Miami and Brooklyn had been added. Jim Crowley of Notre Dame, one of the fabled Four Horsemen, was named commissioner.

Elmer Layden, the NFL commissioner who had been a teammate of Crowley's with the Four Horsemen, accurately portrayed the older league's attitude when he instructed his publicity man, George Strickler, to issue the following statement: "Over the years there has always been talk about new professional leagues sprouting up. As far as I am concerned, the All-America Football Conference should first get a ball, then make a schedule, and then play a game." Historians conveniently shortened Layden's statement to "Tell them to get a football first," but it was a remark that plagued him for the remainder of his term as commissioner. By the time the AAFC did begin playing in 1946, Bert Bell had replaced Layden as commissioner and had become the man who would successfully lead the fight against the upstart league.

Even though the brand of football exhibited by the AAFC was comparable to that of the older league, the new conference suffered from a lack of balance among its members, both on and off the field. The Miami Seahawks failed miserably and quit after one season. The Baltimore Colts, who replaced Miami, enjoyed only mild success. The Chicago Rockets, expected to be one of the league's stronger franchises, ran into stiff competition from both the Bears and Cardinals in Chicago and never did click. In 1949, the Brooklyn Dodgers disbanded and merged with the New York Yankees. Direct competition for fan interest and media support in New York, Chicago, and Los Angeles, plus the high cost of bidding for player talent, was taking its toll. Travel expenses in the coast-to-coast league also proved to be a major burden.

Finally, the AAFC was severely handicapped by a unique situation—one of its teams was simply too good for the rest of the league. With an excess

Above: *Ben Agajanian's unusual kicking shoes (he lost all the toes of his kicking foot in an elevator accident) are attention-getters. Left: Red Badgro, at 78, was the oldest person ever elected to the Pro Football Hall of Fame.*

HANLEY AND NEVERS TO COACH CHICAGO

The enterprise, imagination and check-book of John L. Keeshin has brought together two of the greatest figures in college football history — Dick Hanley, Head Coach of Northwestern University during its hottest rivalry with Knute Rockne and Notre Dame — and Ernie Nevers, Stanford University's all-time, All-America fullbacks. Both men are now in the Marine Reserve Corps, Hanley a Lt. Colonel and Nevers a Major.

John Keeshin, owner of the Keeshin Freight Line, signed Hanley and Nevers to coach his team in the All America Football Conference. This double-barrel wallop came right on the heels of Keeshin's deal, securing Soldier Field for his team, on a ten year lease. It looks like Mr. Keeshin will give football fans around Chicago a new and greater era of gridiron entertainment.

All America Football Conference

Commissioner—JAS. H. CROWLEY, Commander, U. S. N. R. (inactive while in navy).
Vice President—CHRISTY WALSH, Hotel Roosevelt, Hollywood, Cal.
Treasurer — SAM CORDOVANO, 137 Livingston St., Buffalo, N.Y.
Secretary—Mrs. LOU GEHRIG, 277 Park Ave., New York, N.Y.

3 Tribune Phone Numbers — SUPerior 0200 Public Information Service — SUPerior 0260 Sports Bulletin Service — SUPerior 0100 Want Ads—General Business

Chicago Daily Tribune — THE WORLD'S GREATEST NEWSPAPER

PAUL BROWN NAMED CLEVELAND PRO COACH

ARCH WARD, organizer of annual Golden Gloves tournament and many other great sport projects, including the All America Football Conference, outlines purpose and progress of the new major gridiron circuit—

In the WAKE of the NEWS

BY ARCH WARD.
[Chicago Tribune Press Service.]

NEW YORK, Dec. 11.—Admission of Miami into the All-America football conference promises to develop one of the greatest chamber of commerce battles in the history of sport. . . . Associated with Miami in the new professional gridiron circuit is Los Angeles, claimed by its representatives, Don Ameche and Christy Walsh, to be the best sports community in the country. . . . The Miami owners served notice at the third quarterly meeting of the league yesterday that Pasadena's Tournament of Roses parade will be dwarfed by the showmanship of the Orange bowl committee in whose stadium the new Miami team will operate. . . . Plans have been drawn and approved for a new plant that will accommodate 75,000 as soon after the war as materials are available. . . . Heading the Miami group are Harvey Hester, who predicts his club will outdraw every other team in the league, and Doug Wycoff, All-America full back at Georgia Tech nearly two decades ago. . . . Acquisition of Miami gives the All-America conference three cities which hold out the inducement of good December weather, an advantage enjoyed by no other major professional sports organization. . . . In addition to Los Angeles the west coast is represented by San Francisco. . . . The league plans to run its schedule into late December. . . . Cities located on the Great Lakes—Chicago, Cleveland, and Buffalo—will wind up their home season by mid-November to avoid unfavorable climatic conditions which usually prevail at that time of year.

Commissioner James Crowley, a lieutenant commander in the navy, suggested at yesterday's meeting that the eight teams play home and home games with every other club. . . . Crowley will not assume active direction of the league until he completes his services to the navy. . . . The same holds for Comdr. Gene Tunney, owner of the New York club, who will turn over the operation of his interests to a civilian. . . . Tunney will continue to give all his time and energy to the office he holds as chief of the navy's physical training program. . . . Christy Walsh, co-owner of the Los Angeles club, has been named vice president of the conference and will serve as the league's spokesman until Lt. Comdr. Crowley takes over. . . . Sam Cordavano, co-owner of the Buffalo team, has been chosen treasurer and Mrs. Lou Gehrig secretary. . . . Ray Miller, former mayor of Cleveland, has been engaged as legal counsel and he also will serve with John L. Keeshin of Chicago and A. J. Morabito of San Francisco as a committee to draw up a constitution and by-laws. . . . The conference will be incorporated as a nonprofit organization. . . . The various clubs will incorporate or set up partnerships as they choose.

Three months ago the conductor of this column explained his connection with the organization of the All-America conference. . . . We expressed the hope and ambition to give the football fans of the land another organization which would be a source of entertainment and civic interest. . . . We stated that we had agreed to act as organizer and head of the league until it was on its feet and regular officers elected. . . . We said we were serving without pay. . . . Now we wish to add that we have not even accepted a penny of expense money. . . . Our job is finished. . . . America has a new major professional football league. . . . While some spent their time and used up valuable news space sniping at the endeavor, the task went on without interruption. . . . Ten or 20 years from now the details of organization will have been forgotten. . . . They are not important anyway. . . . The important thing is that an institution which will endure has been added to the sporting scene. . . . It is a reputable enterprise directed by men who have been extremely successful in other fields. . . . They have no intention of destroying any existing professional football league, even if they could. . . . They merely have established competition and, after all, isn't that one of the principles which have made America great?

POLICY

ALL-AMERICA FIRES BACK AT GRID CRITICS

Pledges Continued Bids for Players.

Los Angeles, Cal., Dec. 21 [Special].—Christy Walsh, vice president of the All-America Football conference, today fired back at a spokesman for the National Football league who stated recently that clubs in the new conference had been deluding college players into believing that a contract with a team in the All-America was the same as with a team in the National league.

Walsh, co-owner of the Los Angeles team with Don Ameche, issued this statement:

"It is not surprising to note that the strong All-America Football conference has been singled out by the National Football league. The sports loving public owes much to that group of gridiron pioneers whose imagination and courage has brought prestige and prosperity to professional football.

Says It's Only Natural.

"However, for 20 years the National league has enjoyed a monopoly on player talent and major league franchises, it is not to be expected that these wise and able old timers should welcome the young blood, new ideas and competitive 'know how' of the All-America conference.

"A National league spokesman is quoted as having said that prospective players are being the impression that if the player signs with us it would be the same as signing in the N. F. L.

"As spokesman for the All-America conference, I say no such impression ever has been authorized by our club owners. On the contrary, we tell players that our conference has conspicuous advantages to offer a player, including clubs located in the great sunshine states of California and Florida.

Welcomes Inter-League Play.

"When the time comes for inter-league coöperation, which is inevitable, our conference will give respectful consideration to any overture submitted by the National owners.

"Meanwhile, any players not signed or legally obligated to a National league club, will be considered free agents and our owners will pursue every proper means to secure such players as Angelo Bertelli, Bill Daley, Paul Governali and Glenn Dobbs, to mention a few of the outstanding college stars already under contract to clubs in the All-America conference."

A BRILLIANT ADDITION TO ALL-AMERICA'S LIST

Lt. (j. g.) Paul Brown (right), football officer at the Great Lakes Naval Training center and head coach at Ohio State university, signs a five year contract as coach and general manager of the Cleveland club in the new All-America conference. The contract was drawn in Chicago. Arthur McBride, Cleveland taxicab magnate, who owns the franchise, looks on. (TRIBUNE Photo.)

One of the high spots in Lt. Col. Hanley's career, his official welcome as head coach at Northwestern in 1927. He is shown shaking hands with his predecessor, Glenn Thistlethwaite, who had accepted a position at Wisconsin. In the picture are (left to right) the late Knute Rockne of Notre Dame, Thistlethwaite, Athletic Director K. L. (Tug) Wilson of N. U., Hanley, and the late Judge Walter Steffen of Chicago, football coach at Carnegie Tech. (TRIBUNE Photo.)

OHIO STATE CHIEF SIGNS 5 YEAR CONTRACT AT RECORD SALARY

Joins Meagher and Buck Shaw with All-America.

BY ARCH WARD

Lt. (j. g.) Paul Brown, for three years head football coach at Ohio State university, yesterday signed a five year contract as head coach and general manager of the Cleveland team in the All-America conference. He will report for duty when he has completed his service to the United States navy.

Brown, who is football officer at the Great Lakes Naval Training center, is the third big name coach to enroll in professional football's new major league. Lt. Comdr. Jack Meagher of the Iowa Seahawks, who was head football coach and athletic director at Alabama Polytechnic for seven years, and Buck Shaw of Santa Clara university are the others. Meagher has been signed by Miami and Shaw by San Francisco

Owner Calls It "Best Deal."

Terms of Brown's contract were not made public, but according to Arthur McBride, Cleveland taxicab magnate who owns the All-America franchise in that city, it is the best deal ever given a football coach. The agreement was drawn in Chicago.

Brown will have complete charge of the club, including the right to hire and fire all personnel on and off the field. The team will use Cleveland's Municipal stadium, which has a seating capacity of 83,000, as a home base.

"This is the toughest decision I ever have had to make," Brown said after signing the contract. "The people of Ohio and Columbus have been wonderful to me. I have been happy in my work at Ohio State university. It is difficult to leave Athletic Director St. John and other members of the athletic staff as well as my friends in Columbus.

"However, in fairness to my family this is an opportunity I cannot afford to turn down. I have every confidence in professional football and especially in the future of the All-America conference. It has been thoroly organized. It embraces the key cities of the country. I am convinced that professional football and college football will continue to prosper, side by side.

"I welcome the chance to live in Cleveland. It is like home to me. I know it is a fine sports city. We will do everything in our power to give the fans there a team of which they will be proud. We're out to win."

As Buckeye Boss

[Associated Press Photo.]

Lt. (j. g.) Paul Brown as he looked when named head football coach at Ohio State university in 1941.

SOLDIER FIELD, CHICAGO, GOES TO JOHN KEESHIN

☆

JOHN L. KEESHIN, owner of the Chicago franchise in the All America Conference, has sewed up the largest football stadium in the United States — SOLDIER FIELD! Seating capacity—100,000.

Owner Keeshin holds a 10-year contract with the Chicago Park Board, giving him professional football rights in the historic stadium.

Soldier Field is the fifth playing grounds announced by the All America Conference. The Cleveland team has arranged to play in the Cleveland Municipal Stadium, seating 83,000, while the New York entry will play at Triborough Stadium, seating 48,000. At Buffalo, the municipal stadium will accommodate 53,000.

The Orange Bowl, Miami, Florida, will take care of 38,000 spectators and the Miami club has secured exclusive professional football rights for the proposed post-war Orange bowl, seating 75,000.

THANKS TO SPORTS EDITOR

Portions of Chicago Tribune sport page and material from other newspapers (see credit lines) are reproduced with appreciation of the All America Football Conference.

BUCK SHAW - San Francisco | **DICK HANLEY - Chicago - ERNIE NEVERS** | **JACK MEAGHER - Miami**

Considered by many as one of the two greatest coaches in football history on the Pacific Coast, Buck Shaw brought Santa Clara University to the top of the gridiron ladder against all comers. Tony Morabito, San Francisco football owner, and head of vast lumber interests, signed Buck Shaw to coach his club in the All America Conference. Cut courtesy LOS ANGELES TIMES

Because it was one of the most important football pictures in recent years, Associated Press sent the above scene to 150 newspapers, via wire photo. Lt. Col. Dick Hanley (left) looks on while Maj. Ernie Nevers signs football contract, with John L. Keeshin (background). After leaving the Marine Corps, Col. Hanley will be Head Coach of the Keeshin All America team in Chicago, with Maj. Nevers as his assistant.

Dick Hanley and Ernie Nevers are proteges of Glenn Scobey Warner, originator of the historic Warner system and one of the truly grand old men of the gridiron sport. Both men, now famous football figures in their own rights, learned their fundamentals under the personal coaching of the beloved Pop.

As Head Coach at Auburn, Jack Meagher was rated as one of Dixie's outstanding coaches; as Lt. Commander and Head Coach of the Iowa Seahawks he has maintained all the prestige of past performance. Harvey Hester picked Jack Meagher from a list of top-flight prospects but he will not report to Miami until discharged by Navy. (TRIBUNE Photo)

Opposite: *The heroes and history of every era of pro football are remembered in the modern exhibition rotunda.* Above: *The All-America Football Conference posed a major post-World War II threat to the NFL.*

of superior talent, the Cleveland Browns won all 4 league championships and piled up a fantastic 51-4-3 record, including play-off games. San Francisco was a distant second with an excellent 38-14-2 overall mark, but 6 of its losses were to Cleveland. None of the other teams could ever seriously challenge the Browns or the 49ers. When the Cleveland fans grew tired of the weekly slaughters, it became obvious it was time to end the experiment. Peace was announced as a "merger" after the 1949 season, but, in reality, it was "surrender" by the AAFC. Cleveland, San Francisco, and Baltimore were granted NFL franchises, and the players from other AAFC squads were put into a "grab bag" to be selected by established NFL teams. There was no question, however, that the AAFC had indeed "gotten a football" and with it made an indelible mark on pro football.

Now there was just one major question to be answered—what kind of competition would the Browns be for the NFL's best? For four years, while the two leagues were feuding and the Browns were running rampant over all opposition, Cleveland owner Mickey McBride had been calling for a "true championship showdown" between the NFL and AAFC titlists. The end of the interleague war paved the way for just such an opportunity, and Bert Bell saw to it that the long-awaited confrontation came about. The showdown between the Browns and the Philadelphia Eagles was scheduled for the opening game of the 1950 Season.

The game figured to be a titanic struggle. The Browns' overwhelming success in the AAFC was well known, but the Eagles had been almost as successful in the NFL, winning three straight divisional crowns and two consecutive NFL cham-

pionships by shutout scores. The Eagles' three-year record of 28-7-1 was certainly comparable to Cleveland's 35-2-3. Newspapers reported the game was "the most talked about game in NFL history" and, in response, 71,237 turned out at Philadelphia's Municipal Stadium. No previous NFL championship game had come close to drawing as many people.

Philadelphia, a 6-point favorite, scored first on Cliff Patton's field goal, but Otto Graham, the Browns' quarterback, countered with 3 touchdown passes, a 59-yarder to Dub Jones, a 26-yarder to Dante Lavelli, and a 13-yarder to Mac Speedie. Graham then switched to a grinding ground game in the final period en route to a rather easy 35-10 victory.

"I never saw a team with so many guns," a dazed Greasy Neale, the Eagles' coach, admitted after the game.

"This is as good a team as I have ever seen," Bell said as he congratulated Paul Brown, the Cleveland coach.

"Emotions were higher in this game than any I have ever coached," Brown admitted.

Yet Brown and his squad didn't gloat in the locker room postmortems. They knew they had more to prove. The Browns went on to win 10 of 12 games and then posted an 8-3 victory over the New York Giants in a divisional play-off game. Next was the championship battle against the Los Angeles Rams, the team that had deserted Cleveland just before the Browns arrived. The Browns won, 30-28, when their standout tackle and kicking specialist, Lou Groza, booted a 16-yard field goal with 28 seconds to play. A picture of that crucial kick is included among the Hall of Fame's exhibits.

Above: *Cleveland Rams owner Dan Reeves, who moved his team west.* Right: *Otto Graham, who led the Browns to ten championships.*

Paul Brown, who almost single-handedly created one of pro football's great dynasties, wasn't particularly interested in a pro football career when McBride first approached him about taking over the leadership of the Cleveland team in the AAFC. Brown had been highly successful as a coach at Massillon (Ohio) High School, at Ohio State University, and at Great Lakes Navy, and had tentative plans to return to Ohio State when his tour of duty in the Navy was over. McBride, however, persisted, and on February 9, 1945, Brown made the famous jump into pro football. "My salary was to be twenty-five thousand dollars a year plus five percent ownership of the team and a monthly retainer of fifteen hundred dollars for as long as I remained in the Navy," Brown revealed in his autobiography. "Most important to me, I had complete control of the team's operation, with total freedom to sign players and coaches."

Brown utilized that total control to assemble an awesome team. Graham, fullback Marion Motley, guard Bill Willis, end Dante Lavelli, and tackle Lou Groza from Brown's first Cleveland team all have been elected to the Hall of Fame. Several prized mementoes of the original Browns are on display at the Hall. Graham's number 14 jersey is particularly interesting in that, behind the number 14, is the unfaded image of the number 60. Graham's original number was 60, but when the NFL adopted a standard numbering system in 1951, the Cleveland equipment man simply had cut the old numbers off and stitched new numbers on the same jersey. Groza's kicking shoes are on exhibit, as are a bronzed coaching cap belonging to Brown and the first contract signed by Willis.

Of all the Browns' talented stars, Graham enjoyed the most spectacular success. When Brown set out to build his first pro team, he singled out Graham as his quarterback, although the 6-foot 1-inch, 195-pounder had excelled at Northwestern in 1941, 1942, and 1943 as a single-wing tailback who specialized in the run-pass option play. "From my Ohio State days, I remembered his tremendous peripheral vision and his great athletic skill, as well as his ability to throw a football far and accurately with just a flick of his arm," Brown explained. "I felt he was the best possible player to be our quarterback." If, as Brown contended, "the true test of a quarterback is where his team finishes," then Graham does have to rank as the best of them all. He led the Browns for ten years, the first four in the AAFC and the remainder in the NFL, and his team played in ten league championships, winning seven. With Graham at the controls, the Browns won 109 games, lost just 20, and tied 4—representing a remarkable decade of domination by one team that never has been equaled.

If there ever was any doubt the ex-tailback would become an outstanding T-quarterback, those doubts were quickly dispelled. From the Browns' very first victory, a 44-0 shellacking of the Miami Seahawks in 1946, to Graham's final game, when Cleveland defeated Los Angeles, 38-14, for the 1955 NFL championship, Graham always was the master magician with the delicate passing touch and the clear, cool head in the heat of combat. In those ten seasons, he was beaten out of all-league honors just once—in 1950 by fellow Hall of Famer Bob Waterfield. His lifetime statistics show 1,464 pass completions for 23,584 yards and 174 touchdowns. In the Hall of Fame's Top Twenty passing rankings, Graham, with an 86.8 rating, stands as the number-two passer behind 1983's record-breaker, Joe Montana. Unlike all other major rankings, the Hall's Top Twenty display includes statistics from all major pro football leagues, including the AAFC.

Graham, however, gave much more to the Browns than just passing skill. He was universally recognized as a player who not only performed at his absolute peak in the biggest games but who could bring out the best in his teammates as well. "Otto's the kind of guy you want to do your best for," Mike Scarry, the Cleveland center, once said. "If we are not giving him the protection he needs, he quietly mentions in the huddle that he could use a little more help so he doesn't have to rush his passes. That's all. No griping. How can you help playing for a guy like that?" Graham specialized in the long pass, which he threw with uncanny accuracy. It arched high and settled softly in the hands of talented receivers such as Dante Lavelli and Mac Speedie. Lavelli always said his favorite play was to dart out into the secondary, look back at Graham, and yell for him to throw the football. "That hollering really helped me more than once," Graham agreed. "He had a voice that seemed to penetrate, and it was a welcome sound when a couple of those big tackles would be breathing on me."

A team player who rarely complained, Graham did have a running disagreement with Brown over the coach's policy of calling plays from the sidelines. But, for the most part, he kept his sentiments to himself. "He's the coach," Graham always insisted. "He's the boss." Yet there were occasions when he would override Brown's call. In a game against the Eagles, with the Browns in desperate need of a touchdown, Graham ignored Brown's call for a dive play over left tackle and kept the ball himself for a touchdown. "You'd better be right when you override your boss," Graham said afterward. "If you're wrong too often, you could be out on the street looking for a job." Obviously, Graham never had to look for a job and, in fact, agreed as a

favor to his coach to come back for one final season in 1955 after announcing his retirement the year before.

Graham finished his career on a high note befitting his stature. Playing in the championship game before a record crowd of 85,693 in the Los Angeles Coliseum, he passed for two touchdowns and ran for two more, leading Cleveland to its win over the Rams. Then, he again announced his retirement. When a reporter asked Brown if he would try to get Graham to reconsider, the Cleveland coach firmly replied, "No, I imposed on him once. That's enough." Years later, Brown added, "It was an end of an era that could never again be duplicated because, though we tried, we never found another Otto Graham."

While the Browns were winning seven Eastern Division titles in eight years after joining the NFL in 1950, the Detroit Lions and the Los Angeles Rams dominated the Western Conference. There is some validity to the claim that the Lions actually were the best in the NFL because the Detroit team did defeat the Browns in three of four championship game battles between the two teams. However, by the mid-1950's, a new powerhouse was about to grab the spotlight in the NFL West. In 1958, the Baltimore Colts exploded onto the championship scene with an impact that spread interest in pro football to corners of the country that until then had virtually ignored the sport.

The Baltimore team that moved from the AAFC

Opposite: *Dante Lavelli of the Cleveland Browns in 1951 action. His white helmet is on display at the Hall. Top: The helmet of Green Bay Packers ace Tony Canadeo also has a place in the exhibition rotunda. Above: Graham presents his jersey to the Hall's second director, Dick Gallagher.*

115

into the NFL in 1950 had disbanded after just one season, but in its place a new franchise was founded by Carroll Rosenbloom in 1953.

A year later, Rosenbloom hired as his head coach a Cleveland assistant, Wilbur "Weeb" Ewbank, who embarked on a building program targeted for a championship in five seasons. He reached the NFL championship game right on schedule.

In his refurbishing plan, Ewbank held on to the most capable of the talent-thin squad he inherited and, using them as a nucleus, carefully augmented his team with capable free agents and quality draft picks. Two defensive stars, end Gino Marchetti and tackle Art Donovan, were already on hand when Ewbank took over. End Raymond Berry, who eventually wound up with 631 career receptions, joined the team in 1955, and halfback Lenny Moore came aboard a year later. All are now members of the Hall of Fame. All played a vital role in Baltimore's climb to the NFL throne.

The key figure, however, was an obscure quarterback who played college football at the University of Louisville—Johnny Unitas. As a ninth-round draft choice of the Pittsburgh Steelers in 1955, Unitas was so lightly regarded that he was cut before he threw even one pass in game action; from there he went on to play semipro ball in the Pittsburgh area with the Bloomfield Rams for $6 a game. After the season, an interested fan wrote Ewbank telling him of the outstanding passer he had seen on the sandlots. Not wanting to miss any opportunity to strengthen his team, Ewbank checked out the tip and eventually signed Unitas to a $7,000 contract.

Unitas was ticketed for backup duty behind George Shaw and nothing more when the 1956 season got under way. But, in the fourth game of the season, Shaw was severely injured and Ewbank had to go with Unitas.

His first pass was intercepted and returned for a touchdown by the Chicago Bears, but from that point on, he never looked back. Before Unitas retired 18 seasons later, he had become a household name among American sports fans. His career statistics are astonishing—5,186 pass attempts, 2,830 completions, 40,239 yards gained, and 290 touchdown passes. A five-time all-NFL selection, he was named the NFL Player of the Year in 1959, 1964, and 1967. The record book is still clogged with Johnny Unitas notations, perhaps the most remarkable being the fact that Unitas threw at least one touchdown pass in an incredible 47 consecutive games (49 if you count the 1958 and 1959 NFL championship games). That, and Joe Dimaggio's 56-game hitting streak in baseball may be the most difficult feats to match in all of sports' recorded history. This amazing accomplishment is now chronicled in detail in a major new display at the Hall.

For all of his exceptional accomplishments, his last-second heroics in the 1958 NFL championship game against the New York Giants more than anything else place Unitas in the forefront of American sports heroes. In this game, which received broader television coverage than any ever played before, millions of fans saw for the first time all of the marvelous attributes that later earned Unitas the designation as the NFL's top quarterback in its first 50 years. He had courage, confidence, coolness under fire, leadership, play-calling genius, as well as passing skill. Fans from coast to coast soon grew to expect the impossible and, with stunning

Opposite: *The Browns won their fourth AAFC title in 1949. Above: A few years later in 1957, fullback Jim Brown joined the Cleveland team.*

regularity during his long tenure, the 6-foot 1-inch, 195-pound Pittsburgh native provided just that.

The 1958 championship game matched teams of equal ability. Like the Colts, the Giants listed a handful of future Hall of Famers on their roster—linebacker Sam Huff, tackler Roosevelt Brown, halfback Frank Gifford, defensive end Andy Robustelli, and safety Emlen Tunnell. It had taken a 10–0 playoff victory over defending-champion Cleveland for the Giants to win the Eastern championship, while in the West, the Colts edged past the Chicago Bears and the L.A. Rams by just one

game.

Baltimore got off quickly against the Giants, Unitas throwing 15 yards to Berry for a touchdown as the Colts forged a 14-3 halftime lead. New York fought back in the second half and took a 17-14 advantage it still held when the Colts started a last-ditch drive from their own 14 with just 2 minutes to play. Unitas went to the air seven consecutive times. He completed four, three to Berry. With the Colts at the New York 13 and only 7 seconds remaining, Steve Myrha kicked a field goal that sent the game into overtime—a first for the NFL title game series.

Johnny Unitas' strong right arm paced the Colts to victory in the 1958 NFL championship game.

Besieged by reporters in the locker room following the game, Unitas was asked the obvious: "Why take a chance passing with the Colts already in field-goal position?" He answered politely but with calculated aplomb: "When you know what you are doing, you're not intercepted. The Giants were jammed up at the line and not expecting a pass. If Jim had been covered, I'd have thrown the pass out of bounds. It's just that I would rather win a game like this by a touchdown than a field goal."

For some athletes, such statements would smack of cockiness. In Unitas' case, he was just being himself—honest, telling it like he thought it was, and, at the same time, demonstrating a rare perception of the right things to do on a football field.

Unitas was always popular with his teammates, but there never was any question who was running the show on the field. Many an erring Colt felt his sting when things didn't go right. As one Colt suggested when asked what it was like playing with Unitas, "It's like being in the huddle with God."

In many circles, the 1958 championship game has been labeled "The Greatest Game Ever Played." Because of its length, the intense competitiveness, and the brilliant individual performances on both sides, such a description has its merits. Historians agree that the game, because of its nature and the size and presence of the television audience, was pivotal in pro football history, pointing out that the modern surge of popularity for the sport stems from this one game.

Ironically, just one decade later, another landmark event again featured Ewbank and Unitas. This time it was Super Bowl III, matching the Colts, of which Unitas was still a member, and the New York Jets of the American Football League, coached by Ewbank. After leading the Colts to championships in 1958 and 1959, Ewbank had fallen out of favor with the Baltimore ownership and wound up in 1963 as the coach of the Jets in the rival AFL. He had gone right to work, utilizing the same formula that had been so successful in Baltimore, and built another championship team. The only difference was that, with the Jets, it had taken him six years to reach the top.

In a remarkable parallel to the situation in Baltimore a decade earlier, a talented young quarterback also triggered the Jets' rise. Ewbank's new quarterback was Joe Namath from the University of Alabama, who in 1965 had signed a highly publicized $400,000 contract that, more than anything else, had put the Jets and the AFL on the map until merger brought the two leagues together. Merger had spawned the Super Bowl series

New York was stymied after the overtime kickoff, so Unitas got the opportunity to move the ball again, this time from the Colts' 20. With textbook-perfect play selection, he steered the Colts to a first down at the Giants' eight. Alan Ameche hit the line for a yard. Then Unitas stunned the nationwide television audience by passing to tight end Jim Mutscheller at the one-yard line. On third down, Ameche slashed off right tackle for the touchdown that gave the Colts a 23-17 victory. An artist's rendering of that winning touchdown, the Colts' game ball, and a piece of the Yankee Stadium goalpost are included in the Hall of Fame's display·

but, after two games, teams from the AFL had not been able to prove themselves the equals of their NFL counterparts. As thousands gathered in Miami for the third AFL-NFL World Championship, the prevailing mood was that Super Bowl III would be the most uneven pairing of all.

While the Jets had beaten an excellent Oakland team in a 27-23 thriller for the AFL championship, the Colts had whipped 13 of 14 opponents and then swamped Cleveland, 34-0, in the NFL championship game. Many felt the 1968 Colts were the strongest team ever to represent Baltimore. "Any more matches like this," one writer observed, "and the Super Bowl will be headed for oblivion." Echoing this sentiment, 49 of 55 writers polled two days before the game selected the Colts to win; some said the Colts would win by as many as 47 points. Throughout the week before the game, however, there was only one voice challenging the forecast of impending disaster for the Jets. The lone dissenter was Namath, the Jets' brash young quarterback, who, three days before the game, staunchly promised, "We'll win. I guarantee it!"

Ewbank preferred to keep the Colts overly confident and winced when Namath's statement hit the newspaper headlines. "I really wished Joe hadn't said that," the low-key Ewbank said. "Actually, we all thought we would win—we just didn't want the Colts to know. But Joe is an honest person and, when someone asked him about the outcome, he said what he honestly believed. I couldn't criticize him for that." Only after the game was under way did people begin to take Namath's "guarantee" seriously.

The first quarter was played close to the vest, but the Jets broke through with a 12-play, 80-yard drive early in the second period. Namath completed five of six passes during the march, and fullback Matt Snell, who scored from the Colts' four, carried six times into the surprisingly vulnerable right side of Baltimore's defensive line. The Jets clung to that 7-0 lead at halftime. New York, with Namath in command, controlled the ball for all but seven plays in the third quarter, while Jim Turner kicked 32- and 30-yard field goals. Turner then added a third at the start of the final period for a 16-0 bulge. A touch of drama unfolded, but soon fizzled, in the fourth period when Unitas, who had been sidelined most of the season with a bad elbow, entered the game and led the Colts to their only

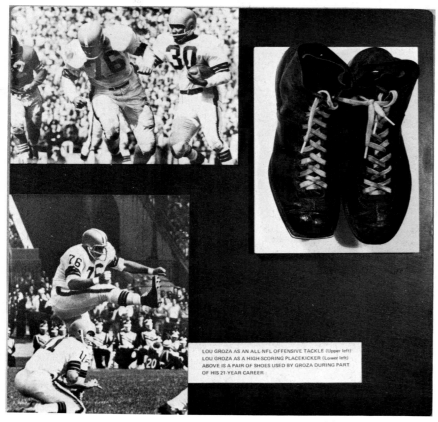

LOU GROZA AS AN ALL-NFL OFFENSIVE TACKLE (Upper left)
LOU GROZA AS A HIGH-SCORING PLACEKICKER (Lower left)
ABOVE IS A PAIR OF SHOES USED BY GROZA DURING PART
OF HIS 21-YEAR CAREER

Opposite: *Johnny Unitas was a Baltimore hero for 17 seasons. He was the first to pass for more than 40,000 yards.* Top: *Front-page headlines from the host cities recapture the excitement of the first five Super Bowl games.* Bottom: *Lou Groza is remembered in this display both as a six-time all-NFL tackle and as a placekicking star who scored 1,068 points.* Center: *The dominance of the Cleveland Browns is chronicled in this All-America Football Conference exhibition.* Above: *A separate panel tells the story of every Super Bowl, but Super Bowl III provided the biggest upset and the most drama.*

touchdown. But this was one time when it was unrealistic to expect even the old master to guide the Colts to a come-from-behind victory.

Once again, Ewbank had presided at a pivotal game in NFL history. The amazing upset assured the integrity of the Super Bowl and did more than anything else to make the series into an American sports classic. The Hall of Fame spotlights Super Bowl III in several displays. Namath's jersey is in the Modern Era exhibit and a picture panel story of the game is in the Pro Football Adventure Room. The banner headline the Miami *Herald* used to proclaim the startling outcome is displayed in the Hall's Super Bowl exhibition.

Players such as Baugh, Hutson, Luckman, and Unitas were, by the nature of their abilities and the timing of their arrival on the NFL scene, able to alter the evolutionary course of pro football. Many players equally as talented didn't have the opportunity to change the course of history during their tenures, but they made their marks simply by doing their jobs superbly. One such craftsman was Jim Brown. For nine seasons with the Cleveland Browns, from 1957 through 1965, Brown's primary job was to run with the football, and he did that better than anyone else, past or present. "I rate Jim Brown as the greatest running back of all time," Chuck Heaton, the Cleveland representative on the Hall's board of selectors, wrote at the time of Brown's induction into the Hall in 1971. "I never expect to see another like him."

Unlike most great athletes, Brown retired at the age of 30, when he was still the number-one running back in the NFL and still in outstanding physical condition. He left behind a record book saturated with outstanding and precedent-setting accomplishments. As a rusher, he accounted for 12,312 yards and 106 touchdowns. He scored 126 touchdowns in all and on rushing, receiving, and kickoff-return plays, he amassed 15,459 yards, or almost 9 miles.

Although the Syracuse star was Cleveland's first draft pick in 1957, he actually was the Browns' second choice. Their preferred choice was quarterback Len Dawson of Purdue, who was picked by Pittsburgh just before Cleveland's drafting turn. This was no case of second best, however. The payoff for the Browns was immediate. In 1957, Brown was named both NFL Rookie of the Year and Player of the Year. And the honors never stopped coming. In 1958 and in 1965, his final season, he was named the league's Most Valuable Player. He was a unanimous all-NFL choice eight times in nine years and played in nine consecutive Pro Bowls, winning Player of the Game honors twice. In his final game, the 1966 Pro Bowl, he scored

three touchdowns. But the most significant statistic of all may be that, despite the constant pounding he absorbed game after game from defenses always stacked against him, the 6-foot 2-inch, 230-pounder never missed a game in nine years. As one admiring opponent once put it, "That Brown. He says he isn't Superman. What he really means is that Superman isn't Jimmy Brown."

In keeping with the Hall's effort to pay tribute to those players who have been the best in the sport, Brown's full game uniform, complete with his famous number 32 Browns' jersey and his bright orange helmet, hangs in the Maturing Years section. Here and in nearby displays, several players who made unique contributions also are recognized with a display of their mementoes. In these sections, exhibits are designed so that artifacts can be easily replaced by new ones as significant events occur or new stars emerge. For example, two unusual kicking shoes on display belonged to handicapped players who played pro football for many years. One is the square-toed shoe of Ben Agajanian, who scored 655 points kicking for 9 teams in 3 leagues. Along with linebacker Hardy Brown, Agajanian is the only player to perform in the AAFC, NFL, and AFL. Agajanian lost all the toes on his kicking foot in an elevator accident while he was at the University of New Mexico, and his kicking shoe was shortened to accommodate his toeless foot. The other shoe is the square-bottom variety worn by Tom Dempsey of the New Orleans Saints when he kicked a record 63-yard field goal in 1970. Dempsey was born without a right hand or right foot, but still scored more than 700 points kicking.

Another interesting story is illustrated by a wristband belonging to Tom Matte. In 1965, halfback Matte of the Baltimore Colts performed some late-season heroics when pressed into emergency service in place of Johnny Unitas and Gary Cuozzo, the club's two injured quarterbacks. Unfamiliar with the plays he would have to call, Matte simply jotted some notes on a card and then enclosed the card in a plastic case attached to a band around his wrist. With his gyp sheet always at hand, Matte led the Colts to a victory over Los Angeles that enabled them to tie Green Bay for the Western Division title. In the ensuing play-off, however, the Packers won in overtime, despite Matte's courageous performance. Matte's wristband is one of the more unusual mementoes exhibited at the Hall.

There are a variety of other artifacts on display close by. One is the pair of badly worn shoulder pads used by Hall of Fame quarterback Y. A. Tittle throughout his 17-year career with the Baltimore Colts of the AAFC and the NFL's San Francisco

49ers and New York Giants. Tittle preferred to use adhesive tape to keep his old pads action-ready rather than break in a stiff new pair. A comparatively new item is the complete uniform worn by defensive end Jim Marshall of the Minnesota Vikings, who played longer as a regular on the line of scrimmage than any other player in history. He spent 19 of his 20 NFL seasons with the Vikings and retired after the 1979 season.

Significant records also are recognized with appropriate mementoes in the Modern Era and nearby sections. For example, there are three footballs with special significance. One is the ball Paul Krause of the Vikings grabbed against the Los Angeles Rams in 1979, when he set an all-time interception record by bringing his career total to 81. Next to the Krause ball is an American Football League model caught by Gino Cappelletti of the Boston Patriots for a touchdown that made him the first—and only—1,000-point scorer in AFL annals. The third football is the one kicked off in 1968 at the start of the one-hundredth game in the storied Green Bay Packers-Chicago Bears series. The rivalry began in 1921 when the Bears were still the Chicago Staleys.

Jerseys worn by record-making stars also have their place. O. J. Simpson's number 32 Buffalo Bills' jersey commemorates his 2,003-yard rushing season in 1973. Still muddy and blood-stained, the shirt was shipped to the Hall immediately after the final game of that historic season and was on display fewer than 72 hours after he had established his record. Fran Tarkenton's number 10 Minnesota Vikings jersey was placed on display after he threw his two-hundred-ninety-first touchdown pass, eclipsing Johnny Unitas' record. Other jerseys displayed in the exhibition rotunda belong to Charley Taylor of the Washington Redskins, a 1984 enshrinee of the Hall of Fame who ranks first among lifetime pass catchers with 649 receptions, and to quarterback Jack Kemp of the Buffalo Bills. Kemp, now active in the House of Representatives, is one of only three former NFL players to serve in the United States Congress. Others were end Lavern Dilwey of the 1927-1934 Green Bay Packers and Winfred Denton of the 1922 Evansville Crimson Giants.

Close by are the eyeglasses worn by Miami Dolphins quarterback Bob Griese—the only quarterback to successfully wear glasses in NFL games—and two rings of more than passing interest. One is a duplicate of the size 19½ Hall of Fame ring presented to Bronko Nagurski—the largest ring size ever made by the Balfour Company. The other ring was presented to Billy Cannon, a halfback from Louisiana State University who was one of the first big-name stars signed by the AFL in the interleague war of the 1960's. Similar rings were given to all members of the 1960 Houston Oilers' team that won the first AFL championship.

A helmet worn by New York Giants linebacker Sam Huff in the 1950's and 1960's is another item of interest. Made of hard plastic, the helmet on display has a large depression near its top, an imperfection caused not by a vicious collision as might be supposed, given Huff's hard-hitting reputation, but instead by an overheated radiator on which Huff once innocently tossed his headgear.

Then there are the two footballs used by the Kansas City Chiefs and Green Bay Packers in Super Bowl I. For the first four Super Bowls, while the AFL and NFL were still separate leagues, the team on offense used its league's official football. The AFL ball was the Spalding J5-V, while the NFL model was the Wilson F1100, better known as The Duke. Both "prolate spheroids" had the same dimensional requirements, but there were slight differences in the "ogive," the line of the missile from the laces to the tip of the ball. The NFL ball was a little more rounded, while the AFL version was more pointed. There were also slight differences in the lacing and in the "tacky surface" of the two balls. But even to the most experienced hands, the balls were difficult to tell apart. Green Bay quarterback Bart Starr agreed to a blindfold test in the week before Super Bowl I and then confidently, but incorrectly, selected the J5-V as the NFL model he had been using throughout his career.

The shoes worn by Tony Dorsett of the Dallas Cowboys when he raced a record 99 yards for a touchdown against the Minnesota Vikings on January 3, 1983, are among the Hall's newest mementoes. Besides its record length, the play was unusual in that the Cowboys had only ten men of their offensive unit when the ball was snapped. Fullback Ron Springs was supposed to have carried the ball, but he thought the formation was "Jayhawk," which called for him to leave the field. Unaware of the manpower shortage until the play began, Dallas quarterback Danny White and Dorsett quickly improvised, and the result was an alltime record longest touchdown on a rushing play.

Occupying a major area in the rotunda is the Professional Football Today exhibition, devoted not only to individuals but also to the 28 teams of the present National Football League. The display was created in 1969 at a time when 14 of the 26 teams in pro football had not even been in existence for as long as 10 years. Thus, for more than half of all pro football teams, there was no sense of individual history, no representation in the Hall's displays. Something obviously was needed to fill the void.

The colorful Professional Football Today display quickly became one of the most popular and most photographed of all the Hall's major areas. Each team's individual display contains a helmet plaque and a picture panel of leading players and team personnel, along with a brief history, all of which is updated yearly.

Then there is the George Blanda display, which consists of items from key moments in the exceptional career of the quarterback-kicker. First, there's the Oakland jersey Blanda wore when he "saved the day" for the Raiders on five consecutive weekends in 1970. Then there's the football he kicked to reach the 2,000-point scoring plateau in his final regular-season game in 1975.

It is appropriate that Blanda is honored near the end of the tour in the exhibition rotunda, which provides as the central theme a rough chronological progression through 90 years of pro football. No other player was actively involved in pro football longer than Blanda, who played 26 seasons and 340 games in a career that began in 1949 and ended shortly before the 1976 season. When he retired, he was almost 49 years old and ranked as history's oldest pro football player. In addition to his exceptional longevity, Blanda achieved a number of significant playing accomplishments. Included were a record 2,002 points scored, a passing accumulation of 26,920 yards and 236 touchdowns, a single-season passing record of 36 touchdowns, 21 championship game records, and 21 entries in the regular-season record manual.

Still, all of those accomplishments might have gone relatively unnoticed had it not been for a five-game string in 1970 when he demonstrated the kind of heroics week after week that ordinarily are found only in fiction. On October 25, 1970, Blanda replaced Daryle Lamonica at quarterback and promptly threw three touchdown passes and kicked a field goal, breaking a 7-7 deadlock and giving the Raiders a 31-14 victory over Pittsburgh. The next week, Blanda kicked a 48-yard field goal with 3 seconds left, enabling Oakland to tie Kansas City, 17-17. Next came a 23-20 triumph over Cleveland made possible by a Blanda touchdown pass with 1:34 to go and his 52-yard field goal as time ran out. Then Oakland beat Denver, 24-19, when the 6-foot 2-inch, 215-pound Youngwood, Pennsylvania, native threw a 20-yard scoring strike with 2:28 to play. Finally, on November 22 against San Diego, Blanda kicked a field goal with 7 seconds left, giving Oakland a 20-17 victory. Never before had one individual so completely held his team's destiny in his hands and feet for such an extended period. Making the feat even more remarkable was the fact that Blanda was 43 years old. He became an instant folk hero. As humorist Erma Bombeck wrote in her daily column, "After George beat Cleveland, my husband announced he was going to jog all the way to the garbage can in the morning."

A twelfth-round draft pick of the Chicago Bears in 1949, Blanda, from the University of Kentucky, enjoyed what amounted to three "standard-length" careers with three different teams. He played ten years with the Bears, through 1958. Except for the 1953 and 1954 seasons when he played as a starter, he was cast in the role of a backup quarterback and kicking specialist. He did not play in 1959, but, in 1960, he moved to the Houston Oilers where, for the next seven years he was a big-play, point-producing quarterback who led the Oilers to their only two AFL titles in 1960 and 1961. In 1967, Blanda joined the Raiders for the nine final seasons that eventually assured his membership in the Hall of Fame.

When his election to the Hall was announced early in 1981, Blanda opened a press conference by saying, "I first of all want to clear something up. I never really retired anywhere. I just got fired from every team I was with. In Chicago, they were going with a youth movement and didn't have a place for me. In Houston, they thought I was too old, and I read in the paper that I had been released. Even at Oakland, where they were so good to me, I walked into [Coach] John Madden's office and he said, 'Hey, no visitors allowed in here.' "

A careful examination of the George Blanda story shows that, when studied separately, its component parts do not smack of pro football immortality. After all, being "fired" from three teams is not the ordinary way to gain election to the Hall of Fame. Blanda's 26-year service record was extraordinary, but no one has ever been elected on the basis of playing time alone. His passing statistics, while impressive, do not compare with the records of many of the great passers in the Hall. Scoring 2,002 points is, to be sure, a memorable feat. But the Hall's board of selectors had repeatedly refused to consider a kicking specialist alone as a serious candidate. However, taken together, all these elements add up to an exceptional career, probably one that will never be duplicated. And that quality—uniqueness—is what Hall of Famers are all about.

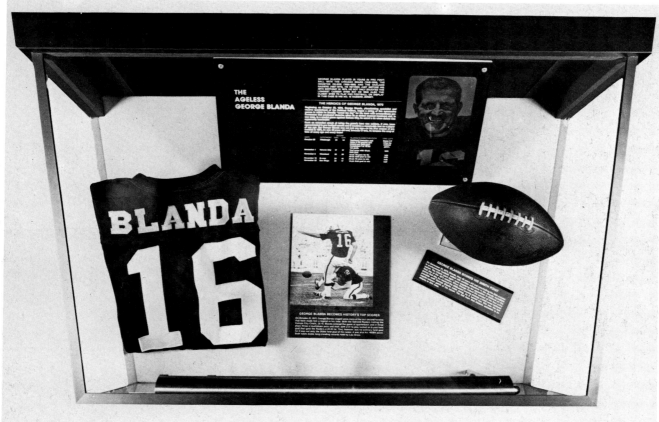

Top: *Supreme Court Justice Byron "Whizzer" White is
featured in this "A Bit out of the Ordinary " display. Above:
George Blanda's unparalleled career is recounted in his
own special exhibition.*

Chapter 6

A Pageant of Photography

The Hall of Fame's Art Gallery is composed of the best photographs of National Football League subjects selected from entries submitted to a nationwide contest conducted each year by the Hall of Fame. These photographs, taken at NFL games by professional photographers regularly assigned to cover them, are judged purely on content—on what the pictures portray and not whom they feature.

So, the Art Gallery is not necessarily about modern-day superstars or record-breaking performances, although there's no way to escape it when the camera's eye has been turned on someone as familiar as Earl Campbell or Don Shula. The photos displayed capture the excitement of play, the emotions of the players, and sometimes, even the "action" on the sidelines. The photos on display are all prizewinners.

The annual photo contest was initiated in 1968 and has become one of the Hall of Fame's most successful and popular projects. The first year of the contest 43 photographers entered 168 photographs. Just a dozen years later, in 1979, 210 photographers submitted 1,086 photographs in four categories—black-and-white action, black-and-white feature, color action, and color feature. Portraiture and experimental photography are judged in the feature categories.

Each year a panel of judges reviews all the entries and names a winner in each individual category; as if that isn't hard enough to do, they then select from those a Photograph of the Year. The pages that follow are a portfolio of prizewinning photographs from the Hall of Fame display.

Page 126: Don Bierman, Chicago Daily News, "Touchdown Dancers." First Place Black and White Action, 1977. Page 127: Joe Elbert, Miami Herald, "Warfield Catch." First Place Black and White Action, 1973.

Above: M. Frederic Stein, Chicago Daily News, "Ring Around the Runner." First Place Black and White Action, 1976. Opposite: Mary Sterling, Sarasota Herald Tribune, "Sweetness." Third Place Color Action, 1979.

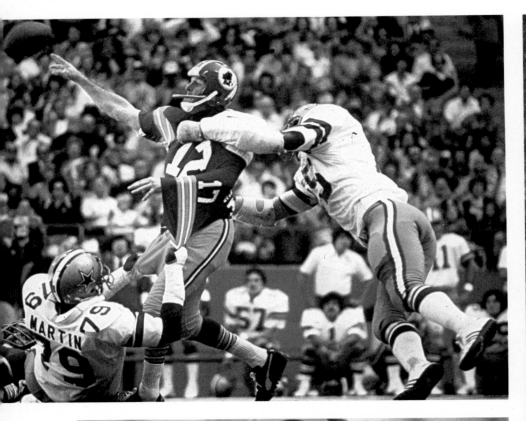

eft: *Phil Huber, Dallas Times Herald. "Kilmer*
pered." First Place Color Action, 1977. Left: Blake Sell, **131**
dena Star-News. "Life at the Bottom." Honorable
ion Color Action,1981.Above: Pete J. Groh, Port Clinton,
News-Herald. "Flakey Fumble." First Place Color
re, 1979.

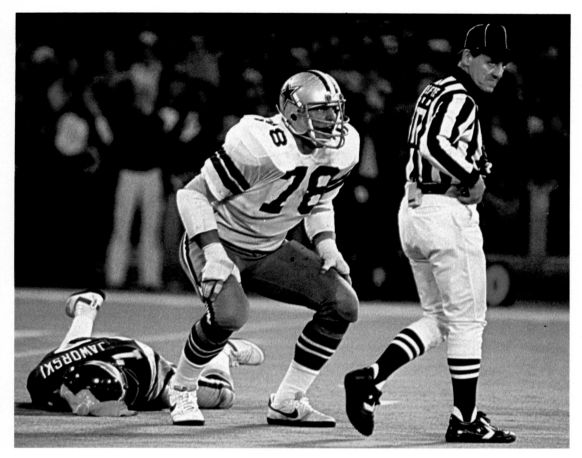

Opposite top: *Walter Iooss. Sports Illustrated. "Full Steam Ahead." Second Place Color Action, 1977.* Opposite bottom: *Ron Scribner, Dallas Cowboys. "The Winning Edge." Second Place Color Action, 1981.* Top: *John Rhodes, Dallas Morning News. "I Don't Believe It." Second Place Color Feature, 1981.* Bottom: *Ron Scribner, Dallas Cowboys, "Mr. Clutch." Honorable Mention Color Action, 1979.*

Above: *Dennis Desprois, San Francisco 49ers, "Super Bowl Ride." First Place Color Feature, 1976.* Left: *Malcolm Emmons, "Angry Coach." First Place Color Feature, 1974.*
Opposite top: *Robert C. Holt III, St. Louis Post-Dispatch, "Up For Grabs." Honorable Mention Color Action, 1978.*
Opposite bottom: *Al Messerschmidt, Miami Beach, "Who's Talking, Who's Listening." Second Place Color Feature, 1980.*

Above: *Charles Trainor, Miami News, "Victory on a Foggy Night." First Place Black and White Action, 1975.* Opposite: *John C. Hillery, Detroit, Michigan, "Walking on Air." Honorable Mention Color Action, 1981.*

Opposite: *Jerry Lodriguss, Metairie, La., "Winning Field Goal." First Place Black and White Feature, 1979.* Above: *Jerry Lodriguss, UPI New Orleans, "Every Which Way But Up." Photograph of the Year, 1980, and First Place Black and White Action.*

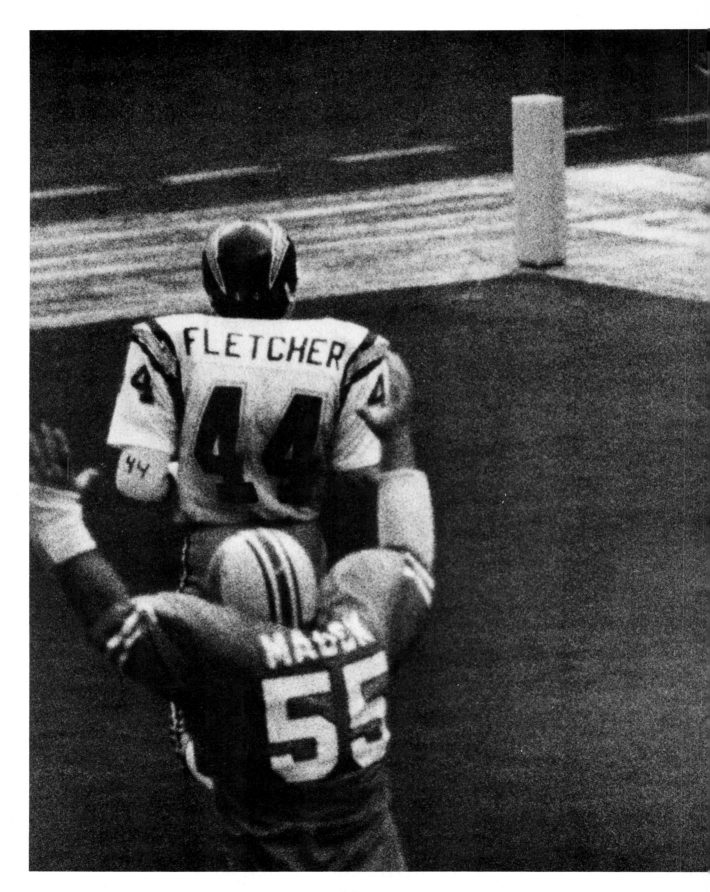

Opposite: *George Honeycutt, Houston Chronicle, "Head-Down Touchdown." First Place Black and White Feature, 1975.* Above: *Vernon J. Biever, Green Bay Packers, "Thank God." First Place Black and White Action, 1969.*

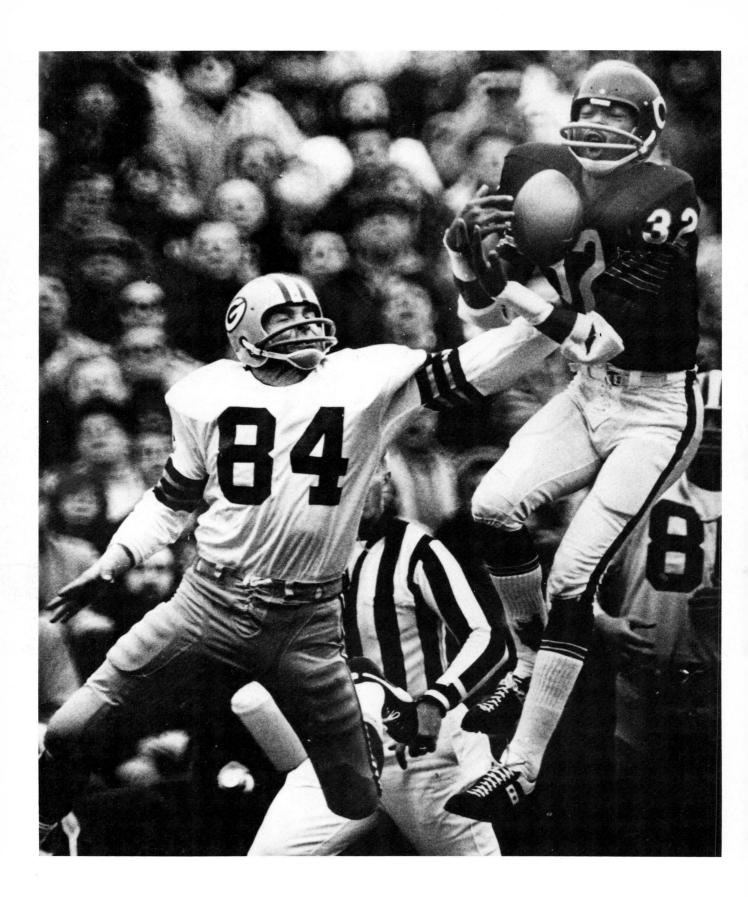

Opposite: *Ron Overdahl, Milwaukee Journal, "Interception."*
First Place Black and White Action, 1972. Above: Lance
Wynn, Tiffin, Ohio Advertiser-Tribune, "Classic Duel." First
Place Black and White Action, 1981.

Opposite: *Michael Delaney, Miami News, "Arrumgumphh!"*
Photograph of the Year, 1982, and First Place Black and
White Action. Above: *David Woo, Dallas Morning News,*
"Arabian Cowboy." First Place Black and White Feature,
1981.

Fawcett Stadium, home of the annual AFC-NFC Hall of Fame preseason opener, is located right across the street from the four-building Pro Football Hall of Fame complex.

Chapter 7

Hall of Famers: "Their Deeds and Dogged Faith"

A player is eligible for the Hall of Fame five years after his retirement, and there is no minimum limit on the number of years he must play in order to be considered. A coach is eligible for election as soon as he announces his retirement; an administrator is eligible even while he continues to work at his job. Anyone can nominate a candidate, merely by making his wishes known to Hall of Fame officials or the 29-member board of selectors that is charged with the task of voting on the nominees. To be elected, a nominee must receive between 80 and 85 percent of the votes cast by the board of selectors, which is made up of one media representative from each of the NFL's 28 cities plus one member of the Pro Football Writers Association of America.

Gale Sayers of the Chicago Bears, voted the NFL's all-time halfback in 1969, is one of a number of players who have been voted into the Hall of Fame the first year of eligibility. Sayers, who entered with the class of 1977, remains the youngest player ever to have been so honored. He was 34 at the time. The oldest enshrinee was Red Badgro, a two-way end with the New York Giants during the 1930's, who came in with the class of 1981. Badgro was 78 when he was elected—he had waited 45 years after having played his last game.

Sayers, Badgro, and the other 121 Hall of Famers are presented here. And, in an attempt to convey as much as possible the feeling of the galleries that are the heart of the Hall, each is represented by the action mural and the biography used in the player's niche to describe his "deeds and dogged faith," to which this area is dedicated.

HERB ADDERLEY

(Michigan State)

CORNERBACK—6-1, 200

1961-1969 Green Bay Packers
1970-1972 Dallas Cowboys

Enshrined in 1980

First-round draft pick, 1961, as offensive back . . . Switched to cornerback late in rookie season . . . Played in five NFL, two NFC title games, four Super Bowls . . . Had 60-yard TD interception in Super Bowl II . . . All-NFL five times, played in five Pro Bowls, seven College All-Star games . . . Career record: 48 interceptions for 1,046 yards, 7 TDs; 120 kickoff returns for 3,080 yards, 2 TDs . . . Born June 8, 1939, in Philadelphia, Pa.

DOUG ATKINS

(Tennessee)

DEFENSIVE END—6-8, 275

1953-1954 Cleveland Browns
1955-1966 Chicago Bears
1967-1969 New Orleans Saints

Enshrined in 1982

All-America tackle at Tennessee . . . Browns' No. 1 draft pick, 1953 . . . Ringleader of powerful Bears' defensive units for 12 years . . . Exceptionally strong, agile, earned legendary acclaim as devastating pass rusher . . . Often leap-frogged blockers to get at passer . . . Scrimmage-line regular for then-record 17 years, 205 games . . . All-NFL three years . . . Played in eight Pro Bowls . . . Born May 8, 1930, in Humboldt, Tenn.

LANCE ALWORTH

(Arkansas)

FLANKER—6-0, 184

1962-1969 San Diego Chargers (AFL)
1970 San Diego Chargers (NFL)
1971-1972 Dallas Cowboys

Enshrined in 1978

1961 Arkansas All-America . . . First AFL star to be enshrined . . . All-AFL seven times, 1963-1969 . . . Played in seven AFL All-Star games . . . Caught passes in 96 straight games . . . AFL receiving leader three years . . . Scored first Dallas TD in Super Bowl VI win . . . Nicknamed "Bambi" for smooth, graceful, spectacular moves . . . Career record: 542 receptions, 10,266 yards, 85 TDs . . . Born August 3, 1940, in Houston, Texas.

MORRIS (Red) BADGRO

(Southern California)

END—6-0, 190

1927 New York Yankees
1930-1935 New York Giants
1936 Brooklyn Dodgers

Enshrined in 1981

Three-sport star at USC . . . Rookie with Red Grange-led 1927 Yankees . . . In pro baseball with St. Louis Browns two years, returned to NFL, 1930 . . . Superior defender, excellent blocker, big-play receiver . . . Tied for NFL pass-receiving title, 1934 . . . All-NFL 1930, 1931, 1933, 1934 . . . Scored first TD in NFL championship game series, 1933 . . . Oldest player ever elected to Hall . . . Born December 1, 1902, in Orillia, Wash.

CLIFF BATTLES

(West Virginia Wesleyan)

HALFBACK—6-1, 201

1932 Boston Braves
1933-1936 Boston Redskins
1937 Washington Redskins

Enshrined in 1968

Phi Beta Kappa scholar, triple-threat grid star at West Virginia Wesleyan . . . NFL rushing champ, 1933, 1937 . . . All-NFL choice, 1933, 1936, 1937 . . . Six-year career rushing—3,542 yards . . . First to gain over 200 yards in one game, 1933 . . . Scored three spectacular TDs in division-clinching win over Giants, 1937 . . . Retired after 1937 season when salary was frozen at $3,000 . . . Born May, 1, 1910, in Akron, Ohio . . . Died April 28, 1981, at age of 70.

CHUCK BEDNARIK

(Pennsylvania)

CENTER-LINEBACKER—6-3, 230

1949-1962 Philadelphia Eagles

Enshrined in 1967

Two-time Pennsylvania all-America . . . Eagles' bonus draft choice, 1949 . . . NFL's last "iron man" star . . . Rugged, durable, bulldozing blocker, bone-jarring tackler . . . Missed only three games in 14 years . . . Eight times all-NFL . . . Played in eight Pro Bowls, MVP in 1954 game . . . Named NFL's all-time center, 1969 . . . Played 58 minutes, made game-saving tackle, 1960 NFL title game . . . Born May 1, 1925, in Bethlehem, Pa.

SAMMY BAUGH

(Texas Christian)

QUARTERBACK—6-2, 180

1937-1952 Washington Redskins

Charter Enshrinee, 1963

Two-time TCU all-America . . . No. 1 draft choice, 1937 . . . Split career between tailback, T-quarterback . . . Premier passer who influenced great offensive revolution . . . All-NFL six years . . . NFL passing, punting, interception champ, 1943 . . . Six-time NFL passing leader . . . History's top punter . . . Career record: 21,886 yards, 186 TDs passing; 44.9-yard punting average, 28 interceptions . . . Born March 17, 1914, in Temple, Texas.

BERT BELL

(Pennsylvania)

LEAGUE ADMINISTRATOR
OWNER

1933-1940 Philadelphia Eagles
1941-1946 Pittsburgh Steelers

Charter Enshrinee, 1963

Weathered heavy financial losses as Eagles' owner, 1933-1940, Steelers' co-owner, 1941-1946 . . . Built NFL image to unprecedented heights as commissioner, 1946-1959 . . . Generalled NFL's war with AAFC . . . Set up farsighted television policies . . . Established strong anti-gambling controls . . . Recognized NFL Players Association . . . Born February 25, 1895, in Philadelphia, Pa. . . . Died October 11, 1959, at age 64.

BOBBY BELL

(Minnesota)

LINEBACKER, DEFENSIVE END
6-4, 225

1963-1974 Kansas City Chiefs

Enshrined in 1983

All-state prep quarterback, all-America tackle at Minnesota . . . Big early prize in AFL-NFL war . . . All-AFL/AFC nine times. All-time AFL choice, 1969 . . . Extremely versatile, determined, rugged, fast, smart . . . Played in last six AFL All-Star games, first three AFC-NFC Pro Bowls . . . Scored eight career touchdowns, one on onside kickoff return . . . Had 25 interceptions for 479 yards, 6 TDs . . . Born June 17, 1940, in Shelby, N.C.

CHARLES W. BIDWILL, SR.

(Loyola of Chicago)

OWNER-ADMINISTRATOR

1933-1947 Chicago Cardinals

Enshrined in 1967

Purchased Cardinals' franchise, 1933 . . . staunch faith in NFL stood as guiding light during dark depression years . . . Dealt AAFC most stunning blow with $100,000 signing of Charley Trippi, 1947 . . . Built famous "Dream Backfield" but died before it could bring him a Cardinals' championship . . . Financial help saved Bears' ownership for George Halas, 1932 . . . Born September 16, 1895, in Chicago, Ill. . . . Died April 19, 1947, at age of 51.

RAYMOND BERRY

(Southern Methodist)

END—6-2, 187

1955-1967 Baltimore Colts

Enshrined in 1973

Formed exceptional pass-catch team with Johnny Unitas . . . Caught then-record 631 passes for 9,275 yards, 68 touchdowns . . . All-NFL in 1958, 1959, 1960 . . . Played in five Pro Bowl games . . . Fumbled only once in 13-season career . . . Set NFL title game mark with 12 catches for 178 yards in 1958 overtime game . . . Colts' 20th-round future choice in 1954 . . . Born February 27, 1933, in Corpus Christi, Texas.

GEORGE BLANDA

(Kentucky)

QUARTERBACK-KICKER—6-2, 215

1949 Chicago Bears
1950 Baltimore Colts
1950-1958 Chicago Bears
1960-1966 Houston Oilers (AFL)
1967-1969 Oakland Raiders (AFL)
1970-1975 Oakland Raiders (NFL)

Enshrined in 1981

Famous for last-minute heroics in five straight 1970 games . . . Scored record 2,002 points . . . Holds or ties for 21 title-game, 16 regular-season marks . . . Passed for 7 TDs one game, 36 in season, 1961 . . . 1961 AFL, 1970 AFC Player of Year . . . Career passing totals: 4,007 attempts, 26,920 yards, 236 TDs . . . 26-season, 340-game career longest ever . . . Played until age of 48 . . . Born September 17, 1927, in Youngwood, Pa.

JIM BROWN

(Syracuse)

FULLBACK—6-2, 228

1957-1965 Cleveland Browns

Enshrined in 1971

Syracuse all-America, 1956 . . . Browns' No. 1 draft pick, 1957 . . . Most awesome runner in history . . . Led NFL rushers eight years . . . All-NFL eight of nine years . . . NFL's Most Valuable Player, 1958, 1965 . . . Rookie of Year, 1957 . . . Played in nine straight Pro Bowls . . . Career marks: 12,312 yards rushing, 262 receptions, 15,459 combined net yards, 756 points scored . . . Born February 17, 1936, in St. Simons, Ga.

ROOSEVELT BROWN

(Morgan State)

OFFENSIVE TACKLE—6-3, 255

1953-1965 New York Giants

Enshrined in 1975

Black all-America at Morgan State, 1951-1952 . . . Giants' 27th pick in 1953 draft . . . Joined Giants as green 20-year old . . . Quickly won starting role, held it for 13 seasons . . . Excellent downfield blocker, classic pass protector, fast, mobile . . . All-NFL eight straight years, 1956-1963 . . . Played in nine Pro Bowl games . . . Named NFL's Lineman of Year, 1956 . . . Born October 20, 1932, in Charlottesville, Va.

PAUL BROWN

(Miami of Ohio)

COACH

1946-1949 Cleveland Browns (AAFC)
1950-1962 Cleveland Browns (NFL)

Enshrined in 1967

Exceptionally successful coach at all levels of football . . . Organized Browns in AAFC, 1946 . . . Built great Cleveland dynasty with 158-48-8 record, four AAFC titles, three NFL crowns, only one losing season in 17 years . . . A revolutionary innovator with many coaching "firsts" to his credit . . . Elected to Pro Football Hall of Fame before Cincinnati Bengals tenure began . . . Born September 7, 1908, in Norwalk, Ohio.

WILLIE BROWN

(Grambling)

CORNERBACK—6-1, 210

1963-1966 Denver Broncos (AFL)
1967-1969 Oakland Raiders (AFL)
1970-1978 Oakland Raiders (NFL)

Enshrined in 1984

Undrafted, cut by Oilers, joined 1963 Broncos, allAFL in second season . . . Traded to Raiders, 1967 . . . Fast, mobile, aggressive . . . All-AFL/AFC seven times . . . All-time AFL team, 1969 . . . Played in five AFL All-Star games, four AFC-NFC Pro Bowls, nine AFL/AFC title games, two Super Bowls . . . Career totals: 54 interceptions, 472 yards, two TDs . . . Scored on 75-yard interception, Super Bowl XI . . . Born December 2, 1940, in Yazoo City, Miss.

DICK BUTKUS

(Illinois)

MIDDLE LINEBACKER—6-3, 245

1965-1973 Chicago Bears

Enshrined in 1979

Two-time Illinois all-America . . . First-round draft pick, 1965 . . . Exceptional defensive star with speed, quickness, instinct, strength . . . Great leader, tremendous competitor, adept at forcing fumbles . . . Had 22 lifetime interceptions, 25 opponents' fumble recoveries . . . Serious knee injury ended brilliant career . . . All-NFL seven years . . . In eight straight Pro Bowls . . . Born December 9, 1942, in Chicago, Ill.

JOE CARR

(No College)

LEAGUE ADMINISTRATOR

1921-39 National Football League

Charter Enshrinee, 1963

Sportswriter, promoter who founded Columbus Panhandles team, 1904 . . . NFL co-organizer, 1920 . . . NFL president, 1921-1939 . . . Gave NFL stability, integrity with rigid enforcement of rules . . . Introduced standard player's contract . . . Barred use of collegians in NFL play . . . Worked tirelessly to interest financially capable new owners . . . Born October 22, 1880, in Columbus, Ohio . . . Died May 20, 1939, at age of 58.

TONY CANADEO

(Gonzaga)

HALFBACK—5-11, 195

1941-1944 Green Bay Packers
1946-1952 Green Bay Packers

Enshrined in 1974

Gonzaga Little all-America, 1939 . . . Multi-talented two-way performer . . . Averaged 75 yards all categories in 116 NFL games . . . Led Packers air game, 1943 . . . Used as heavy-duty runner on return from service, 1946 . . . Became third back to pass 1,000-yard mark in one season, 1949 . . . All-NFL, 1943, 1949 . . . Career record: 4,197 yards rushing, 1,642 yards passing, 186 points, 69 pass receptions . . . Born May 5, 1919, in Chicago, Ill.

GUY CHAMBERLIN

(Nebraska)

END—6-2, 210
COACH

1919 Canton Bulldogs (pre-NFL)
1920 Decatur Staleys
1921 Chicago Staleys
1922-1923 Canton Bulldogs
1924 Cleveland Bulldogs
1925-1926 Frankford Yellowjackets
1927-1928 Chicago Cardinals

Enshrined in 1965

Legendary grid hero at Nebraska . . . Became premier end of the NFL in the 1920s . . . Extremely durable two-way performer . . . Player-coach of four NFL championshop teams: 1922-1923 Canton Bulldogs, 1924 Cleveland Bulldogs, 1926 Frankford Yellowjackets . . . Six-year coaching record 56-14-5 for a remarkable .780 percentage . . . Born January 16, 1894, at Blue Springs, Nebr. . . . Died April 4, 1967, at age of 73.

JACK CHRISTIANSEN

(Colorado State U.)

DEFENSIVE BACK—6-1, 185

1951-1958 Detroit Lions

Enshrined in 1970

Left safety stalwart on three title teams . . . All-NFL six straight years, 1952-1957 . . . Played in five Pro Bowls . . . Formidable defender, return specialist . . . Foes' standard rule: "Don't pass in his area, don't punt to him" . . . NFL interception leader, 1953, 1957 . . . Career marks: 46 steals for 717 yards, 3 TDs; 85 punt returns for 1,084 yards, record 8 TDs . . . Born December 20, 1928, in Sublette, Kans.

GEORGE CONNOR

(Holy Cross, Notre Dame)

TACKLE, LINEBACKER
6-3, 240

1948-1955 Chicago Bears

Enshrined in 1975

All-America at both Holy Cross, Notre Dame . . . Boston Yanks' No. 1 draft pick, 1948 . . . Quickly traded to Bears . . . All-NFL at three positions—offensive tackle, defensive tackle, linebacker . . . All-NFL five years . . . Two-way performer throughout career . . . First of big, fast, agile linebackers . . . Exceptional at diagnosing enemy plays . . . Played in first four Pro Bowl games . . . Born January 21, 1925, in Chicago, Ill.

EARL (Dutch) CLARK

(Colorado College)

QUARTERBACK—6-0, 185

1931-1932 Portsmouth Spartans
1934-1938 Detroit Lions

Charter Enshrinee, 1963

Colorado College all-America, 1928 . . . Called signals, played tailback, did everything superbly well . . . Quiet, quick-thinking, exceptional team leader . . . NFL's last dropkicking specialist . . . All-NFL six of seven years . . . NFL's scoring champ three years . . . Generalled Lions to 1935 NFL title . . . Scored 368 points on 42 TDs, 71 PATs, 15 FGs . . . Player-coach final two seasons . . . Born October 11, 1906, in Fowler, Colo. . . . Died August 5, 1978, at age of 71.

JIMMY CONZELMAN

(Washington of St. Louis)

QUARTERBACK—6-0, 180
COACH-OWNER

1920 Decatur Staleys
1921-1922 Rock Island Independents
1923-1924 Milwaukee Badgers
1925-1926 Detroit Panthers
1927-1930 Providence Steam Roller
1940-1942 Chicago Cardinals
1946-1948 Chicago Cardinals

Enshrined in 1964

Multi-talented athlete, editor, executive, songwriter, orator . . . Began NFL career with Staleys, 1920 . . . Player-coach of four NFL teams in the 1920s, including 1928 champion Providence . . . Player-coach-owner of Detroit team, 1925-1926 . . . Knee injury ended 10-year playing career, 1928 . . . Coached Cardinals to 1947 NFL, 1948 division crowns . . . Born March 6, 1898, in St. Louis, Mo., . . . Died July 31, 1970, at age of 72.

WILLIE DAVIS

(Grambling)

DEFENSIVE END—6-3, 245

1958-1959 Cleveland Browns
1960-1969 Green Bay Packers

Enshrined in 1981

No. 17 draft pick, 1956 . . . Played Army football prior to joining 1958 Browns . . . Career turning point came with 1960 trade to Green Bay, where he became a defensive standout . . . Had speed, agility, size . . . Great team leader, dedicated, intelligent . . . All-NFL five seasons . . . In five Pro Bowls, six NFL title games, two Super Bowls . . . Didn't miss a game in 12-year, 162-game career . . . Born July 24, 1934, in Lisbon, La.

JOHN (Paddy) DRISCOLL

(Northwestern)

QUARTERBACK—5-11, 160

1919 Hammond Pros (pre-NFL)
1920 Decatur Staleys
1920-1925 Chicago Cardinals
1926-1929 Chicago Bears

Enshrined in 1965

Triple-threat on attack, flawless on defense . . . Drop-kicked record four field goals one game, 1925 . . . Drop-kicked 50-yard field goal, 1924 . . . Scored 27 points one game, 1923 . . . 23 precision punts stymied Grange's NFL debut, 1925 . . . Sold by Cards to Bears, 1926, to thwart signing with rival AFL . . . Sparked Bears four years . . . All-NFL six times . . . Born January 11, 1896, in Evanston, Ill. . . . Died June 29, 1968, at age of 72.

ART DONOVAN

(Boston College)

DEFENSIVE TACKLE—6-3, 265

1950 Baltimore Colts
1951 New York Yanks
1952 Dallas Texans
1953-1961 Baltimore Colts

Enshrined in 1968

First Colt to enter Pro Football Hall of Fame . . . Began NFL play as 26-year-old rookie in 1950 . . . Vital part of Baltimore's climb to powerhouse status in 1950's . . . All-NFL, 1954 through 1957 . . . Played in five Pro Bowls . . . Great morale builder on Colts' teams . . . Son of famous boxing referee of same name . . . Played at Boston College after World War II Marines service . . . Born June 5, 1925, in The Bronx, N.Y.

BILL DUDLEY

(Virginia)

HALFBACK—5-10, 176

1942 Pittsburgh Steelers
1945-1946 Pittsburgh Steelers
1947-1949 Detroit Lions
1950-1951 Washington Redskins
1953 Washington Redskins

Enshrined in 1966

Virginia's first All-America, 1941 . . . Steelers' No. 1 draft choice, 1942 . . . Small, slow with unorthodox style, but exceptionally versatile, awesomely efficient . . . Won rare "triple crown" (NFL rushing, interception, punt-return titles), 1946 . . . All-NFL, 1942, 1946 . . . Most Valuable Player, 1946 . . . Gained 8,147 combined net yards, scored 484 points, had 23 interceptions in career . . . Born December 24, 1921, in Bluefield, Va.

154

ALBERT GLEN (Turk) EDWARDS

(Washington State)

TACKLE—6-2½, 260

1932 Boston Braves
1933-1936 Boston Redskins
1937-1940 Washington Redskins

Enshrined in 1969

Rose Bowl star, Washington State all-America, 1930 . . . Joined new Boston team for $150 a game, 1932 . . . Giant of his era . . . Immovable, impregnable 60-minute workhorse . . . Steamrolling blocker, smothering tackler . . . Official all-NFL, 1932, 1933, 1936, 1937 . . . Bizarre knee injury suffered at pre-game coin toss ended career, 1940 . . . Born September 28, 1907, in Mold, Wash. . . . Died January 12, 1973, at age of 65.

TOM FEARS

(Santa Clara, UCLA)

END—6-2, 215

1948-1956 Los Angeles Rams

Enshrined in 1970

Led NFL receivers first three seasons, 1948-1950 . . . Top season mark: 84 catches, 1950 . . . Had three TD receptions in 1950 division title game . . . Caught 73-yard pass to win 1951 NFL title . . . Caught record 18 passes one game, 1950 . . . All-NFL, 1949, 1950 . . . Career mark: 400 catches for 5,397 yards, 38 TDs . . . Precise pattern-runner, specialized in buttonhook route . . . Born December 3, 1923, in Los Angeles, Calif.

WEEB EWBANK

(Miami of Ohio)

COACH

1954-1962 Baltimore Colts
1963-1969 New York Jets (AFL)
1970-1973 New York Jets (NFL)

Enshrined in 1978

Only coach to win world championships in both NFL, AFL . . . His 1958, 1959 Colts won NFL crowns, 1968 Jets AFL, Super Bowl III titles . . . Took first pro head coach job at age of 47 . . . Led both Colts, Jets to championships with patient, effective building programs paced by brilliant quarterbacks . . . Possessed great ability to judge, handle young talent . . . Coached 130 career wins . . . Born May 6, 1907, in Richmond, Ind.

RAY FLAHERTY

(Gonzaga)

COACH

1936 Boston Redskins
1937-1942 Washington Redskins
1946-1948 New York Yankees (AAFC)
1949 Chicago Hornets (AAFC)

Enshrined in 1976

Compiled 80-37-5 coaching record . . . Won four Eastern division, two NFL titles with Redskins, two AAFC divisional crowns with Yankees . . . Introduced behind-the-line screen pass in 1937 NFL title game . . . Two-platoon system with one rushing, one passing unit also a Flaherty first . . . Played end with Los Angeles Wildcats (first AFL), New York Yankees, New York Giants . . . All-NFL, 1928, 1932 . . . Born September 1, 1904, in Spokane, Wash.

LEN FORD

(Morgan State, Michigan)

DEFENSIVE END—6-5, 260

1948-1949 Los Angeles Dons (AAFC)
1950-1957 Cleveland Browns
1958 Green Bay Packers

Enshrined in 1976

Caught 67 passes as two-way end with Dons, 1948, 1949 . . . After AAFC folded, Browns converted him to full-time defensive end, altered defenses to take advantage of his exceptional pass-rushing skills . . . Overcame serious injuries in 1950 to earn all-NFL honors five times, 1951-1955 . . . Played in four Pro Bowls . . . Recovered 20 opponents' fumbles in career . . . Born February 18, 1926, in Washington, D.C. . . . Died March 14, 1972, at age of 46.

BILL GEORGE

(Wake Forest)

LINEBACKER—6-2, 230

1952-1965 Chicago Bears
1966 Los Angeles Rams

Enshrined in 1974

Bears' No. 2 future draft choice, 1951 . . . One of the first great middle linebackers . . . Called Bears' defensive signals eight years . . . Exceptionally astute strategist, on-the-field innovator . . . All-NFL eight years . . . Played in eight straight Pro Bowls, 1955-1962 . . . Career record: 18 interceptions, 16 opponents' fumbles recovered . . . 14 years service longest of any Bear . . . Born October 27, 1930, in Waynesburg, Pa. . . . Died September 29, 1982, at age of 51.

DAN FORTMANN

(Colgate)

GUARD—6-0, 210

1936-1943 Chicago Bears

Enshrined in 1965

Bears' No. 9 pick in first NFL draft, 1936 . . . At 19, became youngest starter in NFL . . . 60-minute line leader, battering-ram blocker . . . Deadly tackler, genius at diagnosing enemy plays . . . All-NFL six straight years, 1938-1943 . . . Phi Beta Kappa scholar at Colgate . . . Earned medical degree while playing in NFL . . . Born April 11, 1916, in Pearl River, N.Y.

FRANK GIFFORD

(Southern California)

HALFBACK, FLANKER—6-1, 195

1952-1960 New York Giants
1962-1964 New York Giants

Enshrined in 1977

All-America at USC . . . No. 1 draft pick, 1952 . . . Starred on both offense, defense, 1953 . . . All-NFL four years . . . NFL Player of Year, 1956 . . . In seven Pro Bowls, playing defensive back, halfback, flanker . . . Retired in 1961, came back as flanker, 1962 . . . Totaled 9,753 combined yards . . . Record includes 3,609 yards rushing, 367 receptions, 484 points . . . Born August 16, 1930, in Santa Monica, Calif.

SID GILLMAN

(Ohio State)

COACH

1955-1959 Los Angeles Rams
1960 Los Angeles Chargers (AFL)
1961-1969 San Diego Chargers (AFL)
1971 San Diego Chargers (NFL)
1973-1974 Houston Oilers

Enshrined in 1983

Innovative coach, dynamic administrator . . . Recognized as leading authority on passing theories, tactics . . . 18-year pro record: 123-104-7 . . . First to win divisional titles in both NFL, AFL . . . Won 1963 league, five division crowns in AFL's first six years . . . Major factor in developing AFL's image, impetus, respect . . . AFC Coach of Year, 1974 . . . Played in first College All-Star Game, 1934 . . . Born October 26, 1911, in Minneapolis, Minn.

HAROLD (Red) GRANGE

(Illinois)

HALFBACK—6-0,185

1925 Chicago Bears
1926 New York Yankees (AFL)
1927 New York Yankees (NFL)
1929-1934 Chicago Bears

Charter Enshrinee, 1963

Three-time all-America, 1923-1925 . . . Earned "Galloping Ghost" fame as whirling dervish runner at Illinois . . . Joined Bears on Thanksgiving Day, 1925 . . . Magic name produced first huge pro football crowds on 17-game barnstorming tour . . . With manager, founded rival American Football League, 1926 . . . Missed entire 1927 season with injury . . . Excelled on defense in latter years . . . Born June 13, 1903, in Forksville, Pa.

OTTO GRAHAM

(Northwestern)

QUARTERBACK—6-1, 195

1946-1949 Cleveland Browns (AAFC)
1950-1955 Cleveland Browns (NFL)

Enshrined in 1965

College tailback, switched to T-quarterback in pros . . . Guided Browns to 10 division or league crowns in 10 years . . . Topped AAFC passers four years, NFL two years . . . All-league 9 of 10 years . . . Four TD passes in 1950 NFL title win . . . Had three TDs running, three TDs passing in 1954 NFL title game . . . Career passes for 23,584 yards, 174 TDs . . . Scored 276 points on 46 TDs . . . Born December 6, 1921, in Waukegan, Ill.

FORREST GREGG

(Southern Methodist)

TACKLE, GUARD—6-4, 250

1956 Green Bay Packers
1958-1970 Green Bay Packers
1971 Dallas Cowboys

Enshrined in 1977

No. 2 draft pick, 1956 . . . Lombardi called him "best player I ever coached" . . . Versatile, durable, hard-working, intelligent . . . Played guard in emergencies . . . Played in 188 straight games, 1956-1971 . . . All-NFL eight straight years, 1960-1967 . . . Played in nine Pro Bowls . . . Played on seven NFL championship teams, three Super Bowl Winners . . . Born October 18, 1933, in Birthright, Texas.

LOU GROZA

(Ohio State)

OFFENSIVE TACKLE, PLACEKICKER
6-3, 250

1946-1949 Cleveland Browns (AAFC)
1950-1959 Cleveland Browns (NFL)
1961-1967 Cleveland Browns

Enshrined in 1974

Last of "original" Browns to retire . . . Regular offensive tackle, 1947-1959 . . . Back injury forced layoff, 1960 . . . Kicking specialist only, 1961-1967 . . . All-NFL tackle six years . . . NFL Player of Year, 1954 . . . In nine Pro Bowls . . . Last-second field goal won 1950 NFL title game . . . Scored 1,608 points in 21 years . . . Played in four AAFC, nine NFL title games . . . Born January 25, 1924, in Martins Ferry, Ohio.

GEORGE HALAS

(Illinois)

FOUNDER, OWNER, COACH

1920 Decatur Staleys
1921 Chicago Staleys
1922-1983 Chicago Bears

Charter Enshrinee, 1963

Truly "Mr. Everything" of pro football . . . Founded Decatur Staleys, attended league organizational meeting in 1920 . . . Only person associated with NFL throughout first 50 years . . . Coached Bears for 40 seasons, won seven NFL titles . . . 326 coaching wins most by far in pro history . . . Recorded many "firsts" in pro coaching, administration . . . Also played end for 11 seasons . . . Born February 2, 1895, in Chicago, Ill. . . . Died on October 31, 1983, at age of 88.

JOE GUYON

(Carlisle, Georgia Tech)

HALFBACK—6-1, 180

1919 Canton Bulldogs (pre-NFL)
1920 Canton Bulldogs
1921 Cleveland Indians
1922-1923 Oorang Indians
1924 Rock Island Independents
1924-1925 Kansas City Cowboys
1927 New York Giants

Enshrined in 1966

Thorpe's teammate at Carlisle . . . All-America tackle at Georgia Tech, 1918 . . . Triple-threat halfback in pros . . . Extremely fierce competitor . . . Played with Thorpe on four NFL teams . . . TD pass gave Giants win over Bears for 1927 NFL title . . . Professional baseball injury ended gridiron career, 1928 . . . Born November 26, 1892, on White Earth Indian Reservation, Minn. . . . Died November 27, 1971, at age of 79.

ED HEALEY

(Dartmouth)

TACKLE—6-3, 220

1920-1922 Rock Island Independents
1922-1927 Chicago Bears

Enshrined in 1964

Three-year end at Dartmouth . . . Left coaching job to seek tryout with Rock Island in new league, 1920 . . . Converted to tackle as pro . . . Sold to Bears for $100, 1922—first player sale in NFL . . . Became perennial all-pro with Bears . . . Rugged, two way star . . . Called "most versatile tackle ever" by Halas . . . Starred in Bears' long barnstorming tour after 1925 season . . . Born December 28, 1894, in Indian Orchard, Mass. . . . Died December 9, 1978, at age of 83.

MEL HEIN

(Washington State)

CENTER—6-2, 225

1931-1945 New York Giants

Charter Enshrinee, 1963

Played 25 years in school, college, pro . . . 1930 all-America . . . Wrote to three NFL clubs offering his services . . . Giants bid high at $150 per game . . . 60-minute regular for 15 years . . . Injured only once, never missed a game . . . All-NFL eight straight years, 1933-1940 . . . NFL's Most Valuable Player, 1938 . . . Flawless ball-snapper, powerful blocker, superior pass defender . . . Born August 22, 1909, in Reading, Calif.

ARNIE HERBER

(Wisconsin, Regis College)

QUARTERBACK—6-0, 200

1930-1940 Green Bay Packers
1944-1945 New York Giants

Enshrined in 1966

Joined Packers as 20-year-old rookie . . . Threw TD pass first pro game . . . Exceptional long passer . . . Teamed with Don Hutson for first great pass-catch combo . . . NFL passing leader, 1932, 1934, 1936 . . . Triggered four Packers' title teams . . . Left retirement to lead 1944 Giants to NFL Eastern crown . . . Lifetime passes gained 8,033 yards, 66 TDs . . . Born April 2, 1910, in Green Bay, Wis. . . . Died October 14, 1969, at age of 59.

WILBUR (Pete) HENRY

(Washington and Jefferson)

TACKLE—6-0, 250

1920-1923 Canton Bulldogs
1925-1926 Canton Bulldogs
1927 New York Giants
1927-1928 Pottsville Maroons

Charter Enshrinee, 1963

Three-year Washington and Jefferson all-America . . . Signed with Bulldogs same day NFL organized, 1920 . . . Largest player of his time, bulwark of Canton's championship lines, 1922-1923 . . . 60-minute performer, also punted, kicked field goals . . . Set NFL marks for longest punt (94 yards), longest dropkick field goal (50 yards) . . . Born October 31, 1897, at Mansfield, Ohio . . . Died February 7, 1952, at age of 54.

BILL HEWITT

(Michigan)

END—5-11, 191

1932-1936 Chicago Bears
1937-1939 Philadelphia Eagles
1943 Phil-Pitt

Enshrined in 1971

First to be named all-NFL with two teams—1933, 1934, 1936 Bears, 1937 Eagles . . . Famous for super-quick defensive charge . . . Fast, elusive, innovative on offense . . . Invented many trick plays to fool opposition . . . Middle man on forward-lateral that gave Bears 1933 NFL title . . . Played without helmet until rules change forced use . . . Born October 8, 1909, in Bay City, Mich. . . . Died January 14, 1947, at age of 37.

CLARKE HINKLE

(Bucknell)

FULLBACK—5-11, 201

1932-1941 Green Bay Packers

Enshrined in 1964

One of most versatile stars in NFL annals . . . Fullback on offense, linebacker on defense . . . Famous for head-on duels with Nagurski . . . Did everything well—ran, passed, punted, placekicked, caught passes . . . Savage blocker, vicious tackler, adept pass defender . . . All-NFL four years . . . Rushed 3,860 yards, scored 373 points, averaged 43.4 yards on punts . . . Top NFL scorer, 1938 . . . Born April 10, 1910, in Toronto, Ohio.

ROBERT (Cal) HUBBARD

(Centenary, Geneva)

TACKLE—6-5, 250

1927-1928 New York Giants
1929-1933 Green Bay Packers
1935 Green Bay Packers
1936 New York Giants
1936 Pittsburgh Pirates

Charter Enshrinee, 1963

Most feared lineman of his time . . . Rookie star with Giants' great defensive team, 1927 . . . Played end with Giants, switched to tackle with Packers . . . Anchored line for Packers' title teams, 1929-1931 . . . Excelled as a blocker, backed up line on defense . . . Extremely fast, strong . . . All-NFL six years, 1928-1933 . . . Named NFL's all-time offensive tackle, 1969 . . . Born October 31, 1900, in Keytesville, Mo. . . . Died October 17, 1977, at age of 76.

ELROY (Crazylegs) HIRSCH

(Wisconsin, Michigan)

HALFBACK, END—6-2, 190

1946-1948, Chicago Rockets (AAFC)
1949-1957 Los Angeles Rams

Enshrined in 1968

Led College All-Stars' upset of Rams, 1946 . . . Became key part of Rams' revolutionary "three-end" offense, 1949 . . . Led NFL in receiving, scoring, 1951 . . . 10 of 17 TD catches, 1951, were long-distance "bombs" . . . Mixed sprinter speed with halfback elusiveness . . . Named all-time NFL flanker, 1969 . . . Career record: 387 catches for 7,209 yards, 60 TDs; 405 points scored . . . Born June 17, 1923, in Wausau, Wis.

SAM HUFF

(West Virginia)

LINEBACKER—6-1, 230

1956-1963 New York Giants
1964-1967 Washington Redskins
1969 Washington Redskins

Enshrined in 1982

All-America guard at West Virginia . . . No. 3 draft pick, 1956 . . . Inspirational leader, brilliant diagnostician with great speed, tackling ability . . . Noted for hard-hitting duels with premier running backs . . . Had 30 career interceptions . . . Played in six NFL title games, five Pro Bowls . . . All-NFL four years . . . Top NFL lineman, 1959 . . . Redskins' player-coach, 1969 . . . Born October 4, 1934, in Morgantown, W.Va.

LAMAR HUNT

(Southern Methodist)

LEAGUE FOUNDER
OWNER

Kansas City Chiefs (Dallas Texans)
Starting in 1960

Enshrined in 1972

Continually frustrated in attempts to gain NFL franchise . . . Developed idea, became driving force behind organization of rival American Football League, 1959 . . . Founded Dallas Texans, 1960 . . . Moved team to Kansas City, 1963, where solid club, organization provided AFL with stability, strength during AFL-NFL war . . . Spearheaded merger negotiations with NFL, 1966 . . . Born August 2, 1932, in El Dorado, Ark.

DAVID (DEACON) JONES

(South Carolina State, Mississippi Vocational)

DEFENSIVE END—6-4, 272

1961-1971 Los Angeles Rams
1972-1973 San Diego Chargers
1974 Washington Redskins

Enshrined in 1980

Obscure 14th-round draft pick, 1961 . . . Among first of fast, tough, mobile defensive linemen . . . Noted for clean but hard-hitting play . . . Specialized in quarterback "sacks," a term he invented . . . Innovative, quick-thinking, flamboyant . . . Unanimous all-league six straight years, 1965-1970 . . . Played in eight Pro Bowls . . . NFL defensive player of year, 1967-1968 . . . Born December 9, 1938, in Eatonville, Fla.

DON HUTSON

(Alabama)

END—6-1, 180

1935-1945 Green Bay Packers

Charter Enshrinee, 1963

Alabama all-America, 1934 . . . NFL's first "super end" . . . Also placekicked, played safety . . . NFL receiving champ eight years . . . Topped scorers five times . . . All-NFL nine years . . . Most Valuable Player, 1941,1942 . . . Had 488 catches for 7,991 yards, 99 TDs . . . Scored 823 points . . . Caught passes in 95 straight games, 1937-1945 . . . Named NFL's all-time end, 1969 . . . Born January 31, 1913, in Pine Bluff, Ark.

SONNY JURGENSEN

(Duke)

QUARTERBACK—6-0, 203

1957-1963 Philadelphia Eagles
1964-1974 Washington Redskins

Enshrined in 1983

Exceptional passer, superb team leader, intelligent, determined, competitive, poised against pass rush . . . Career 82.8 passing rating third best ever . . . Won three NFL individual passing titles . . . Surpassed 3,000 yards in five seasons, 300 yards in 25 games, 400 yards in five games . . . Career totals: 2,433 completions, 32,224 yards, 255 touchdowns . . . Excelled in spite of numerous injuries . . . Born August 23, 1934, in Wilmington, N.C.

WALT KIESLING

(St. Thomas of Minnesota)

GUARD—6-2, 245
COACH

1926-1927 Duluth Eskimos
1928 Pottsville Maroons
1929-1933 Chicago Cardinals
1934 Chicago Bears
1935-1936 Green Bay Packers
1937-1938 Pittsburgh Pirates
1939 Pittsburgh Pirates (coach)
1940-1942 Pittsburgh Steelers (coach)
1954-1956 Pittsburgh Steelers (coach)

Enshrined in 1966

34-year career as pro player, assistant coach, head coach . . . Rugged two-way lineman with six NFL teams . . . All-NFL, 1932 . . . Starred on Bears' unbeaten juggernaut, 1934 . . . Also co-head coach of 1943 Phil-Pitt, 1944 Card-Pitt teams . . . Assistant with Packers, Steelers 14 seasons . . . Led Steelers to first winning season, 1942 . . . Born May 27, 1903, in St. Paul, Minn. . . . Died March 2, 1962, at age of 58.

FRANK (Bruiser) KINARD

(Mississippi)

TACKLE—6-1, 210

1938-1944 Brooklyn Dodgers
1946-1947 New York Yankees (AAFC)

Enshrined in 1971

Two-time Mississippi all-America . . . Dodgers' second-round draft pick, 1938 . . . Small for tackle position, but tough, aggressive, fast, durable . . . Out with injuries only once . . . 60-minute performer . . . Outstanding blocker, smothering tackler . . . First man to earn both all-NFL all-AAFC honors . . .all-NFL, 1940, 1941, 1943, 1944 . . . All-AAFC, 1946 . . . All-service, 1945 . . . Born October 23, 1914, in Pelahatchie, Miss.

EARL (Curly) LAMBEAU

(Notre Dame)

FOUNDER, COACH

1919-1949 Green Bay Packers
1950-1951 Chicago Cardinals
1952-1953 Washington Redskins

Charter Enshrinee, 1963

Founded pre-NFL Packers in 1919 . . . Coach-general manager for Packers until 1949 . . . Credited with keeping pro football alive in Green Bay . . . First coach to make forward pass an integral part of the offense . . . 33-year NFL coaching record: 231-133-23 with six championships in Green Bay . . . Played halfback for 11 years until 1929 . . . Born April 9, 1898, in Green Bay, Wis. . . . Died June 1, 1965, at age of 67.

DICK (Night Train) LANE

(Scottsbluff Junior College)

DEFENSIVE BACK—6-2, 210

1952-1953 Los Angeles Rams
1954-1959 Chicago Cardinals
1960-1965 Detroit Lions

Enshrined in 1974

Joined Rams as free agent after four years in Army . . . Set NFL interception record (14) as rookie, 1952 . . . All-NFL five years . . . Named to six Pro Bowls . . . Selected all-time NFL cornerback, 1969 . . . Career interception record: 68 for 1,207 yards, five TDs . . . Gambler on field who made spectacular plays . . . Deadly open-field tackler . . . Very fast, agile, aggressive . . . Born April 16, 1928, in Austin, Texas.

YALE LARY

(Texas A&M)

DEFENSIVE BACK—5-11, 189

1952-1953 Detroit Lions
1956-1964 Detroit Lions

Enshrined in 1979

Major contributor to three Lions' championships . . . 11-year fixture at right safety, exceptional punter, long-distance threat on kick returns . . . Lifetime marks show 50 interceptions, 44.3-yard punting average, three NFL punting crowns, three TDs on punt returns . . . All-NFL four years . . . In nine Pro Bowls . . . Third-round draft pick, 1952 . . . Career interrupted by Army service . . . Born November 24, 1930, in Fort Worth, Texas.

BOBBY LAYNE

(Texas)

QUARTERBACK—6-2, 190

1948 Chicago Bears
1949 New York Bulldogs
1950-1958 Detroit Lions
1958-1962 Pittsburgh Steelers

Enshrined in 1967

Texas all-America, 1947 . . . Led Lions to four divisional, three NFL titles in 1950s . . . Exceptional field leader, at best in clutch . . . Last-second TD pass won 1953 NFL title game . . . Also kicked field goals . . . All-NFL, 1952, 1956 . . . NFL scoring champ, 1956 . . . Career record: 1,814 completions for 26,768 yards, 196 TDs; 2,451 yards rushing; 372 points scored . . . Born December 19, 1926, in Santa Anna, Texas.

DANTE LAVELLI

(Ohio State)

END—6-0, 199

1946-1949 Cleveland Browns (AAFC)
1950-1956 Cleveland Browns (NFL)

Enshrined in 1975

Played only three college games, served in U.S. Infantry before turning pro . . . Top AAFC receiver as rookie, scored winning TD in title game, 1946 . . . Caught 11 passes in 1950 NFL championship . . . All-AAFC, 1946-1947 . . . All-NFL, 1951, 1953 . . . In three Pro Bowls . . . Caught 386 passes for 6,488 yards, 62 TDs . . . Had record 24 catches in six NFL title games . . . Nicknamed "Glue Fingers" . . . Born February 23, 1923, in Hudson, Ohio.

ALPHONSE (Tuffy) LEEMANS

(Oregon, George Washington)

HALFBACK, FULLBACK—6-0, 200

1936-1943 New York Giants

Enshrined in 1978

Second-round pick in first NFL draft. . . 1936 College All-Star Game MVP . . . Aggressive, dedicated do-everything team leader . . . Player-coach in final 1943 season . . . Led NFL rushers as rookie, 1936 . . . All-NFL, 1936, 1939 . . . Career totals—3,142 yards rushing, 2,324 yards passing, 442 yards receiving . . . Had 16 TD passes, 14-yard punt return average . . . Born November 12, 1912, in Superior, Wis. . . . Died January 19, 1979, at age of 66.

BOB LILLY

(Texas Christian)

DEFENSIVE TACKLE—6-5, 260

1961-1974 Dallas Cowboys

Enshrined in 1980

Cowboys' first-ever draft choice (1961), first Pro Bowl pick (1962), first all-league (1964), first Hall of Famer (1980) . . . Foundation of great Dallas defensive units . . . Had unusual speed, strength, intelligence, recovery ability . . . All-NFL/NFC eight years . . . Named to 11 Pro Bowls . . . Played in five NFL/NFC title games, two Super Bowls . . . Missed just one game in 14 years . . . Born July 29, 1939, in Olney, Texas.

SID LUCKMAN

(Columbia)

QUARTERBACK—6-0, 195

1939-1950 Chicago Bears

Enshrined in 1965

No. 1 draft pick, 1939 . . . Columbia tailback who became first great 'T'-quarterback as pro . . . Performance in 73-0 title win, 1940, started mass rush to T-formation . . . Superb signal-caller, ball-handler . . . All-NFL five times, Most Valuable Player, 1943 . . . Threw seven TD passes one game, 1943 . . . Had five TD passes, 1943 title game . . . Career passing: 14,683 yards, 139 TDs . . . Born November 21, 1916, in Brooklyn, N.Y.

VINCE LOMBARDI

(Fordham)

COACH

1959-1967 Green Bay Packers
1969 Washington Redskins

Enshrined in 1971

Began head coaching career at age 45 . . . Transformed Green Bay into winner in two seasons . . . Acclaimed NFL Man of the Decade in the 1960s . . . Gave Packers 89-29-4 record, five NFL titles, first two Super Bowl crowns in nine years . . . Led 1969 Redskins to first winning record in 14 years . . . Noted taskmaster, never had a losing season . . . Born June 11, 1913, in Brooklyn, N.Y. . . . Died September 3, 1970, at age of 57.

WILLIAM ROY (Link) LYMAN

(Nebraska)

TACKLE—6-2, 252

1922-1923 Canton Bulldogs
1924 Cleveland Bulldogs
1925 Canton Bulldogs
1925 Frankford Yellowjackets
1926-1928 Chicago Bears
1930-1931 Chicago Bears
1933-1934 Chicago Bears

Enshrined in 1964

Very agile, large for his day . . . Pioneered more sophisticated defensive play with shifting, sliding style . . . Starred on four title teams: 1922-1923 Canton, 1924 Cleveland, 1933 Bears . . . Joined Bears for barnstorming tour after 1925 season . . . Played on only one losing team in 16 seasons of college, pro ball . . . Born November 30, 1898, in Table Rock, Nebr. . . . Died December 16, 1972, at age of 74.

TIM MARA

(No College)

FOUNDER, ADMINISTRATOR

1925-1959 New York Giants

Charter Enshrinee, 1963

Paid $2,500 for Giants' franchise, 1925, thus giving NFL vital showcase in nation's largest city . . . Withstood heavy financial losses until Grange debut in Polo Grounds turned tide . . . Bore brunt of fight against rival AFL, 1926, and AAFC, 1946-1949 . . . Built Giants into perennial powerhouse with three NFL, eight divisional titles . . . Born July 29, 1887, in New York City . . . Died February 17, 1959, at age of 71.

GEORGE PRESTON MARSHALL

(Randolph-Macon)

FOUNDER ADMINISTRATOR

1932 Boston Braves
1933-1936 Boston Redskins
1937-1969 Washington Redskins

Charter Enshrinee, 1963

Acquired Boston franchise, 1932 . . . Moved team to Washington, 1937 . . . Flamboyant, controversial, innovative master showman . . . Pioneered gala halftime pageants, organized first team band . . . Sponsored progressive rules changes, splitting NFL into two divisions with title playoff, 1933 . . . Produced six division, two NFL titles in 1936-1945 period . . . Born October 11, 1897, in Grafton, W.Va. . . . Died August 9, 1969, at age of 71.

GINO MARCHETTI

(San Francisco)

DEFENSIVE END—6-4, 245

1952 Dallas Texans
1953-1964 Baltimore Colts
1966 Baltimore Colts

Enshrined in 1972

Named top defensive end of NFL's first 50 years . . . New York Yanks' No. 2 draftee, 1952—team moved to Dallas for Gino's rookie season . . . Selected for record 11 straight Pro Bowls but missed one game because of injury suffered in 1958 NFL overtime title game . . . All-NFL seven years, 1957 to 1962, 1964 . . . All-around great defender, best known for vicious pass rushing . . . Born January 2, 1927, in Smithers, W.Va.

OLLIE MATSON

(San Francisco)

HALFBACK—6-2, 220

1952 Chicago Cardinals
1954-1958 Chicago Cardinals
1959-1962 Los Angeles Rams
1963 Detroit Lions
1964-1966 Philadelphia Eagles

Enshrined in 1972

San Francisco U. defensive all-America . . . U.S. Olympic medal winner in track, 1952 . . . No. 1 draft pick, 1952 . . . All-NFL four years, 1954-1957 . . . Traded to Rams for nine players, 1959 . . . Career ledger: 12,844 combined net yards, 5,173 yards rushing, 222 receptions, 438 points, record nine TDs on punt, kickoff returns . . . Played in five Pro Bowl games . . . MVP in 1956 Pro Bowl . . . Born May 1, 1930, in Trinity, Texas.

GEORGE McAFEE

(Duke)

HALFBACK—6-0, 177

1940-1941 Chicago Bears
1945-1950 Chicago Bears

Enshrined in 1966

Phenomenal two-way star, a long-distance scoring threat on any play . . . Scored 234 points, gained 5,022 combined net yards, intercepted 21 passes in eight seasons . . . NFL punt-return champ, 1948 . . . Holds career punt-return average record—12.78 yards . . . Left-handed passer, kicker . . . Pioneered use of low-cut shoes . . . All-NFL, 1941 . . . Navy service came at peak of career . . . Born March 13, 1918, in Ironton, Ohio.

HUGH McELHENNY

(Washington)

HALFBACK—6-1, 198

1952-1960 San Francisco 49ers
1961-1962 Minnesota Vikings
1963 New York Giants
1964 Detroit Lions

Enshrined in 1970

Washington U. all-America . . . 49ers' No. 1 draft pick, 1952 . . . Scored 40-yard TD on first pro play . . . Had phenomenal first season, winning all-NFL, Rookie of Year honors . . . Played in six Pro Bowls . . . MVP of 1958 Pro Bowl . . . Gained 11,375 combined net yards in 13 years . . . Record includes 5,281 yards rushing, 264 pass receptions, 360 points . . . Nicknamed "The King" . . . Born December 31, 1928, in Los Angeles, Calif.

MIKE McCORMACK

(Kansas)

TACKLE—6-4, 250

1951 New York Yanks
1954-1962 Cleveland Browns

Enshrined in 1984

Drafted by 1951 New York Yanks . . . Played in first of six Pro Bowls as a rookie . . . In U.S. Army, 1952-1953 . . . Traded to Browns in 10-player deal while in service . . . Played defensive middle guard, 1954 Browns . . . Stole ball to set up key Browns' TD, 1954 NFL title game . . . Excelled as offensive right tackle for eight years, 1955-1962 . . . Equally adept as rushing blocker, pass protector . . . Born June 21, 1930, in Chicago, Ill.

JOHN (Blood) McNALLY

(St. John's of Minnesota)

HALFBACK—6-0, 185

1925-1926 Milwaukee Badgers
1926-1927 Duluth Eskimos
1928 Pottsville Maroons
1929-1933 Green Bay Packers
1934 Pittsburgh Pirates
1935-1936 Green Bay Packers
1937-1939 Pittsburgh Pirates

Charter Enshrinee, 1963

Famed "vagabond halfback," totally unpredictable funster on and off the field . . . Assumed "Johnny Blood" alias from Valentino movie title, "Blood and Sand" . . . Superb runner with breakaway speed, exceptional pass receiver . . . Scored 37 TDs, 224 points in 15 seasons with five NFL teams . . . Official all-NFL, 1931 . . . Pittsburgh player-coach, 1937-1939 . . . Born November 27, 1904, in New Richmond, Wis.

MIKE MICHALSKE

(Penn State)

GUARD—6-0, 209

1926 New York Yankees (AFL)
1927-1928 New York Yankees (NFL)
1929-1935 Green Bay Packers
1937 Green Bay Packers

Enshrined in 1964

All-America at Penn State . . . Rookie year with 1926 American Football League Yankees . . . Anchored Packers' championship lines, 1929, 1930, 1931 . . . 60-minute workhorse who specialized in blitzing on defense . . . Pioneered idea of using fullbacks at guard to capitalize on size, speed . . . All-NFL, 1929, 1930, 1931, 1935 . . . First guard elected to Pro Football Hall of Fame . . . Born April 24, 1903, in Cleveland, Ohio . . . Died October 26, 1983, at age of 80.

BOBBY MITCHELL

(Illinois)

WIDE RECEIVER, HALFBACK
6-0, 195

1958-1961 Cleveland Browns
1962-1968 Washington Redskins

Enshrined in 1983

Blessed with exceptional speed, balance, faking ability . . . Split career as Browns halfback, Redskins flanker . . . Noted for spectacular long-distance scoring plays . . . Amassed 14,078 combined net yards . . . Scored 91 touchdowns, caught 521 passes, had eight kick return TDs . . . Topped NFL receivers, 1962 . . . Surpassed 50 catches six years . . . All-NFL two times . . . Played in four Pro Bowl games . . . Born June 6, 1935, at Hot Springs, Ark.

WAYNE MILLNER

(Notre Dame)

END—6-0, 191

1936 Boston Redskins
1937-1941 Washington Redskins
1945 Washington Redskins

Enshrined in 1968

Two-time Notre Dame all-America . . . Hero of famous Ohio State upset, 1935 . . . Fierce competitor at best in crucial games . . . Caught 55-yard, 77-yard TD passes in 1937 NFL championship . . . Starred on four Redskins' divisional title teams . . . Top Redskin receiver at retirement with 124 catches . . . Career interrupted by Navy service . . . Player-coach in final 1945 season . . . Born January 31, 1913, in Roxbury, Mass. . . . Died November 19, 1976, at age of 63.

RON MIX

(Southern California)

OFFENSIVE TACKLE—6-4, 255

1960 Los Angeles Chargers (AFL)
1961-1969 San Diego Chargers (AFL)
1971 Oakland Raiders

Enshrined in 1979

Picked AFL over Colts, who drafted him No. 1 . . . All-AFL tackle eight times, once as guard . . . In seven AFL All-Star, five AFL title games . . . Consistent, finely conditioned, intense with excellent speed, strength . . . Noted for quick charge, accomplished blocking on both passing, running plays . . . Had only two holding penalties in 10 years . . . Nicknamed "The Intellectual Assassin" . . . Born March 10, 1938, in Los Angeles, Calif.

167

LEONARD (Lenny) MOORE

(Penn State)

FLANKER-RUNNING BACK
6-1, 198

1956-1967 Baltimore Colts

Enshrined in 1975

No. 1 draft choice, 1956 . . . Rookie of Year, 1956 . . . Started as a flanker, moved to running back in 1961 . . . Amassed 11,213 combined net yards, 5,174 yards rushing, 363 receptions for 6,039 yards . . . Scored 113 TDs, 678 points . . . All-NFL five years . . . Played in seven Pro Bowls . . . Comeback Player of Year, 1964 . . . Scored touchdowns in record 18 straight games, 1963-1965 . . . Born November 25, 1933, in Reading, Pa.

GEORGE MUSSO

(Millikin)

TACKLE, GUARD—6-2, 270

1933-1944 Chicago Bears

Enshrined in 1982

Typified superior line play of Bears' greatest era . . . 60-minute star, specialized in big play as middle guard on defense . . . Started as $90-per-game tackle on offense, switched to guard in fifth year . . . First to win all-NFL at two positions—tackle (1935), guard (1937) . . . Inspirational team leader, captained Bears nine seasons . . . Played in seven NFL championship games . . . Born April 8, 1910, in Collinsville, Ill.

MARION MOTLEY

(South Carolina State, Nevada)

FULLBACK—6-1, 238

1946-1949 Cleveland Browns (AAFC)
1950-1953 Cleveland Browns (NFL)
1955 Pittsburgh Steelers

Enshrined in 1968

Deadly pass blocker, peerless runner on Browns' famed trap play . . . Also played linebacker early in career . . . All-time AAFC rushing champ . . . Top NFL rusher, 1950 . . . All-AAFC three years, all-NFL in 1950 . . . Lifetime rushing: 828 carries, 4,720 yards . . . 5.7-yard career average all-time record . . . Caught 85 passes, scored 234 points in nine years . . . Played in 1951 Pro Bowl . . . Born June 5, 1920, in Leesburg, Ga.

BRONKO NAGURSKI

(Minnesota)

FULLBACK—6-2, 225

1930-1937 Chicago Bears
1943 Chicago Bears

Charter Enshrinee, 1963

Joined Bears after legendary college career at Minnesota . . . Became pro football's symbol of power, ruggedness . . . A bulldozing runner on offense, a bone-crushing linebacker on defense . . . Gained 4,031 yards in 9 seasons . . . All-NFL, 1932, 1933, 1934 . . . His two TD passes clinched Bears' 1933 title win . . . Helped 1943 Bears to NFL crown after 6-year retirement . . . Born November 3, 1908, in Rainy River, Ontario.

EARLE (Greasy) NEALE

(West Virginia Wesleyan)

COACH

1941-1950 Philadelphia Eagles

Enshrined in 1969

Extensive college coaching career preceded entry into NFL in 1941 . . . Quickly built second-division Eagles into a contender . . . Produced three straight Eastern division crowns and NFL championships in 1948 and 1949 . . . Both NFL titles came by shutout scores . . . Using an assumed name, played end with the pre-NFL Canton Bulldogs . . . Born November 5, 1891, in Parkersburg, W.Va. . . . Died November 2, 1973, at age of 81.

RAY NITSCHKE

(Illinois)

MIDDLE LINEBACKER—6-3, 235

1958-1972 Green Bay Packers

Enshrined in 1978

No. 3 draft pick 1958 . . . First Green Bay defender from 1960s to be enshrined . . . Exceptional team leader, tough, strong, fast . . . Savage defender on rushes, cat-like quick against passes . . . Named NFL's all-time top linebacker, 1969 . . . All-NFL three years . . . Intercepted pass for TD in 1964 Pro Bowl . . . Had 25 career interceptions . . . MVP in 1962 NFL title game . . . Born December 29, 1936, in Elmwood Park, Ill.

ERNIE NEVERS

(Stanford)

FULLBACK—6-1, 205

1926-1927 Duluth Eskimos
1929-1931 Chicago Cardinals

Charter Enshrinee, 1963

Stanford all-America, 1925 Rose Bowl hero . . . Lured from pro baseball career by Eskimos . . . Truly a do-everything iron man, playing 1,714 of 1,740 minutes in 29-game 1926 season . . . Missed 1928 with injuries, returned with Cardinals, 1929 . . . Scored record 40 points in one game against Bears, 1929 . . . All-league all five NFL seasons . . . Player-coach two years each in Duluth, Chicago . . . Born June 11, 1903, in Willow River, Minn. . . . Died May 3, 1976, at age of 72.

LEO NOMELLINI

(Minnesota)

DEFENSIVE TACKLE—6-3, 284

1950-1963 San Francisco 49ers

Enshrined in 1969

Two-time Minnesota all-America . . . 49ers first-ever NFL draft choice, 1950 . . . Played every 49ers game for 14 seasons, 174 regular-season and 266 pro games in all . . . Excellent defensive pass rusher, bulldozing offensive blocker . . . All-NFL six times, two years on offense, four years on defense . . . Named NFL's all-time defensive tackle . . . Played in 10 Pro Bowl games . . . Born June 19, 1924, in Lucca, Italy.

MERLIN OLSEN

(Utah State)

DEFENSIVE TACKLE—6-5, 270

1962-1976 Los Angeles Rams

Enshrined in 1982

All-America, Outland Trophy winner, Phi Beta Kappa at Utah State . . . Rams' No. 1 draft pick, 1962 . . . Big, fast, agile, smart . . . Stabilizing leader of famed Fearsome Foursome defensive line . . . Named to record 14 straight Pro Bowls . . . All-NFL, 1966-1970 . . . All-NFC, 1973 . . . Rookie of the Year, 1962 . . . Picked on Rams' all-time team, 1970 . . . Played in 208 games, last 198 in a row . . . Born September 15, 1940, in Logan, Utah.

STEVE OWEN

(Phillips University)

TACKLE—6-2, 235
COACH

1924-1925 Kansas City Cowboys
1926-1953 New York Giants

Enshrined in 1966

Great defensive star of the 1920s . . . Captained Giants' 1927 title team which held foe to record low 20 points . . . Coached Giants 23 years from 1931 to 1953 . . . Coaching record: 150-100-17, eight divisional, two NFL title teams . . . A-formation offense, umbrella defense, two-platoon system among his many coaching innovations . . . Born April 21, 1898, at Cleo Springs, Okla. . . . Died May 17, 1964, at age of 66.

JIM OTTO

(Miami)

CENTER—6-2, 255

1960-1969 Oakland Raiders (AFL)
1970-1974 Oakland Raiders (NFL)

Enshrined in 1980

Anchored Raiders' offensive line for 15 years . . . Noted for pride, dedication, leadership, intelligence . . . Sure-handed ball-snapper, superior blocker with wide range . . . Overcame numerous injuries to play 308 games, including six AFL/AFC title games, Super Bowl II, 12 all-star contests . . . AFL's only all-league center . . . Named to all-time AFL team, 1969 . . . Also all-AFC in 1970, 1971, 1972 . . . Born January 5, 1938, in Wausau, Wis.

CLARENCE (Ace) PARKER

(Duke)

QUARTERBACK—5-11, 168

1937-1941 Brooklyn Dodgers
1945 Boston Yanks
1946 New York Yankees (AAFC)

Enshrined in 1972

All-America tailback at Duke . . . Dodgers' No. 1 draftee in 1937, but signed Philadelphia Athletics baseball contract, expecting to play pro football briefly . . . All-NFL, 1938, 1940 . . . NFL's Most Valuable Player, 1940 . . . Triple-threat, two-way back who paced Dodgers to their greatest seasons in 1940, 1941 . . . Spearheaded Yankees to AAFC Eastern title in 1946 . . . Born May 17, 1912, in Portsmouth, Va.

JIM PARKER

(Ohio State)

GUARD, TACKLE—6-3, 273

1957-1967 Baltimore Colts

Enshrined in 1973

First full-time offensive lineman named to Pro Football Hall of Fame . . . Exceptional blocker, specialized in protecting quarterback . . . All-NFL eight straight years, 1958-1965 . . . Played half of 11-year career at tackle, half at guard . . . Played in eight Pro Bowl games . . . No. 1 draft choice in 1957 . . . Two-time all-America, Outland Trophy winner at Ohio State . . . Born April 3, 1934, in Macon, Ga.

PETE PIHOS

(Indiana)

END—6-1, 210

1947-1955 Philadelphia Eagles

Enshrined in 1970

Indiana all-America, 1943 . . . No. 3 draft pick in 1945 even though he couldn't play until 1947 . . . 60-minute star on Eagles' title teams, 1948-1949 . . . Caught winning TD pass in 1949 NFL championship . . . All-NFL six times in nine seasons . . . Played in first six Pro Bowls . . . Three-time NFL receiving champ, 1953-1955 . . . Career record: 373 catches for 5,619 yards, 378 points . . . Born October 22, 1923, in Orlando, Fla.

JOE PERRY

(Compton Junior College)

FULLBACK—6-0, 200

1948-1949 San Francisco 49ers (AAFC)
1950-1960 San Francisco 49ers (NFL)
1961-1962 Baltimore Colts
1963 San Francisco 49ers

Enshrined in 1969

Didn't play college football . . . Spotted playing service football by pro scouts . . . Signed as free agent by 49ers . . . Extremely quick runner who earned nickname "The Jet" . . . First to gain over 1,000 yards two straight years, 1953-1954 . . . Career record: 12,505 combined net yards, 9,723 yards rushing, 260 receptions, 513 points . . . Played in three Pro Bowls . . . Born January 27, 1927, in Stevens, Ark.

HUGH (Shorty) RAY

(Illinois)

TECHNICAL ADVISOR ON RULES
SURPERVISOR OF OFFICIALS

Enshrined in 1966

Only 5-6, 136, but a giant of pro football . . . NFL Supervisor of Officials, 1938-1952 . . . Worked tirelessly to improve officiating techniques . . . Streamlined rules to improve tempo of play, increase safety . . . Visited each team annually to educate players, coaches . . . Said to have made 300,000 notations as technical observer . . . Born September 21, 1884, in Highland Park, Ill. . . . Died September 16, 1956, at age of 71.

DAN REEVES

(Georgetown)

OWNER-ADMINISTRATOR

1941-1945 Cleveland Rams
1946-1971 Los Angeles Rams

Enshrined in 1967

One of game's greatest innovators . . . Opened up West Coast to major sports by moving Rams to Los Angeles, 1946 . . . Experiments in game TV paved way for modern NFL policies . . . First post-war NFL owner to sign a black (Kenny Washington), 1946 . . . First to employ full-time scouting staff . . . Founded famous kids attendance program at Rams' games . . . Born June 30, 1912, in New York City . . . Died April 15, 1971, at age of 58.

ANDY ROBUSTELLI

(Arnold College)

DEFENSIVE END—6-0, 230

1951-1955 Los Angeles Rams
1956-1964 New York Giants

Enshrined in 1971

Rams' 19th-round draft pick, 1951 . . . On winning team 13 of 14 years . . . In eight NFL title games, seven Pro Bowls . . . All-NFL seven years, two with Rams, five with Giants . . . Named NFL's top player by Maxwell Club, 1962 . . . Exceptionally smart, quick, strong . . . Superb pass rusher . . . Recovered 22 opponents' fumbles in career . . . Missed only one game in 14 years . . . Born December 6, 1925, in Stamford, Conn.

JIM RINGO

(Syracuse)

CENTER—6-2, 230

1953-1963 Green Bay Packers
1964-1967 Philadelphia Eagles

Enshrined in 1981

No. 7 draft choice, 1953 . . . All-pro status preceded Packers' dynasty years . . . All-NFL six times . . . Played in 10 Pro Bowls, three NFL championship games . . . Small for offensive lineman, but quick, determined, intelligent, superb team leader . . . Excellent down-field blocker, pass protector . . . Ignored numerous injuries to start in then-record 182 straight games, 1954-67 . . . Born November 21, 1931, in Orange, N.J.

ART ROONEY

(Georgetown, Duquesne)

FOUNDER-ADMINISTRATOR

Pittsburgh Steelers (Pirates)
Starting in 1933

Enshrined in 1964

One of most revered of all sports personalities . . . Bought new Pittsburgh Pirates franchise for $2,500 in 1933 . . . Renamed team Steelers in 1940 . . . His faith in pro football a guiding light during the dark depression years . . . Startled NFL with $15,000 signing of fabled Whizzer White in 1938 . . . Organized, operated Western Pennsylvania semi-pro grid teams before 1933 . . . Born January 27, 1901, in Coulterville, Pa.

GALE SAYERS

(Kansas)

HALFBACK—6-0, 200

1965-1971 Chicago Bears

Enshrined in 1977

Kansas all-America . . . Exceptional break-away runner . . . Scored rookie record 22 TDs, 132 points, 1965 . . . Led NFL rushers, 1966, 1969 . . . Named all-time NFL halfback, 1969 . . . All-NFL five years . . . Player of Game in three Pro Bowls . . . Career totals: 9,435 combined net yards, 4,956 yards rushing, 336 points . . . NFL lifetime kickoff return leader . . . Born May 30, 1943, in Wichita, Kans.

BART STARR

(Alabama)

QUARTERBACK—6-1, 200

1956-1971 Green Bay Packers

Enshrined in 1977

17th-round draft pick, 1956 . . . Precision passer, poised team leader . . . Led Packers to six division, five NFL, two Super Bowl titles . . . NFL Most Valuable Player, 1966 . . . MVP in Super Bowls I, II . . . Three-time NFL passing champion . . . In four Pro Bowls . . . Career passing totals: 24,718 yards, 152 TDs, record 57.4 completion percentage . . . Born January 9, 1934, in Montgomery, Ala.

JOE SCHMIDT

(Pittsburgh)

LINEBACKER—6-0, 222

1953-1965 Detroit Lions

Enshrined in 1973

Pittsburgh all-America, 1952 . . . Lions' No. 7 draft pick, 1953 . . . Mastered new middle linebacking position which evolved in the 1950's . . . A superb field leader . . . Exceptional at diagnosing foe's plays . . . All-NFL eight years . . . Played in Pro Bowl nine straight years, 1955-1963 . . . Team captain nine years . . . Lions' MVP four times . . . Had 24 career interceptions . . . born January 18, 1932, in Pittsburgh, Pa.

ERNIE STAUTNER

(Boston College)

DEFENSIVE TACKLE—6-2, 235

1950-1963 Pittsburgh Steelers

Enshrined in 1969

No. 2 draft pick, 1950 . . . Bulwarked strong Pittsburgh defense for 14 years . . . Saw spot service at offensive guard . . . Known for excellent mobility, burning desire, extreme ruggedness, unusual durability . . . All-NFL, 1956, 1958 . . . Played in nine Pro Bowls, winning Best Lineman Award, 1957 . . . Recovered 21 opponents' fumbles, scored three safeties in career . . . Born April 20, 1925, in Prinzing-by-Chan, Bavaria.

KEN STRONG

(New York University)

HALFBACK—5-11, 210

1929-1932 Staten Island Stapletons
1933-1935 New York Giants
1936-1937 New York Yanks (AFL)
1939 New York Giants
1944-1947 New York Giants

Enshrined in 1967

NYU all-America, 1928 . . . Excelled in every phase of game—blocking, running, passing, punting, placekicking, defense . . . Scored 17 points to pace Giants to 1934 title in famous "Sneakers" game . . . All-NFL, 1934 . . . Scored 64 points to top NFL, 1933 . . . Served as place-kicking specialist only, 1944-1947 . . . Led NFL in field goals, 1944 . . . Scored 479 points in 14 NFL years . . . Born August 6, 1906, in West Haven, Conn. . . . Died October 5, 1979, at age of 73.

CHARLEY TAYLOR

(Arizona State)

WIDE RECEIVER—6-3, 210

1964-1975 Washington Redskins

1977 Washington Redskins

Enshrined in 1984

Top lifetime receiver with 649 catches for 9,140 yards, 79 TDs . . . Other career stats: 10,883 combined net yards, 90 TDs, 540 points . . . No. 1 draft pick, 1964 . . . Rookie of Year running back, 1964 . . . Shifted to split end, 1966 . . . NFL receiving champion, 1966, 1967 . . . Had 50 or more catches seven seasons . . . All-NFL/NFC three years . . . Played in eight Pro Bowls . . . Born September 28, 1941, in Grand Prairie, Texas.

JOE STYDAHAR

(West Virginia)

TACKLE—6-4, 230

1936-1942 Chicago Bears
1945-1946 Chicago Bears

Enshrined in 1967

Bears' No. 1 choice in first-ever NFL draft, 1936 . . . 60-minute performer who bulwarked Bears' line in famous "Monsters of the Midway" era . . . Played on five divisional and three NFL championship teams . . . Named to official all-NFL team four years, 1937-1940 . . . Often played without helmet early in career . . . Later coached 1950-1952 Rams, 1953-1954 Cardinals . . . Born March 17, 1912, in Kaylor, Pa. . . . Died March 23, 1977, at age of 65.

JIM TAYLOR

(Louisiana State)

FULLBACK—6-0, 216

1958-1966 Green Bay Packers
1967 New Orleans Saints

Enshrined in 1976

LSU all-America, 1957 . . . Packers' No. 2 draft pick, 1958 . . . 1,000-yard rusher five straight years, 1960-1964 . . . Rushed for 8,597 yards, caught 225 passes, amassed 10,538 combined net yards, scored 558 points . . . Led NFL rushers, scorers, had record 19 TDs rushing, 1962 . . . Excelled in 1962 NFL title game . . . Ferocious runner, rugged blocker, prime disciple of "run to daylight" doctrine . . . Born September 20, 1935, in Baton Rouge, La.

JIM THORPE

(Carlisle)

HALFBACK—6-1, 190

1915-1917 Canton Bulldogs (pre-NFL)
1919 Canton Bulldogs (pre-NFL)
1920 Canton Bulldogs
1921 Cleveland Indians
1922-1923 Oorang Indians
1924 Rock Island Independents
1925 New York Giants
1926 Canton Bulldogs
1928 Chicago Cardinals

Charter Enshrinee, 1963

All-America halfback at Carlisle, 1912 Olympic decathlon champion . . . First big-name athlete to play pro football, signing with pre-NFL Canton Bulldogs in 1915 . . . Named "The Legend" on the all-time NFL team . . . Voted top American athlete of first half of 20th century . . . First president of American Professional Football Association, 1920 . . . Born May 28, 1888, in Prague, Okla. . . . Died March 28, 1953, at age of 64.

Y. A. TITTLE

(Louisiana State)

QUARTERBACK—6-0, 200

1948-1949 Baltimore Colts (AAFC)
1950 Baltimore Colts (NFL)

1951-1960 San Francisco 49ers
1961-1964 New York Giants

Enshrined in 1971

AAFC rookie of Year, 1948 . . . Joined 49ers in 1951 after Colts disbanded . . . Career record: 2,427 completions, 33,070 yards, 242 TDs, 13 games over 300 yards passing . . . Paced 1961, 1962, 1963 Giants to division titles . . . Threw 33 TD passes in 1962, 36 in 1963 . . . NFL's Most Valuable Player, 1961, 1963 . . . All-NFL, 1957, 1962, 1963 . . . Played in six Pro Bowls . . . Born October 24, 1926, in Marshall, Texas.

GEORGE TRAFTON

(Notre Dame)

CENTER—6-2, 235

1920 Decatur Staleys
1921 Chicago Staleys
1923-1932 Chicago Bears

Enshrined in 1964

Turned pro after one year at Notre Dame . . . First center to play for Staleys (Bears) . . . 60-minute star, excelled on defense . . . First center to rove on defense . . . First to snap ball with one hand . . . Colorful, aggressive, smart . . . Defiantly wore No. 13 . . . Nicknamed "The Brute" . . . Named top NFL center of the 1920s . . . Born December 6, 1896, in Chicago, Ill. . . . Died September 5, 1971, at age of 74.

CHARLEY TRIPPI

(Georgia)

HALFBACK, QUARTERBACK—6-0, 185

1947-1955 Chicago Cardinals

Enshrined in 1968

Cards' No. 1 future draft pick, 1945 . . . Georgia all-America, 1946 . . . Played in four Chicago All-Star games as collegian . . . $100,000 signee during AAFC-NFL war, 1947 . . . Final link in Cards' famed "Dream Backfield" . . . Scored two TDs in 1947 NFL title win . . . All-NFL, 1948 . . . Extremely versatile—played halfback five years, quarterback two years, defense two years . . . Born December 14, 1922, in Pittston, Pa.

EMLEN TUNNELL

(Toledo, Iowa)

DEFENSIVE BACK—6-1, 200

1948-1958 New York Giants
1959-1961 Green Bay Packers

Enshrined in 1967

Signed as free agent, 1948 . . . Known as Giants "offense on defense," keyed famed "umbrella defense" of 1950s . . . Gained more yards (923) on interceptions, kick returns than NFL rushing leader, 1952 . . . Set career marks in interceptions (79 for 1,282 yards), punt returns (258 for 2,209 yards) . . . All-NFL four years . . . Played in nine Pro Bowls . . . Named NFL's all-time safety, 1969 . . . Born March 29, 1925, in Bryn Mawr, Pa. . . . Died July 22, 1975, at age of 50.

JOHNNY UNITAS

(Louisville)

QUARTERBACK—6-1, 195

1956-1972 Baltimore Colts
1973 San Diego Chargers

Enshrined in 1979

Cut by 1955 Steelers, free agent with 1956 Colts, soon became legendary hero . . . Exceptional field leader, thrived on pressure . . . Led Colts to 1958, 1959 NFL crowns . . . All-NFL five seasons, Player of Year three times . . . MVP three times in 10 Pro Bowls . . . Completed 2,830 passes for 40,239 yards, 290 TDs . . . Threw at least one TD pass in 47 straight games . . . Had 26 games over 300 yards passing . . . Born May 7, 1933, in Pittsburgh, Pa.

CLYDE (Bulldog) TURNER

(Hardin-Simmons)

CENTER-LINEBACKER—6-2, 235

1940-1952 Chicago Bears

Enshrined in 1966

Hardin-Simmons Little all-America . . . Bears' No. 1 draft pick, 1940 . . . Rookie starter at age of 20 . . . Terrific blocker, superb pass defender, flawless ball-snapper . . . Had halfback speed . . . Led NFL with eight interceptions, 1942 . . . Stole 16 passes in career . . . All-NFL six times . . . Anchored four NFL championship teams . . . Intercepted four passes in five NFL title games . . . Born November 10, 1919, in Sweetwater, Texas.

NORM VAN BROCKLIN

(Oregon)

QUARTERBACK—6-1, 190

1949-1957 Los Angeles Rams
1958-1960 Philadelphia Eagles

Enshrined in 1971

Oregon all-America, 1948 . . . Rams' No. 4 draftee, 1949 . . . Led NFL in passing three years, punting twice . . . Career mark: 1,553 completions for 23,611 yards, 173 TDs . . . 73-yard pass gave Rams 1951 title . . . Passed for 554 yards one game, 1951 . . . Generalled Eagles to 1960 NFL crown . . . NFL's Most Valuable Player, 1960 . . . Threw eight TD passes in eight Pro Bowl games . . . Born March 15, 1926, in Eagle Butte, S.D. . . . Died May 2, 1983, at age of 57.

STEVE VAN BUREN

(Louisiana State)

HALFBACK—6-1, 200

1944-1951 Philadelphia Eagles

Enshrined in 1965

No. 1 draft pick, 1944 . . . All-NFL four of first five years . . . Provided Eagles a battering-ram punch . . . Won NFL rushing title four times . . . 1944 punt return, 1945 kickoff return champ . . . Scored only TD in 7-0 title win, 1948 . . . Rushed for record 196 yards in 1949 finale . . . Career mark: 5,860 yards rushing, 464 points scored . . . Surpassed 1,000 yards in rushing twice . . . Born December 28, 1920, in La Ceiba, Honduras.

BOB WATERFIELD

(UCLA)

QUARTERBACK—6-2, 200

1945 Cleveland Rams
1946-1952 Los Angeles Rams

Enshrined in 1965

Cleveland Rams' No. 3 future draft pick 1944 . . . NFL's Most Valuable Player as rookie, 1945 . . . Two TD passes keyed Rams' 1945 title win . . . All-NFL three years, NFL passing champ twice . . . Career marks include 11,849 yards, 98 TDs passing; 573 points on 13 TDs, 315 PATs, 60 FGs; 42.4-yard punting average . . . Also played defense first four years, intercepted 20 passes . . . Born July 26, 1920, in Elmira, N.Y. . . . Died March 25, 1983, at age of 62.

PAUL WARFIELD

(Ohio State)

WIDE RECEIVER—6-0, 188

1964-1969 Cleveland Browns
1970-1974 Miami Dolphins
1976-1977 Cleveland Browns

Enshrined in 1983

No. 1 pick both Browns, Bills, 1964 . . . Cleveland fixture before 1970 trade to Miami . . . Key element in Dolphins' offense . . . Mere presence on field forced defensive adjustments . . . Fast, super-smooth, precise pattern runner, sure-handed, excellent blocker . . . Caught 427 passes for 8,565 yards, 85 touchdowns . . . 20.1-yard per-catch average best ever . . . All-NFL five years . . . In seven Pro Bowls . . . Born November 28, 1942, in Warren, Ohio.

ARNIE WEINMEISTER

(Washington)

DEFENSIVE TACKLE—6-4, 235

1948 New York Yankees (AAFC)
1949 Brooklyn-New York Yankees (AAFC)
1950-1953 New York Giants

Enshrined in 1984

One of first defensive players to captivate the masses . . . Big, extremely fast with lateral mobility, great ability to diagnose plays . . . Began pro play in AAFC, moved to NFL with 1950 merger . . . Played two ways in AAFC, exclusively on defense in NFL . . . Became the dominant defensive tackle of his time . . . All-AAFC, 1949 . . . All-NFL, 1950-1953 . . . Named to first four Pro Bowls . . . Born March 23, 1923, in Rhein, Saskatchewan.

BILL WILLIS

(Ohio State)

MIDDLE GUARD—6-2, 215

1946-1949 Cleveland Browns (AAFC)
1950-1953 Cleveland Browns (NFL)

Enshrined in 1977

All-America tackle at Ohio State . . . Played two ways, but excelled as defensive middle guard . . . Lightning quickness his constant trademark that earned him job in first pro scrimmage . . . Touchdown-saving tackle against Giants preserved Browns' 1950 NFL title drive . . . All-AAFC three years . . . All-NFL, 1950-1953 . . . In first three NFL Pro Bowls . . . Born October 5, 1921, in Columbus, Ohio.

ALEX WOJCIECHOWICZ

(Fordham)

CENTER-LINEBACKER—6-0, 235

1938-1946 Detroit Lions
1946-1950 Philadelphia Eagles

Enshrined in 1968

Two-time Fordham all-America, center of famed "Seven Blocks of Granite" line . . . Lions' No. 1 draft pick, 1938 . . . Played four games first week as pro . . . Authentic "iron man" for 8½ years with Lions . . . Joined Eagles as defensive specialist strictly . . . Known for exceptionally wide center stance . . . Outstanding pass defender with 16 lifetime interceptions . . . Born August 12, 1915, in South River, N.J.

LARRY WILSON

(Utah)

FREE SAFETY—6-0, 190

1960-1972 St. Louis Cardinals

Enshrined in 1978

Two-way star at Utah, No. 7 draft pick, 1962 . . . Cat-like defender, exceptional team leader . . . Became NFL's top free safety, made "safety blitz" famous . . . All-NFL six times . . . Played in eight Pro Bowl games . . . Had steals in seven straight games, led NFL interceptors, 1966 . . . Once intercepted pass with both hands in casts . . . Had 52 career interceptions . . . Born March 24, 1938, in Rigby, Idaho.

1977 Hall of Fame enshrinee Gale Sayers and presenter George Halas.

Left to right: *Hall of Fame class of 1983, Bobby Mitchell, Sonny Jurgensen, Paul Warfield, Bobby Bell, Sid Gillman.*

Hall of Famer Steve Van Buren plows through the Chicago Cardinals line for the only touchdown in the Philadelphia Eagles' 7–0 victory in the blizzard-dominated 1948 NFL championship game.

Chapter 8

Mementoes of Fame

The ice tongs Red Grange used while he was working his way through college . . . An Indian headdress from the Washington Redskins' marching band, organized by George Preston Marshall . . . The telegram announcing pro football's most astounding trade—Ollie Matson for nine players . . .

The desk, complete with cigar burns, at which Bert Bell worked as league commissioner . . .

The players' bench from Lambeau Field used in the last Vince Lombardi-coached Green Bay game . . .

These are some of the unique items on display in the Enshrinee Mementoes Room, entered as the visitors leaves the Enshrinement Galleries. In this room, each Hall of Famer is remembered one more time by memorabilia or pictures scavenged from his playing days.

It may be the shoes in which Bronko Nagurski thundered through the line or the jersey that draped across Ernie Stautner's broad shoulders, a uniform worn by Leo Nomellini, a picture of Steve Van Buren.

While their mementoes are anything but as unusual as Grange's ice tongs or Bell's desk, these four players represent a unique group in the Mementoes Room. Of the 123 players who have been inducted into the Hall of Fame, just 5 were born in foreign countries: Van Buren (Honduras), Nomellini (Italy), Stautner (Germany), and Nagurski and 1984 enshrinee Arnie Weinmeister (Canada).

Van Buren's odyssey may have been the most unusual, starting as it did in La Ceiba, Honduras, where he was born in 1930, to parents of Spanish and English descent. Both parents died when Van Buren was a young boy and he came to America as an orphan to live with grandparents near New Orleans. His two brothers and three sisters were distributed among the homes of other relatives.

"When we were split up, we grew apart," Van Buren once explained. "There was nothing warm about my youth."

It wasn't until he reached Warren Easton High School that he first learned about the game his classmates called football. "I had absolutely no in-interest in football until I was fifteen years old," he says. "In Honduras, I was too young to play much except simple running games, and we'd never heard of football. When I was fifteen and in high school, I used to watch the other boys play. It seemed like a good game, so I went out for the team. But I weighed only a hundred twenty-five pounds, and all the coach would let me do was run up and down the field with the others. When it came to playing, he told me to forget it. He was afraid I'd get hurt."

After a year in high school, Van Buren left to work in an iron foundry. Then, realizing his life would be limited without an education, he returned to school—but with weight and muscle added to his body from working in the foundry. "This time," Van Buren recalls, "when I went out for the team, the coach wasn't afraid for me."

181

Neither was Bernie Moore, the coach at Louisiana State University, where Van Buren went to college. Moore took one look at the well-built recruit and made him a blocking back. It wasn't until his junior year that Van Buren began to carry the ball with any regularity, and in his senior season he gained 832 yards rushing. Nevertheless, Van Buren did not make any all-America team and, in general, pro clubs didn't seem to be overly impressed with his potential. The Philadelphia Eagles, however, were convinced by Moore of Van Buren's ability to run with the ball and made him their number-one draft choice in 1944. They never regretted it. Coach Earle (Greasy) Neale made the following comparison with Grange after Van Buren had won three consecutive rushing titles in 1947, 1948, and 1949: "Grange was an elusive runner who had a great blocker in front of him. Steve is as elusive as Red ever was—and he doesn't need a blocker."

That certainly was true. While Van Buren lined up as a halfback in the Eagles' offense and could be elusive, he also was the battering-ram type who would lower his head and gain yardage straight up the middle in fullback fashion. Winning 4 rushing titles in a 9-year career, Van Buren became only the second runner in history to surpass the 1,000-yard mark and set a record of 1,146 yards in 1949 that stood for almost a decade before it was eclipsed. When he retired following the 1951 season, he had amassed an NFL-record 5,860 yards, an impressive 4.4 average, and 71 touchdowns. But there are probably no better examples of his talents than his performances in the 1948 and 1949 championship games. In the first, played in Philadelphia during a blizzard that blanketed the field with snow and left the Eagles and Chicago Cardinals locked in a 0-0 tie for three quarters, Van Buren barreled over the goal line from five yards out in the final period for the only score in a 7-0 victory. A year later, the Eagles met the favored Rams in the rain-soaked Los Angeles Coliseum, but Van Buren paved the way for a 14-0 upset by carrying 31 times for 196 yards—both NFL championship game records that lasted for more than 20 years.

Nomellini and Stautner, though born in different countries, had startlingly parallel careers after reaching the United States. Nomellini was born in Lucca, Italy, in the shadow of the Leaning Tower of Pisa. In 1928, when he was four, his parents left "for the land of opportunity" and settled in Gilman, Illinois, where his father opened a candy store. Stautner was born in Prinzing-by-Chan, Bavaria, close to the Czechoslovakian border, where his father worked as a military policeman. The same year Nomellini left Italy, the Stautners left Germany because, as Stautner puts it, "Dad foresaw the Hitler thing." The Stautners settled in Albany, New York. Both Nomellini and Stautner arrived in the United States at the same time and at the same age. Both went from high school directly into the Marines. Both were stationed at the Cherry Point, North Carolina, Marine base and played on the same team there. Nomellini, called Lion, was the left tackle. Stautner, called Horse, was the right tackle. Both went on to play four years of college ball and began their pro careers in 1950. Both played 14 years in the NFL, both spent their entire careers with one team. Both were elected to the Hall of Fame in their first year of eligibility. And neither would be enshrined today if he had listened to his parents. Neither the Nomellinis nor the Stautners encouraged their sons to play football.

Nomellini says his interest in football began when he saw the movie about the great Notre Dame coach Knute Rockne, which starred Pat O'Brien as Rockne and Ronald Reagan as the fabled player George Gipp. "One thing that has stayed with me to this day," Nomellini says, "is the scene where Gipp (not yet a member of the team) walks by the bench, picks up the ball, and kicks it eighty yards in civilian clothes. I was impressed with the spirit of Notre Dame." His parents, however, looked the other way—because they had to.

"I played sandlot football, but not high school football," Nomellini explains. "I worked. My folks weren't rich. It was the Depression. My parents said, 'You'll hurt yourself [playing football], ruin your clothes.' But what it really was, if you could make twenty dollars working after school, it was much more productive."

Shortly after Pearl Harbor, Nomellini enlisted in the Marines, played service football for the Cherry Point Leathernecks, and built enough of a reputation to secure a scholarship from the University of Minnesota. Freshmen were eligible in the postwar era, and so in the first college game Nomellini ever saw, he was a starting guard for the Gophers. Later, as a tackle, he was an all-American. He also participated in track, putting the shot, and running the anchor leg on the 440-yard-relay team. In addition, he won the Big Ten heavyweight wrestling championship (he wrestled professionally in the off-season during his NFL career). The San Francisco 49ers were duly impressed and in 1950 made Nomellini their first draft choice.

He received no bonus when he signed, but that didn't bother him at all. "I'd have played football for nothing in those days," he explains. How im-

Top: *A treasure of mementoes from every age of pro football fills the spacious Exhibition Rotunda.* Bottom: *Action translites and unique "infinity" boxes are gathered for a colorful welcome to the Hall's display areas.*

Above: *Mini displays of each of the current NFL teams are combined in the popular Professional Football Today exhibit.* Upper right: *The Modern Era display is designed to accommodate quick changes made necessary by significant events in the ever-changing pro football scene.* Near right: *Johnny Unitas' exceptional feat of throwing at least one touchdown pass in 47 straight games is chronicled in detail* Far right: *O. J. Simpson's 2,003-yard rushing season in 1973 is commemorated in another display area.*

The Modern Era

UNITAS' EXCEPTIONAL FEAT

The George Blanda display honors pro football's oldest player.

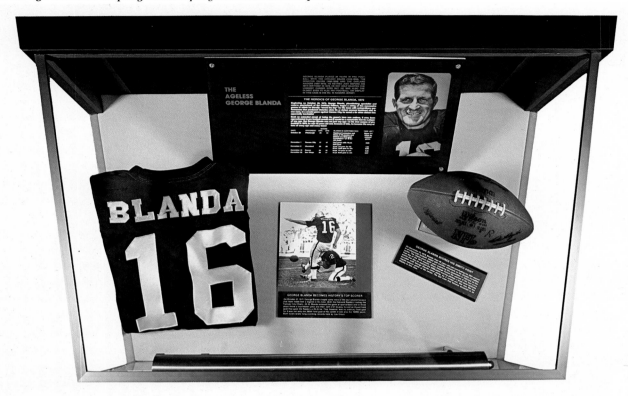

Weeb Ewbank's coaching cap from Super Bowl III and the shoes Tony Dorsett wore on a record 99-yard run are featured in this contemporary area.

The regally finished Enshrinement Gallery.

The Pro Football Photo-Art Gallery.

The striking changes made in the football uniform from the 1920's to the present are traced in this colorful exhibit.

Above: *The Enshrinee Mementoes Room. Here enshrinees are honored in special sections reserved for the teams for which they played.* Left: *The Pro Football Adventure Room, the Hall's largest exhibition area, with more than 15 displays.*

Overleaf: *Fans are invited to actively participate in history with numerous closed circuit television screens, selective slide machines, and football quiz boards.*

portant football was to him became evident when he and his wife, Ruth, were divorced. At the divorce hearing, Ruth testified, "Leo loves football more than he does me and the children. He lives, eats, and sleeps it. It's a passion that has devoured him. His day began with an end run to the front porch for the newspaper and then he would straight-arm all opposition till he tore out the sports section." His dedication to the sport is also reflected statistically. From the day he joined the 49ers in 1950 until he retired following the 1963 season, he never missed a game, playing in 266 in succession, including preseason, regular season, and postseason action.

Besides being durable, Nomellini was a tireless and versatile performer. From 1951 through 1955, he played both offense and defense and never once donned his pads, because "I wanted to be loose and mobile." Loose and mobile, the 6-foot 3-inch, 260-pounder became one of the few players ever selected all-NFL both on offense and defense. He gained all-NFL offensive honors in 1951 and 1952, then added all-NFL defensive laurels in 1953, 1954, 1957, and 1959. In what many still consider his most amazing season, 1955, he did not make an all-NFL team either offensively or defensively, but he played 60 minutes in every game. He preferred to play defense, however. "I could use my hands on defense," he explained. "If I could get my mitts on a guy, I could handle him. Offense was more difficult. I used to have to lead the plays. And it really got my goat when I'd miss some little squirt." A Pro Bowl selection 10 of his 14 years, there obviously weren't too many squirts he missed.

Like Nomellini, Stautner also began to play football on the sandlots, at our Lady of the Angels grade school. "It was a tough neighborhood," Stautner remembers. "One day I came home with my ankles so banged up I had to go to the doctor. We didn't have money for doctor bills, I realize now. My old man ruled the family—what he said, that was it and no question. My dad pointed the big finger at me and laid down the law. 'Keine mehr Fussbal,' he yelled. 'Keine mehr yamerung.'" That meant no more football—no more complaining. But Stautner interpreted it just a little differently. He decided what his father meant was if he did no more complaining, his father wouldn't know he was playing.

Armed with his own interpretation of his dad's admonition, Stautner continued to play. But it never was easy to explain the facial cuts and bleeding noses he often brought home. "Had another fight in school today, Papa," he'd explain. And Papa would look at his son curiously and respond, "So

many fights at a nice Catholic school—I can't understand." Papa understood when his son's cover was blown during his junior year in high school. It was then that Ernie Stautner's name found its way into the newspaper because he had been named all-Albany. "People started calling the house to compliment my dad," Stautner recalls, "and pride took over. Besides, I'd established my independence pretty good by then so he said okay."

Stautner also reaffirmed his independence by joining the Marines and playing for the Cherry Point Leathernecks. That was followed by a college career at Boston College, during which he became an All-American and a selection by the Pittsburgh Steelers in the third round of the 1950 draft. The Steelers admittedly were taking a gamble, because Stautner carried only 235 pounds on a 6-foot 1-inch frame—too small for a defensive lineman, according to those charged with the task of knowing such things. As a matter of fact, Coach Steve Owen of the New York Giants told Stautner, "I don't think you have the size for the pros, son. Our smallest tackle weighs two forty-eight and you're considerably shy of that." The Steelers, however, saw something in Stautner the Giants didn't, and wound up with a defensive tackle who was a nine-time Pro Bowler thoroughly respected by those who had to handle him.

"The man ain't human," said guard Jim Parker of the Baltimore Colts, who at 275 pounds had a 40-pound edge on Stautner. "He's too strong to be human. He keeps coming, coming, coming. Every time he comes back, he's coming harder."

That, of course, was by design. Stautner knew what he was battling. "There's only one way I can stick around here [in the NFL]," he said. "I gotta be mean. At my size, I can't afford to play any other way. Unless I'm meaner than these big guys, unless I can intimidate them I'd have no chance in the world against them." Stautner did intimidate them with tremendous arm strength, which he attributed to growing up as a farmboy. "My dad and my brother and I, we would mow ten tons of hay, using an old German scythe," Stautner explains. "People are always saying they love the smell of new-mown hay. Not me. I hate it. All it smells like to me is hard work. But it gave me muscles. It built up my forearms and at two hundred thirty-five pounds that was the way I stayed in the NFL so many years, using my forearms."

Nagurski was born Bronislau Nagurski in Canada of parents who left the Polish Ukraine early in the 1900's to seek a new way of life. Nagurski's parents settled in the town of Rainy River on the Canadian side of a river by the same name that was the border between Canada and the United

States. When Bronislau was four, the Nagurskis moved to International Falls, Minnesota, some sixty miles away. "It was," said Nagurski, "sort of like moving from the country to the city." Nagurski's father ran a grocery store in International Falls and little Bronislau started school as Bronko when his mother realized so many people were having difficulty pronouncing his given name. When he began to play football, Bronko's parents objected, as had Nomellini's and Stautner's, but not enough to deter him.

"I started playing football right after kindergarten," the 70-year-old Nagurski said in an interview conducted in 1978. "We'd just throw the ball around sandlots—there wasn't much else to do in town during your spare time. In a way, my parents sort of wished I didn't play—they thought their little boy would get hurt. But they didn't raise serious objections."

Nagurski first played football on an organized basis in high school, but the nearest rival for International Falls was a hundred miles away, and the team played only three or four games a year. "The roads were very poor," Nagurski pointed out, "and there were hardly any autos." Not much reason to cheer, either. Despite the fact he was an outstanding fullback, Nagurski never was able to lead International Falls High to even one victory.

Nevertheless, Nagurski had no difficulty getting into the University of Minnesota. How? Why? The Nagurski story has been so embellished through the years that there probably is no accurate answer available, only the stories that have become part of football's folklore. This is the story told by Red Grange, Nagurski's teammate with the Chicago Bears, long after both had retired:

> . . . Doc Spears, who had been Bronko's coach at Minnesota, came down in Florida visiting me, and I asked him how he ever came across Bronko. Spears said that he had gone up to International Falls to see another kid. . . . He thought his name was Smith. Spears told me that just outside of International Falls he saw this young kid pushing a plow. There was no horse or anything else, just the kid pushing the plow. Spears asked the kid where he could find this Smith, and the boy, who happened to be Bronko, just picked up the plow and pointed in the direction. Spears said then he knew he'd better get this kid with the plow.

Whether you believe that story or not, there's no way to question the words of those who testified about his ability, including Grange. "There was something strange about tackling Nagurski," said Grange. "When you hit him at the ankles, it is almost like getting an electric shock. If you hit him above the ankles, you are likely to get killed."

"Defense him?" said Steve Owen of the Giants "There's only one way—shoot him before he leaves the dressing room."

"He was seventy-five percent of an opposing team's worry," said the Giants' Harry Newman. "I was never hit so hard in my life as one time when I tried to stop him in the open field. I hit him as hard as I could and all it did was throw him off pace a little."

"Here's a check for ten thousand dollars, Nagurski," owner G. A. Richards of the Detroit Lions once told him. "Not for playing for the Lions, because you belong to the Bears, but just to quit the game and get the hell out of the league. You are ruining my team."

There is no completely accurate statistical report on Nagurski because a portion of his career occurred before records were kept. Unofficially, the 6-foot 2-inch, 230-pounder is credited with 4,031 yards gained rushing in 872 attempts, a 4.6 average. Grange, however, gives what may be an accurate picture of the triple threat Nagurski was as a bull-like rusher, blistering blocker, and bone-jarring tackler. "He could do everything on offense and defense," Grange said. "He was sort of like a combination of Jim Brown on offense and Dick Butkus on defense. When you played defense against him you never had to look him up. He would come straight for you. He never tried to evade anyone. He was a great blocker as well as a powerful runner and one of the really great linebackers. He could have been an all-Pro defensive star today as a linebacker."

Nagurski and Grange played in the same backfield for the Bears from 1930 to 1934, when Grange retired. Nagurski, however, played three more seasons before quitting at age 29. There was some question as to why he bowed out at the time, but the suspicion was that he may have started to make more money wrestling than he could make playing pro football. Six years later, however, when manpower shortages brought about by World War II caused the Bears to call for help, Nagurski returned to the lineup. And, while he concentrated primarily on the tackle position, there is no record of any other player ever making as successful a comeback after such a long layoff. Nagurski was pressed into service as a fullback as the season drew to a close, and his last hurrah with the ball tucked under his arm came during the NFL championship game against Washington. The Bears and Redskins were locked in a 7-7 tie when Nagurski smashed three yards for the touchdown that put Chicago ahead to stay.

Nagurski's shoes are just one of a number of items on display in the Bears' section of the Mementoes Room. There's also a jersey worn by Gale

Top: *Four San Francisco 49ers who are now Hall of Famers are featured in this display. Leo Nomellini's No. 73 full uniform is a major artifact.*

Above: *Ernie Stautner's Pittsburgh Steelers jersey found a home in the Hall of Fame after it was retired by Steelers president Dan Rooney.*

Sayers, the Grange of the 1960's; a pair of shoes worn by George McAfee, the Grange of the 1940's; and the ice tongs used by the Grange of the 1920's. The Bears and Green Bay Packers have the most crowded displays in the Mementoes Room. The Bears' contingent consists of a total of 24 players who played for the club at one time or another—20 who made their major contributions in Chicago. The Packers are next in line with 16 players who played primarily in Green Bay, and another 3 who spent the majority of their playing careers with other teams. Included among the artifacts in the Packers' team display, besides the bench used during Vince Lombardi's last Green Bay game, are a jersey worn by the great middle linebacker of the Lombardi era, Ray Nitschke, and a blanket that used to be draped over the shoulders of Clarke Hinkle, who may be the most underrated player in the Hall of Fame.

It was Hinkle's misfortune to join the Packers in 1932 at a time when Nagurski was riding high for the Bears. Despite the fact they had some titanic individual battles, Nagurski's fame and the Bears' success always seemed to assure that Hinkle would be overshadowed. It remains that way today—many of those who visit the Hall of Fame are fully aware of Nagurski's exploits with Minnesota and the Bears; few are aware of Hinkle's achievements at Bucknell and Green Bay.

The Bears and Packers began playing an uninterrupted series that now spans seven decades on November 27, 1921. Since that day, when the Bears won, 20-0, as Pete Stinchcomb ran for two touchdowns and Dutch Sternaman passed to George Halas for the other, there have been more games played (127 through 1983) than in any other series ever—high school, college, or pro. Few, if any, series have had as many memorable moments—and there is no more vivid example of the intensity brought to the field by the Bears and Packers than the Nagurski-Hinkle collisions.

The two Hall of Famers—each in their middle fifties—met in New York City in 1966, and Nagurski immediately took over as press agent for Hinkle. Asked to comment on a statement made by those who played against him that he couldn't be brought down by just one man, Nagurski pointed to Hinkle and said, "There's just one fellow who did it more than once. Toughest man I ever played against—and we collided in at least twenty-five games." Hinkle, somewhat embarrassed by the kind words, tried to turn the tables. "One time I hit Bronko and needed seven stitches to patch up a cut on my chin," he said.

"How about the time you broke my nose while I was tackling you?" Nagurski countered. "What did you hit me with, a sixteen-pound shot?"

"The ball," Hinkle replied, laughing. "It was the only thing handy."

"I always tried to get to Bronko before he got to me," said Hinkle, who was a fullback and linebacker while Nagurski was a fullback and tackle. "I played Bronko pretty even, nose to nose. But I learned never to stand still and wait for him, because he would have killed me." In 1934, one almost did in the other. Playing in Green Bay, the Packers had the ball on their own 20, third-and-14. Hinkle went into punt formation, common practice on third down in those years. Hinkle always had the option to kick, run, or pass—and this time he chose to run. He picked a hole at right tackle and then cut toward the sidelines, only to find that Nagurski had him cornered. Nagurski rarely left his feet while tackling; he merely used his shoulder or hip or forearm to wipe out a runner. Hinkle, fully aware of that tactic, decided to beat him to the punch. A second before Nagurski would have made contact, Hinkle pivoted, lowered his shoulder, and smashed into his pursuer. The collision left Nagurski wobbly—a rarity in itself—and unable to walk off the field under his own power. It also left him with a fractured rib and the broken nose he still remembered when they met in New York City 32 years later.

Hinkle played for the Packers for ten seasons and excelled at almost everything a player can do on a football field. He was a runner who would barrel straight ahead into the toughest line, and he could turn the corner with the speediest runners of the day. He was an excellent faker who many times drew the defense to him while leaving either Arnie Herber or Cecil Isbell time to unload a long pass to Don Hutson. He blocked savagely, both for the run and the pass, could also catch the ball, and threw it well enough on the option play to complete 24 out of 54 attempts for 316 yards and 2 touchdowns. He also was the Packers' punter, and kicked extra points and field goals. In addition, he was an outstanding linebacker who always insisted only one receiver ever got behind him. He always liked to point out, "I played twenty years in the league, ten on offense, ten on defense."

Hinkle was all-NFL four times, totaled 3,860 yards rushing, punted for a 43.4 average, and wound up with 42 touchdowns and 367 points scored. He led the league in scoring with 58 points in 1938 and was the NFL field-goal leader in both 1940 and 1941. "Clark Hinkle was the greatest all-around player of all time," said teammate Charles "Buckets" Goldenberg after Hinkle retired. "He

didn't hit as hard straight on as Nagurski and he didn't have Bronk's size [Hinkle was 6 feet, 205 pounds]. But he could do so many things well." And what did the opposition say? "No one in the whole league bruised me more than did Hinkle," said Bears' running back John Sisk. "After we had played the Packers, I'd be black and blue down to my toenails. All I'd want is peace and quiet. Hinkle had a lot of leg action. I broke my shoulder twice tackling Mr. Hinkle!"

In Green Bay, where so much of the social activity of the town revolves around the Packers, arguments inevitably arise about whether the great Green Bay teams of the 1930's—Hinkle's era—were just as good as, possibly even better than, the teams that were so powerful during the Lombardi era. Inevitably, when comparisons are made about offensive units, Hinkle is compared to Lombardi's battering-ram fullback, Jim Taylor. Then, when it's time to talk defense, Hinkle is compared to Nitschke, the premier linebacker of Lombardi's legions. Taking note of that, the Milwaukee *Journal* decided to underscore the situation in summing up a story about Hinkle following a 1965 club reunion. The headline read: HINKLE'S SUCCESSOR WAS NAMED TAYLOR AND NITSCHKE!

The bench from Lambeau Field that sits in the Packers' display as mute testimony to Lombardi's coaching genius was used during the now-famous Ice Bowl Game for the NFL championship played between the Packers and the Dallas Cowboys on December 31, 1967. There are those who believe that the game—due to the circumstances under which it was played—is the most memorable in NFL history. Whether it was or not, it did represent the culmination of Lombardi's amazing career in Green Bay. Lombardi had taken over the Packers after a 1-10-1 1958 season that had been the worst in the team's history. The Packers had slipped so far they hadn't been over .500 since 1947 and hadn't won a division title since 1944. But Lombardi turned them around and became a symbol for excellence that transcended sports. In 9 seasons, his Packers rolled to a 98-30-4 record, won 6 division titles, 5 NFL championships—a record 3 in succession—and 2 Super Bowls.

No game during those nine seasons, however, can compare with the 1967 NFL championship game, played on an afternoon when the thermometer read 13 degrees below zero, with a wind-chill factor of minus 37. It was the coldest New Year's Eve in the recorded history of Green Bay—and conditions were so severe that consideration was given to postponing the game. The Packers and Cowboys, however, took to the frozen field, and the

Packers won 21-17 in the final seconds after completing a 68-yard drive. The play that won the game has been repeated so often on television and seen so much on film it is indelibly etched in our minds. Green Bay quarterback Bart Starr takes the snap from center and plunges into the line for the winning touchdown, squeezing into the end zone in the space provided by Jerry Kramer's block on Jethro Pugh.

There are no such memories attached to Grange's ice tongs; the tongs are simply one of the three most unusual items on display in the Hall of Fame, along with the vertical striped socks worn by the Denver Broncos of the early 1960's, and the oversized trophy presented to wide receiver Harold Carmichael of the Philadelphia Eagles when he caught a pass in his one-hundred-sixth consecutive game. The tongs, as a matter of fact, don't even have a pro pedigree—they were used by Grange during his college career at Illinois. In order to make money during his summers away from school, Grange worked on an ice truck in his hometown of Wheaton, Illinois, earning $37.50 a week toting chunks of ice for the "refrigerators" in use at the time.

As soon as Grange catapulted to national fame by scoring 5 touchdowns in a game against Michigan—4 in the space of 12 minutes on jaunts of 95, 56, 44, and 67-yards—pictures of him with a block of ice slung across his shoulder appeared in a number of newspapers. Although he would become more generally known as the Galloping Ghost, those pictures labeled him the Wheaton Iceman and were accepted at first only as a press agent's gimmickery. Nothing could have been further from the truth. Grange worked on Luke Thompson's ice truck because he had to. "I never got a penny for going to school at Illinois, not when I went or anytime while I was there," Grange explained. "So, I had to make some money in the summers, through high school and college. A bunch of us kids used to hang around the truck, and one day Mr. Thompson offered to give a dollar to whichever one of us could lift a seventy-five pound cake of ice on his shoulder. I did it and got the buck, and the next Saturday when Mr. Thompson needed a helper, he asked me if I wanted to work for him. From then on I worked for him every summer."

Grange always felt the job was perfect for an athlete looking for an off-season conditioning program. "At first," he said. "I did it just for the money, but later on I kept it up because I knew it had a lot to do with keeping me in shape. The work was great for an athlete, great for my arms and legs and shoulders. Working all summer on that ice wagon, I'd go back to school in the fall with legs as hard as iron. At one time or another, I was offered all sorts of soft jobs in the summertime. I turned them all down. The ice truck was just right for me." Grange, as a matter of fact, even went back to Wheaton in 1926 after earning nearly a hundred thousand dollars while barnstorming. "A lot of my friends thought I had lost my mind," Grange says with a laugh whenever he's reminded of that. "They thought it was quite a comedown for a guy who made all that money. I was convinced that I needed the ice truck to stay in condition, for I was still a football player, not a banker." But there was one difference—Grange now drove to work in a $5,500 Lincoln Phaeton. That seemed to unsettle Luke Thompson just a bit. "Red," he said, "please don't park that thing in front of my place. It kind of confuses me as to who is working for whom around here."

George Halas, the owner-coach of the Bears, knew what he had in Grange, and he knew what the Chicago Cardinals had in Ollie Matson. That's why he was so surprised—as were many others in the NFL—when his crosstown rivals decided to trade Matson to the Los Angeles Rams. "I don't know how the Cardinals could have traded him," Halas said. "He's a 'wonder player,' and you just don't trade away your 'wonder players.' There are too few of them in the league—[Jim] Brown of Cleveland, maybe [Jon] Arnett of Los Angeles, certainly Matson. There isn't any value really great enough to make you give them up."

The Rams had admired Matson from the moment Coach Hampton Pool saw him score on a 91-yard pass play and a 74-yard run while playing for the Fort Ord Army team in an exhibition game against Los Angeles. That admiration still existed when Pete Rozelle, the Rams' general manager, sent his telegram to the NFL office on February 28, 1959, advising of the nine-for-one trade.

The telegram on display in the Cardinals' section of the Mementoes Room advised that the Rams were surrendering seven players—halfback Don Brown; fullback Larry Hickman; defensive linemen Frank Fuller, Art Hausner, Glenn Holtzmann; tackle Ken Panfil; and end John Tracey—plus a player to be named later and a draft choice in the Matson deal. The two other players turned out to be 1960 draft choices, guard Mike McGee and end Silas Woods.

Despite the fact that paying such a price for one player was virtually unprecedented, Rams fans were exuberant about the trade, envisioning an NFL title, which, unfortunately, never came. Nevertheless, the trade has to be considered a success from the Los Angeles viewpoint merely because only one of the nine players—John Tracey—still was playing when Matson retired after the 1966 season.

From the time Matson stepped into the NFL in 1952—in his first pro game against the Bears he ran a kickoff back 100 yards and also scored on a 34-yard interception return—he was the kind of "wonder player" Halas revered. Because of that status there always was pressure on Matson to produce—not only rushing, receiving, and returning, but by leading his teams into the NFL throne room. Matson always rejected the theory that he could dramatically alter a team's finish. "I never think about the pressure," he said, "because no one man can take a team to a championship. It takes thirty-five ballplayers [the roster limit at the time], all doing their best." His words were prophetic. In 14 seasons with the Cardinals, Rams, Detroit Lions, and Philadelphia Eagles, he never played on a championship team—and rarely played for a winner. Only two teams for which he played finished above .500, and the combined won-lost record of the four teams during his years with them was 58-117-5.

Because Matson played on teams with few weapons, opposition defenses were able to key on him without too much concern, and he paid a stiff physical price for every yard he gained. But he never complained and always produced, driving himself to prove the one rap against him—that he wouldn't be able to withstand the punishment a player has to take in the NFL—was totally unjustified. "Everybody used to tell me, 'You're not a football player, you're a track man,'" Matson explained. And it was certainly true that Matson was a track man; he won the bronze medal for the 400-meter run in the 1952 Olympics. But he was not only quick, he was tough, and often was used as a heavy-duty ballcarrier. As a matter of fact, he wore many hats during his career—halfback, fullback, blocking back, tight end, split end—and always fought for every yard. "I've never seen him flinch from a tackle," said Clark Shaughnessy, the astute defensive coach of the Bears. "No matter how bad his team was being beaten, I've never seen him fold up."

With defenses keyed to stop him and his teams rarely strong enough to alleviate the pressure, Matson never achieved his goal of leading the NFL in rushing. While still with the Cardinals, he finished second in 1956 with 924 yards (another 350 yards were nullified by penalty). He was unable to gain that much yardage for the Rams—his best was 863 yards in 1959, the year he was acquired. Still his career record is exceptional and shows his amazing versatility. Rushing, receiving, returning, he gained 12,844 yards overall—more than 7¼

miles—and, while he never was the rushing leader, he won the punt-return title in 1954 and the kick-off-return crown in 1957. In all, he rushed for 5,173 yards, caught passes for 3,285 yards, returned kickoffs for 3,746 yards and punts for 595 yards. He scored 73 total touchdowns—40 by rushing, 23 receiving, 9 returning, and 1 on a fumble recovery.

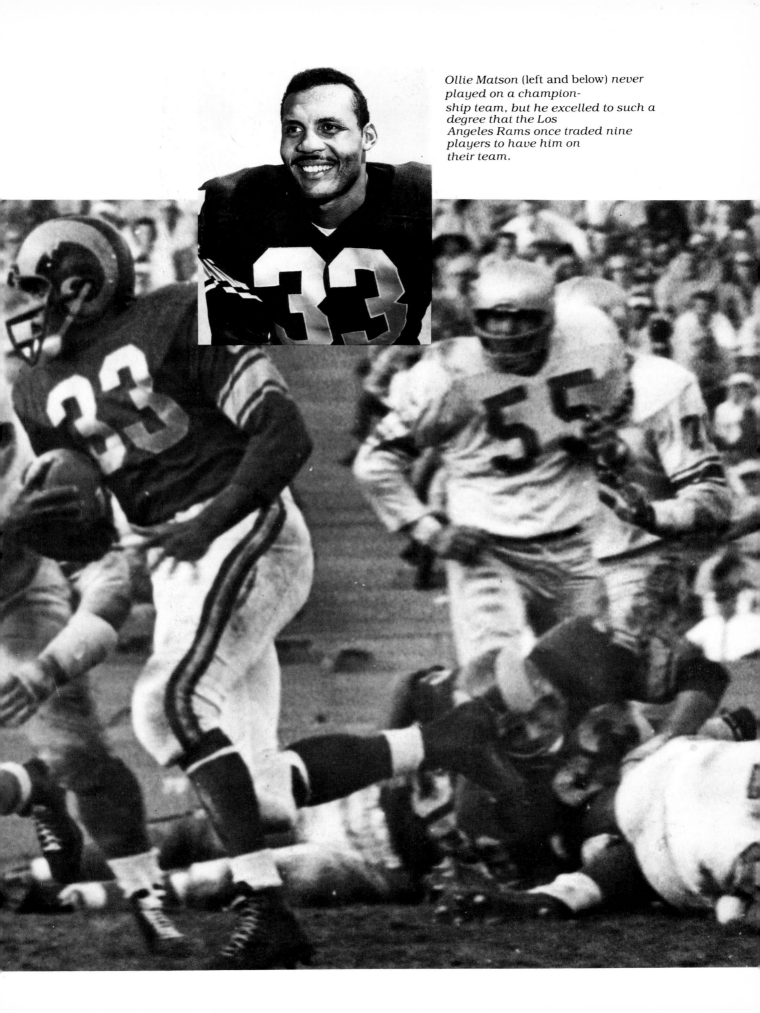

Ollie Matson (left and below) *never played on a championship team, but he excelled to such a degree that the Los Angeles Rams once traded nine players to have him on their team.*

SAFETY JACK CHRISTIANSEN

NFL Opponents Had a Standard Rule: "When playing Detroit and on offense, don't pass the football in Chris' area. When punting, don't kick to him!" On display at the left is a game ball given to Chris after a hero's role against Los Angeles in 1957.

JACK CHRISTIANSEN WAS SUPERB IN A KICK RETURN ROLE AS THIS NINE-PICTURE SEQUENCE OF A 70-YARD PUNT RETURN AGAINST LOS ANGELES IN 1951 WILL ATTEST.

A game ball he won against the Los Angeles Rams and a nine-picture sequence of a 70-yard punt return against the same team six years earlier highlight the Jack Christiansen display in the Detroit Lions portion of the Enshrinee Mementoes Room.

Chapter 9

Heroes and Showmen

The Rozelle telegram advising of Ollie Matson's trade was read by Commissioner Bert Bell at his desk in the NFL's offices in Philadelphia. The desk, pockmarked by burns, clearly indicated how Bell would puff on a cigar, then absentmindedly place it down while handling the weighty issues of his office. Bell first became involved in NFL affairs in 1933 when he and co-owner Lud Wray acquired the defunct Frankford (Pennsylvania) Yellowjackets and moved the franchise from the suburbs into downtown Philadelphia. Bell renamed the team Eagles after the blue eagle that was the symbol of the National Recovery Administration. It wasn't long before he made his first major contribution to the NFL—proposing an annual college player draft. In 1946, he was elected commissioner to succeed Elmer Layden, then proceeded to secure his niche in the NFL with a number of decisions that helped catapult the sport into an astounding period of growth.

Bell's father, John C. Bell, Sr., was a back on the University of Pennsylvania teams of 1882, 1883, and 1884 and later a trustee of the school and head of its athletic association. By the time he was six years old, Bert Bell already was being taken to Penn games. He eventually played quarterback for the Quakers, then became an assistant coach at the university. But he wasn't pushed—he jumped. "All I ever wanted was football," Bell said. "Football's my life."

The pros soon became his life. It is questionable whether the NFL's owners knew exactly the kind of a man they were seeking—or getting—when they handed the reins of leadership to Bell.

But it soon became evident that he was a tireless worker, not only willing to tackle the tough issues but to deal with them intelligently as well.

The toughest case to be dropped on his desk may have occurred the first year he was in office. It happened just before the 1946 NFL championship game between the New York Giants and Chicago Bears when Bell was notified that two Giants' stars—quarterback Frank Filchock and halfback Merle Hapes—had been approached by gamblers about "fixing" the point spread in the game. Neither had accepted, but both had made the mistake of not reporting the bribe attempt. Bell acted swiftly. He suspended Hapes before the game, and while Filchock was allowed to play, he was suspended when additional evidence became available. The rulings by Bell marked the beginning of tough anti-gambling measures that were a hallmark of Bell's regime and have remained integral to NFL policy through the Pete Rozelle years. Still, Bell's most lasting contribution to the sport was his handling of the league's television policy.

Television was comparatively new on the American sports scene during Bell's tenure as commissioner, but Bell anticipated its potential for creating fans throughout the country. He also was wary of its inherent dangers. "Television creates interest, and this can benefit pro football," he said. "But it's only good as long as you can protect your home gate. You can't give fans a game for free on television and also expect them to pay to go to the ball park to see the same game." That posture led to the adoption of the policy that still is the cornerstone of the NFL's television code—the televising of road games to the fans in their home cities and the blacking out of home games (now amended to per-

199

mit telecasting of home games if stadiums are sold out 72 hours before kickoff).

Another key administrator who began his NFL career in the 1930's was George Preston Marshall, a one-time actor and laundry entrepreneur. Marshall acquired the Boston franchise in 1932, and in 1933 joined forces with George Halas in urging the passage of several progressive new rules and pioneering the idea of splitting the NFL into two divisions with an annual championship game. In 1937, Marshall moved his franchise to Washington and built one of the league's legitimate powerhouses. His Redskins won six division titles and two NFL championships by 1946. But Marshall's most significant legacy was his showmanship—he was the first owner to promote his team through the use of professional publicity and he developed the Redskins' marching band and the concept of the halftime show. In so doing, he dramatically altered the sport, bringing color and drama to an event which until then had been merely a contest among men.

Marshall felt the NFL couldn't be successful by appealing only to a male clientele. He wanted women to attend games, too. "For the women, football alone is not enough," he said. "I always try to present halftime entertainment to give them something to look forward to—a little music, dancing, color, something they can understand and enjoy. The thing is that if you get the women to come out, you'll get the men, too. The women will bring them. And the women add class to a sports gathering." He also spoke of his vision of football as spectacle. "Football is a game of pageantry," he said. "It derives as spectacle from the gladiator shows of the Romans of history. It is strictly amphitheater. Its great success is due to the color surrounding it. It needs music and bands. Football without a band is like a musical without an orchestra."

So Marshall instituted a marching band for the Redskins, 110 musicians decked out in $25,000 worth of Indian costumes—burgundy and gold with white feather headdresses (imported from Hollywood, reported Marshall's wife, the silent screen star Corinne Griffith). A full-dress uniform, replete with headdress, and a drum from the band is on display in the Redskins' section of the Mementoes Room. Marshall was so enraptured with the concept of sport as spectacle that there were those who suggested that his band members were as important to him as his players.

Jack Mara of the New York Giants probably thought so in 1960 when an unexpected blizzard struck Washington a few hours before a Redskins-Giants game. Marshall immediately began a frantic search to get equipment to clear off the field before game time. Two hours before kickoff, however, snow still blanketed the field. Mara, obviously concerned, was looking dejectedly at the field when Marshall appeared, a smile on his face. "They're coming," said Marshall. "They'll be here in plenty of time."

"The snowplows?" Mara asked.

"No," said Marshall, his brow furrowing at Mara's lack of understanding. "The overshoes for the band."

The best example of Marshall's penchant for publicity revolves around his portrayal of his star quarterback, Sammy Baugh, as a pistol-packing cowboy despite the fact Baugh was a city guy from Sweetwater, Texas. Marshall, however, couldn't be deterred from the vision he had. When Baugh agreed to go to Washington for contract talks, Marshall made one small request. "Before you come up here, Sam," he said, "be sure to go out and buy a ten-gallon hat and some of those Texas boots. Get the best. I'll give you the money for them when you get here."

"Sure," Baugh said, "but what size?"

"What size?" asked a puzzled Marshall. "Don't you know what size you wear?"

"Sure," said Baugh, "but I thought they were for you."

"No, no, no," stammered Marshall. "I want you to be wearing them when you step off the plane."

"I never wore no such getup in my life," Baugh protested.

"Well, you'll be wearing them from now on," Marshall replied. "Up here you're a rootin', tootin' cowboy."

Besides Marshall's band equipment, Bell's desk, and the other rare items on display in the Mementoes Room, there are a number of prosaic items. And, while they may be less dramatic than the Matson telegram or Red Grange's ice tongs, they have a certain fascination for the sport's historians, either because of the situation they highlight or the player they commemorate. Among those items are helmets that were worn by Pete "Fats" Henry, Bobby Layne, and Y. A. Tittle; a 1928 Providence Steam Roller trophy presented to Jimmy Conzelman; a game ball awarded to Jack Christiansen; and the championship blazer worn by Chuck Bednarik.

The Henry helmet on display is the one he wore during the Canton Bulldogs' reign of terror in 1922 and 1923, when they put together successive unbeaten seasons and an overall 21-0-3 record while becoming the NFL's first two-time champions. Most fans who have a passing knowledge of the Bulldogs' history tend to think of their success in terms of Jim Thorpe. But Thorpe was no longer a

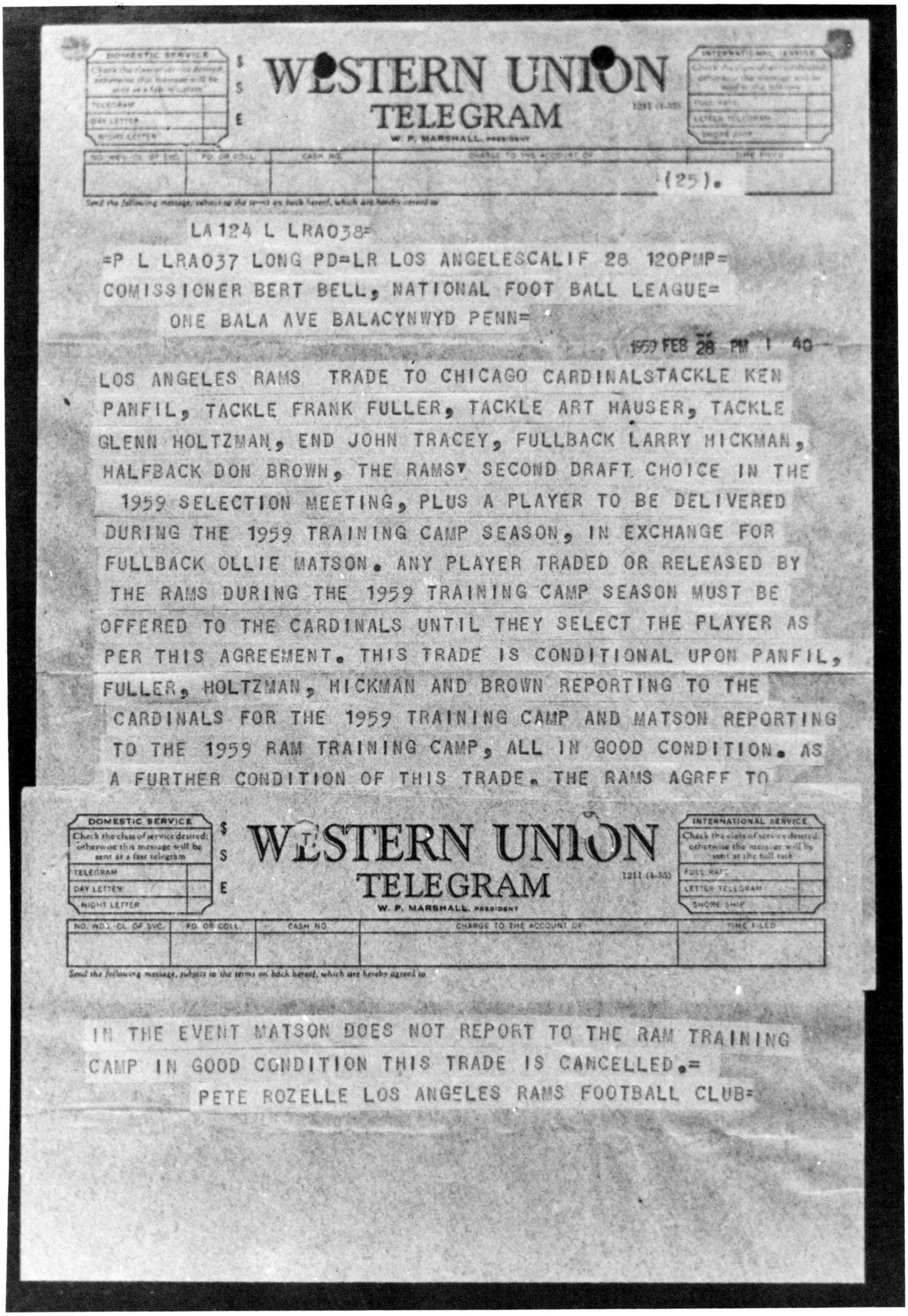

WESTERN UNION TELEGRAM

W. P. MARSHALL, PRESIDENT

{25}.

LA124 L LRA038=

=P L LRA037 LONG PD=LR LOS ANGELESCALIF 28 120PMP=

COMISSIONER BERT BELL, NATIONAL FOOT BALL LEAGUE=

ONE BALA AVE BALACYNWYD PENN=

1959 FEB 28 PM 1 40

LOS ANGELES RAMS TRADE TO CHICAGO CARDINALSTACKLE KEN
PANFIL, TACKLE FRANK FULLER, TACKLE ART HAUSER, TACKLE
GLENN HOLTZMAN, END JOHN TRACEY, FULLBACK LARRY HICKMAN,
HALFBACK DON BROWN, THE RAMS' SECOND DRAFT CHOICE IN THE
1959 SELECTION MEETING, PLUS A PLAYER TO BE DELIVERED
DURING THE 1959 TRAINING CAMP SEASON, IN EXCHANGE FOR
FULLBACK OLLIE MATSON. ANY PLAYER TRADED OR RELEASED BY
THE RAMS DURING THE 1959 TRAINING CAMP SEASON MUST BE
OFFERED TO THE CARDINALS UNTIL THEY SELECT THE PLAYER AS
PER THIS AGREEMENT. THIS TRADE IS CONDITIONAL UPON PANFIL,
FULLER, HOLTZMAN, HICKMAN AND BROWN REPORTING TO THE
CARDINALS FOR THE 1959 TRAINING CAMP AND MATSON REPORTING
TO THE 1959 RAM TRAINING CAMP, ALL IN GOOD CONDITION. AS
A FURTHER CONDITION OF THIS TRADE, THE RAMS AGREE TO

WESTERN UNION TELEGRAM

W. P. MARSHALL, PRESIDENT

IN THE EVENT MATSON DOES NOT REPORT TO THE RAM TRAINING
CAMP IN GOOD CONDITION THIS TRADE IS CANCELLED.=

PETE ROZELLE LOS ANGELES RAMS FOOTBALL CLUB=

*This is the telegram received by Commissioner Bell's office
that detailed the historic trade that sent Ollie Matson from the
Chicago Cardinals to the Los Angeles Rams in exchange for
nine players.*

Above left: *Bert Bell, who served as NFL Commissioner from 1946 until his death in 1959, handled all of his league business at a very small, cigar-burned desk that is on display at the Hall.* Left: *Pete Henry's 1920-style helmet occupies a place in the Canton Bulldogs section of the Enshrinee Mementoes Room.* Above: *Sammy Baugh's No. 33 Redskins jersey and a plaster cast replica of his throwing hand are on exhibit in the Triple Crown display case in the modern Exhibition Rotunda. Also displayed is an Indian headdress from the famous Washington Redskins marching band.*

member of the Bulldogs when they were the kings of the NFL. The major stars of that team were player-coach Guy Chamberlin, tackle Link Lyman, and Henry. And no one was bigger—literally or figuratively. For Henry not only carried 250 pounds on a 6-foot frame he deployed at the tackle spot opposite Lyman, he was a headline maker with a number of skills.

Henry's signing by the Bulldogs in 1920 was worthy of front-page news in the sports section of the Canton *Repository*. He was such a big-name star after his outstanding college career at Washington and Jefferson College that *The Repository* played the news of his joining the Bulldogs far more significantly than it did the formation meeting of the NFL, which occurred at the same time. A good-natured, easygoing performer, Henry played 60 minutes of every game and, besides blocking and tackling, handled the Bulldogs' kicking chores with record-setting ability. In a 1923 game against Akron, he was credited with a 94-yard punt and a 50-yard dropkick field goal against Toledo.

But, it was as a defensive tackle who dominated the line of scrimmage that Henry created the most lasting impression. Lou Little, who secured his own place in history as the coach at Columbia University, liked to regale football people with a story about his confrontation with Henry while he was playing for the Buffalo All-Americans in 1920 and 1921. The game plan devised by Tommy Hughitt, the Buffalo quarterback and coach, called for the All-Americans to run straight at Henry. "Everyone rack him up at once," Hughitt told his troops. "We'll show him who's boss." On Buffalo's first possession, Hughitt put his plan to work with Little and another guard, Swede Youngstrom, blocking on Henry. "Henry met the play head-on," Little recalled. "Using those huge hands of his and that tremendous active body as only he could, Pete telescoped Heinie Miller, the end; Youngstrom; and myself, hurling all three of us into Lud Wray, our center. Then he plunged through and hit Hughitt, the ballcarrier, like one of those baby tanks. Needless to add, Hughitt directed all plays to the other side of the line the rest of the game."

Another situation involved Charlie Berry, a former all-America end at Lafayette College and a baseball star with the Philadelphia Athletics who had been convinced by the Pottsville Maroons to give pro football a try after the baseball season ended. Berry did, joining the Maroons just in time to face the Bulldogs and Henry. As an end, it was Berry's assignment to block Henry, but, while he tried, he didn't meet with much success. "It was like bouncing off a rubber ball," Berry said. "I never

budged him once. After five minutes, I felt as though I had just finished a full sixty-minute game." Noting the beating Berry was taking, Pottsville quarterback Jack Ernst asked him, at one point in the game, if he would like to try and get even by attempting a field goal. Berry agreed to give it a whirl. Henry broke through and blocked it.

The Bobby Layne helmet on exhibit is unique for two reasons—it does not have a face mask and it is the one he wore for his last two seasons in the NFL as a member of the Pittsburgh Steelers. Layne played with only one piece of protective equipment—extremely light shoulder pads—but he never pretended any macho motive, despite his reputation as a tough Texan. Asked specifically about not using a face mask, he replied, "I tried them and I'd wear one every day in practice. But every time I'd look up, I'd see that bar. It bothered my vision. If I could have worn one I would. I damned sure wasn't trying to be brave or anything like that. It would have saved a lot of cheeks and broken noses." As for the significance of his last two seasons, Layne admitted he shouldn't have played them. "I went about two seasons too long," he said. "I think most do. You've got to understand it's hard to quit. You don't realize you're getting too old. You can think and you can still throw, but that's not the trouble. It's not your arm . . . it's your legs. You start getting slower. It was fortunate that [Coach] Buddy [Parker] sat me down and told me that I was going back to pass and they [defensive linemen] were getting back about the same time."

The punch line is typical Bobby Layne. He liked to laugh, liked to enjoy himself—there are a number of stories about his off-the-field activities that are legend—and he reveled in playing quarterback. Parker gave him his first big chance when both were with the Detroit Lions, and it was during this time that Layne established his Hall of Fame credentials. In all, Bobby spent 15 seasons in the NFL, accumulating 26,768 yards with 1,814 completions and 196 touchdowns. Layne's stardom reached its apex after Parker took over as coach in 1951, Layne's fourth season in the NFL. For the next three years, the Lions achieved greater success than at any other time in their history, before or since. With Layne directing the attack, Detroit won division titles in 1952, 1953, and 1954 and punctuated the first two by beating the Cleveland Browns—the dominant power of the decade—for the NFL championship. Nothing ever meant more to Layne than those two titles because he believed then, and still does, that the true measure of a quarterback's stature is whether he can take his team to the top. "You've got winners and you've got losers," he emphasized. "The rest are even. When a person sits down and tries to list the winning quarterbacks, it would shock you [to see who's omitted]. I'm talking about winning championships."

Layne, of course, proved himself a winner by his own definition in 1952 and 1953. In the first showdown with the Browns, he scored the first touchdown and completed 7 of 10 passes in a 17-7 victory. Then, when the two teams met the following season in Detroit's Briggs Stadium, Layne put together his most memorable afternoon. The Browns, who had lost only one game during the regular season, seemed to have the game locked up when 3 field goals by Lou Groza produced a 16-10 lead that still was holding up with just 3 minutes left in the game. Then the Lions took over at their 20, Layne stuck his head in the huddle, and drawled in his best Texas twang, "Y'all block and ol' Bobby'll pass you raht to the champeenship. Bobby'll get you six big ones." He was as good as his word. In just 60 seconds, Layne completed 4 of 6 passes, the last a 33-yarder to end Jim Doran that nudged Detroit in front, 17-16.

Layne and the Lions reportedly accomplished all their heroics with a carefree attitude that most likely would quickly exhaust the patience of today's discipline-oriented coaches. They often frequented night spots and competed in games of "Buzz" and "Cardinal Puff"—which history doesn't accurately describe but which research indicates left at least some of the players "hymn-singing drunk." "We always had a good time," Layne says. "I don't think players today have fun the way they used to. Buddy Parker had a different attitude from most coaches. He didn't care what you did, just as long as you didn't embarrass the club. But you have to realize pro ball is a job. If you don't work you're going to get fired. Nobody is going to jeopardize his career. But by the time a man is thirty, he knows what he can do and can't do. We were grown men. Some of us needed eight hours' [sleep] and some four."

Layne was one of the latter, but he denies that *all* the stories about him are true. "If they were," he says, "I wouldn't have been around for fifteen years." He doesn't, however, totally deny all his character references. "Sure, when I was in New York I'd go to Toots Shoor's (a sports hangout) to have dinner. I'd go in the restaurant and it would be ten or eleven P.M. I'd finish my meal and go home. But someone would see me and he'd tell one drunk who'd tell another drunk and the last drunk says, 'I'll bet on the other team because Layne was out to five-thirty.' " Layne took the opportunity to answer any and all critics of his late-night habits after the Lions were clobbered by the Browns, 56-10, in the 1954 NFL championship game. Pointing out that

the team's curfew prior to the game had been ten P.M., Layne said, "I think it shows it takes more than an early bedtime to win a ball game."

Y. A. Tittle spent 17 seasons in the pros, from 1948 to 1964, passed for 33,070 yards, threw for 242 touchdowns, and—unlike Layne—never achieved championship status. He had three consecutive shots at the end of his career with the New York Giants, but couldn't bring it off. The Giants lost 37-0 to Green Bay in 1961, 16-7 to the Packers in 1962, and, far more disturbingly to Tittle, dropped a 14-10 decision to the Chicago Bears in 1963—a game in which two of his passes were intercepted to set up both Chicago touchdowns. Tittle was so distraught after the loss that in anguish he slammed his blue Giants' helmet twice against the frozen turf of Chicago's Wrigley Field, cracking the headgear. Then, providing one of the most memorable pictorials in NFL history, he picked up the battered helmet and, his bald head bowed, trudged off the field to the bench, where he began to weep. The Tittle helmet on display in the Mementoes Room is the one he cracked that bitter day in Chicago.

But, while the cracked helmet was the result of the frustrations enveloping Tittle, it also serves to remind us of the tough competitor he was. Tittle played the entire second half of that game on wobbly knees after being beaten to the ground late in the first half by Chicago linebacker Larry Morris. Despite his courage in returning after halftime, Tittle blamed himself for the loss. "I contributed greatly to our defeat," he said, describing the game as "the greatest disappointment of my life in football." Others, including teammate Frank Gifford, saw it differently, pointing to Tittle's decision to continue to play despite the severity of his injuries. "I'll never know how Y. A. did it," Gifford said. "I'll remember that show of courage long after I have forgotten the score."

The Giants had acquired Tittle from the San Francisco 49ers prior to the 1961 season for an obscure guard named Lou Cordileone—one of the better trades in the club's history. Tittle shared the quarterbacking duties with Charley Conerly during the 1961 season as the Giants posted a 10-3-1 record, then took total control. The Giants won 23 of 28 games in 1962 and 1963, and Tittle had two of the best years ever recorded by any NFL quarterback. In 1962, he tied an NFL record for most touchdown passes in a game with 7 and wound up with a record-breaking season total of 33 while producing 3,224 yards. In 1963—at 37—he led the NFL in passing, gaining 3,145 yards, with a touchdown record of 36 and a completion percentage of 60.2. But a year later, after a disappointing 2–10–

2 season, Tittle announced his retirement.

Jimmy Conzelman is one of a select group of Hall of Famers who during their careers participated at every level possible—as player, coach, and owner. He also is the only one who ever began his coaching career in the middle of a game. Conzelman began his playing career as a member of George Halas' 1920 Decatur Staleys, then moved on to play for the Rock Island Independents in 1921. A year later he also was coaching. Conzelman was unceremoniously awarded the added duties after a first half in which Rock Island's opponents ran play after play with considerable success over the right tackle spot, a position manned by his predecessor as player-coach of the team. That enraged the club's owner. No one was aware how enraged, however, until the second half when a substitute replaced the embarrassed tackle, stepped into the huddle, and told Conzelman, "The owner says you are the new coach."

Conzelman remained in Rock Island through the 1922 season, then moved on to Milwaukee, where he doubled as player-coach for the Badgers until, in his second season, he was asked by NFL Commissioner Joe Carr to take on ownership of a new Detroit franchise. "The franchise fee is a thousand dollars," Carr told him, "but I'll let you have it for a hundred." Conzelman quickly agreed, named the team the Panthers, and put together a squad that compiled an 8-2-2 record—third best in the 20-team league. Lack of fan support, however, made it a losing proposition, and Conzelman was forced to give it up. This time he headed for Providence, where he became player-coach of the Steam Roller and in his second year in 1928 produced an NFL championship. The trophy commemorating that championship is the one that is on display as an unusual tribute to Conzelman. In the third game of the season Conzelman suffered a knee injury that ended his playing career. Nevertheless, at the end of the year, he was presented the trophy as the team's Most Outstanding Player.

The trophy is exhibited in the St. Louis (nee Chicago) Cardinals' section of the Mementoes Room—and there is little doubt that, while Providence always was a fond memory for Conzelman, he is best remembered as the coach of the 1947-1948 Cardinals. Conzelman's Cardinals were a talent-rich team with a "Dream Backfield," but the club was plagued by tragedies that ultimately forced Conzelman to quit.

He hadn't coached a pro football team since leaving Providence at the end of the 1930 season when, in 1940, George Halas recommended him to Cardinals' owner Charles Bidwill. Conzelman remained with the Cardinals through 1942, then left

The No. 22 jersey Bobby Layne wore with distinction, and Dutch Clark's warmup jacket are treasured mementoes in the Detroit Lions display.

to join baseball's St. Louis Browns before returning in 1946 for his last—and most successful—tour of duty in the NFL. The Cardinals, who were 1-9 in 1945, began to turn it around under Conzelman in 1946 with a 6-5 mark and then rolled into the NFL championship game in 1947, after compiling a 9-3 record behind the Dream Backfield. That backfield consisted of quarterback Paul Christman, Elmer Angsman, Pat Harder, and Charlie Trippi.

The Cardinals defeated the Philadelphia Eagles for the 1947 title on two long-distance touchdowns each by Trippi and Angsman, Trippi scoring on a 44-yard run and a 75-yard punt return and Angsman scoring on a pair of 70-yard runs. The Cardinals were even stronger in 1948, posting an 11-1-0 record, but lost the championship game to Philadelphia, 7-0, in a defensive struggle played in a blinding blizzard that may have handicapped the Cardinals more than the Eagles.

Conzelman was voted the NFL's Coach of the Year for 1947 but, despite the honor and the successful season that followed, he was unable to fully enjoy what he had achieved. Bidwill died in the spring of 1947—before he could ever see his Dream Backfield in action—and during the season halfback Jeff Burkett was killed in a plane crash. Then, in 1948, tackle Stan Mauldin collapsed and died in the Cardinals' dressing room. Those events seemed to depress Conzelman more than the team's success lifted him and, at the end of the year, he left the NFL for the last time.

While Conzelman's "first"—becoming a coach during a game—belongs on the humorous side of history's ledger, Jack Christiansen stands on the other side of the balance sheet, representing a major departure in drafting theory. When the Detroit Lions picked him in the 1951 draft, Christiansen became the first player ever selected for the sole purpose of playing defense. Up until that time, players were drafted for the offensive unit; those who didn't make it joined the defensive team. It wasn't long after Christiansen began running the Lions' secondary that Coach Buddy Parker admitted his philosophy had been completely altered. "If I had to lose four good backs, I'd rather give up the men on offense," Parker said. "You can always get someone to run the ball, but good defensive backs are hard to find."

Good defensive backs often turn games around, and the Los Angeles Rams learned that when they went against Detroit in the Lions' 1957 home opener. The Detroit secondary intercepted 6 passes attempted by Norm Van Brocklin—2 by Christiansen—permitted a total of just 5 completions and scored the Lions' only touchdown in a

10-7 victory. The game ball was presented to Christiansen and is on display in the Mementoes Room.

It was another unexpected honor for Christiansen, who was fortunate even to be playing football following a bizarre shooting incident in high school that could have cost him his life and did threaten his athletic career. Christiansen was born in Sublette, Kansas, in 1928, but two years later, just as the Great Depression was descending upon the country, his father was killed in a grain-elevator accident. Christiansen and his sister wound up at the Good Fellows Orphanage in Canon City, Colorado, where he attended grade, junior, and senior high school. And it was there, on a Halloween night his senior year in high school, that Christiansen and a group of boys were mistaken by a policeman for a gang that had been causing trouble. The policeman fired a warning shot into the ground, but the bullet ricocheted into Christiansen's left arm, missing his heart by inches. Doctors advised Christiansen not to play basketball or football and, when he entered Colorado A&M, he participated only in track—until football Coach Bob Davis convinced him his great speed would be an asset on the football field.

Christiansen never had any trouble with his arm—doctors were concerned it might not be able to take the pounding it would have to withstand—but when the 1951 draft came around, he had a number of liabilities. He had played at an obscure school and he weighed just 162 pounds, obviously not enough, despite his speed, to make him an NFL running back candidate. Nevertheless, the Lions decided to risk a sixth-round draft choice for a guy they could use at defensive back. It was one of the key decisions in a building program that enabled Detroit to win four division titles and three NFL championships during the decade. The Lions of that era revolved around quarterback Bobby Layne and running back Doak Walker, but "Chris' Crew"—the defensive secondary of Christiansen, Yale Lary, Jim David, and Carl Karilivacz—was the major element of a defensive unit that set Detroit apart from the rest of the NFL's teams.

The defensive secondary was named Chris' Crew simply because Christiansen was its leader—a superb safetyman who intercepted 46 passes in his 8 seasons and led the league with 12 in 1953 and 10 in 1957. Both years, it should be emphasized, the Lions won the NFL championship. Christiansen was all-NFL every year except his first and last, but rival players didn't need to be told about the honors he was receiving. Their coaches were telling them all about Christiansen. "Detroit had the defense and Chris was their leader," said Mac Speedie, an outstanding receiver for the Cleveland Browns. "We had a standard rule when we played the Lions—don't throw in Chris' area." There is no greater honor ever accorded a defensive back than that admonition by a rival coach to his players.

Chuck Bednarik may be the most famous "last" in sports history, a 6-foot 3-inch, 235-pounder who played both offense and defense in the NFL long after unlimited substitution led to players who specialized in either offense or defense. A center and linebacker, Bednarik became "The Last of the 60-Minute Men" during the 1960 season when, after three seasons playing only at center, he was forced into double duty again when injuries struck while the Philadelphia Eagles battled for the NFL championship. At age 35, when many players are looking forward to reducing playing time, Bednarik was in action 394½ minutes of the 12-game regular season and underscored his achievement by playing 58 minutes as the Eagles defeated the Green Bay Packers, 17-13, in the NFL championship game. In honor of that victory, each member of the Eagles was given a green blazer. Bednarik's hangs in the Mementoes Room.

Bednarik joined the Eagles in 1949 and immediately went to work playing 60 minutes a game. He continued to do so even as the era of specialization dawned and players began to play on only one unit or the other. He soon became known as pro football's Iron Man. After missing the first 2 regular-season games his rookie season, Bednarik missed only 1 other game in his 14-year tenure with the Eagles. Counting preseason and postseason games, Bednarik played 256 games during that period and, starting with his sophomore season, earned all-NFL honors 7 successive years—the first time as a center and the next 6 as a linebacker. Whenever anyone asked Bednarik what the secret of his success was, he would answer, "I always played with a certain amount of cockiness. You must have absolute confidence. You must feel that you are the best at your position at all times."

But, despite all his heroics over such a long period of time, it was his performances in 1960 that are most often remembered—undoubtedly because he was involved in one of the most controversial moments in NFL history. During a critical game between the Eagles and New York Giants, Bednarik made a jarring tackle on Frank Gifford that left the Giants' halfback sprawled on the field unconscious. The tackle, creating a fumble, gave the Eagles the ball with a seven-point lead and fewer than two minutes left to play, causing Bednarik to celebrate with a victory dance. The crowd, not fully aware why Bednarik was jumping for joy, assumed it was because he had knocked out Gif-

ford—and erupted in violent vocal disapproval. "I play hard to win—that's why I show my emotions as I do," Bednarik explained afterward. "I'm very sorry about Frank, but not the play. It was a good, clean tackle."

A similar super-tackle provided the turning point against the Packers in the championship game. This time the runner was Green Bay's Golden Boy, Paul Hornung, who found himself in front of Bednarik at one point—and the next thing he knew he had been slammed to the ground so hard he had to leave the game. Later in the day, Bednarik added a game-saving tackle to his collection when he grabbed and held onto Jimmy Taylor as the pile-driving fullback tried to churn across the Eagles' goal line with time running out. Bednarik played two more seasons for the Eagles, but what he did during that period was totally dwarfed by what he had achieved in 1960. Considering his age—and the fact he had to play against players who were resting on either offense or defense—his achievement is singular, even among a roll call of Hall of Famers. Bednarik loved every minute of it— with one exception. "I felt pretty silly," he noted, "standing out in the middle of the field all alone when the offense and defense would change."

These two helmets were worn through many NFL seasons by two Hall of Famers. Above: the headgear of Y. A. Tittle, broken when he angrily slammed his helmet on the frozen ground. Right: This helmet belonged to Bobby Layne during his days with the Pittsburgh Steelers.

207

*A tackle for Duquesne while he was in college, Ray Kemp
played for the Pittsburgh Pirates in 1933. He was one of the
last two blacks to play in the National Football League until
1946.*

Chapter 10

"We're Here to Play Football"

It was fewer than six months after Kenny Washington died in 1971 that Jackie Robinson revealed his thoughts about his UCLA teammate in a national publication. Washington and Robinson had played in the same backfield for the 1939 Bruins, but, while Robinson had gone on to secure an exalted place in history, Washington had been overlooked.

"I'm sure," wrote Robinson, "that he had a deep hurt over the fact that he never had become a national figure in professional sports. Many blacks who were great athletes years ago grow old with this hurt. . . . It would be a shame if he were to be forgotten. I know I never will forget him."

Everyone knows that Robinson broke baseball's color line and serves as a role model for black children aspiring to play professional baseball, but few know that Kenny Washington broke pro football's racial barriers—and did it one year earlier.

Books on blacks in professional sports usually focus on Jackie Robinson. Even books on professional football rarely mention the role of Washington or any of the other black pioneers in the National Football League. The Pro Football Hall of Fame, however, has painstakingly researched the subject and amassed the evidence required for the presentation now in place in the Hall's fourth wing, in a room dedicated to The Pro Football Adventure.

The room contains displays on the Super Bowl, the Miami Dolphins' 1972 perfect season, the formation of the American Football Leagues, and the top twenty lifetime statistical leaders. And it spotlights the usual collection of memorabilia—from a vertical striped stocking saved from the Great Sock Barbecue held by the Denver Broncos to the world's largest trophy, the 22-foot 10-inch monster of polished wood and gleaming brass that is a tribute to the pass-catching streak put together by Harold Carmichael of the Philadelphia Eagles. But nothing seems quite as significant as the research resulting in the display about the 21 black players who in different periods of pro football's history opened doors so that the Jim Browns, O. J. Simpsons, and Earl Campbells would later walk into an arena that would accept them for what they are—football players.

It was not that way when Kenny Washington left UCLA after his senior season in 1939, having displayed exceptional abilities by leading the nation's college players in total yardage with 1,370. That brought him to Chicago for the College All-Star Game, against the Green Bay Packers, and ultimately led to a meeting with George Halas. "I remember George Halas of the Bears asking me to stay around Chicago to see what he could do," Washington said in recalling that period of his career. Halas apparently was trying to see what he could do about an agreement that supposedly existed among the owners not to sign black players, a pact that reportedly had been in force since the end of the 1933 season. "I waited about a week," Washington remembered, "and then I was told that he couldn't use me." Barred from playing in the NFL, Washington joined the Hollywood Bears of the Pacific Coast League and, from 1940 to 1945, played with the minor league team for $50 to $100 a game.

It has to be emphasized that Kenny Washington, like Jackie Robinson, was no ordinary player. Both were exceptional athletes—and there are those (including Washington and Robinson) who felt that Washington might have been the better of the two, even at baseball. "Next to me, Jackie was the best competitor I ever saw," Washington said, "but when he became a baseball star it kind of shook me. I outhit him by at least two hundred points at UCLA." Said Robinson, "Kenny's future in baseball seemed much brighter after his brief exposure to the college game than did mine. In 1937, Kenny batted four fifty-four."

But it was as a football player that Washington made headlines, beginning in 1937, when he took over as the tailback for a team that was to become the best in UCLA history up to that time. Washington set university records for rushing (1,915 yards) and passing (1,300 yards) during his career, many of his passes winding up in the arms of Robinson when he joined the team in 1939 as a junior after two years at Pasadena City College. Robinson played right halfback that season.

In an article he wrote for *Gridiron*, Robinson pointed out:

> I took over Kenny's tailback position my senior season of 1940, but there wasn't much to work with. We finished one and nine. But that 1939 season was something special, and it was all because of Kenny Washington. To start off, let me say that Kenny Washington was the greatest football player I have ever seen. He had everything needed for greatness—size, speed, and tremendous strength. Kenny was probably the greatest long passer ever. [There are any number of stories about the exceptional distances Washington could throw a football.] He could throw sixty yards on the fly consistently. . . . On the long ones, nobody could ever touch him. The Montana game was probably the best I saw Kenny play in 1939. We won twenty to six, and Kenny scored all three of our touchdowns. He ran for a hundred sixty-four yards in eleven carries, a fourteen point seven average, and completely dominated play. Over the years, people downgraded Kenny's speed, but he could run a hundred yards in ten seconds flat—in full uniform. For that era, and for his size—six-foot-one, a hundred ninety-five pounds—that was good running."

Kenny Washington, however, remained on the outside looking in until 1946—and he might not have crossed the line even then if it hadn't been for Dan Reeves. Reeves owned the Cleveland Rams, but wasn't driven by the same motives that inspired Branch Rickey, the owner of the Brooklyn Dodgers who signed Robinson. Reeves, however, was a pioneer in his own fashion, and sensed that the West Coast presented opportunities for the NFL that most owners still were reluctant to explore. His decision to move his Rams to Los Angeles for the 1946 season—and the circumstances surrounding the franchise shift—led to the signing of Washington.

The key to moving West as far as Reeves was concerned was the acquisition of the Los Angeles Coliseum as a playing site. But the rival All-America Football Conference also was trying to lease the stadium. "The AAFC people said we shouldn't be dealing with the NFL—they had an unwritten rule of no colored," recalls Bill Nicholas, at the time the general manager of the Coliseum. Nicholas doesn't volunteer much more, but it appears the Coliseum commission insisted Washington be given a tryout if the commission were to offer the Rams a lease. "One of the conditions definitely was Washington trying out for the team," says Bob Snyder, the Rams' backfield coach who actually signed Washington. "They put it in such a way, when you're battling for your life, you say sure."

While the Coliseum people first initiated the subject of the Rams signing Washington, Snyder believes it is likely that the team would have tried to sign him anyway. "If the commission hadn't asked us, we would have tried to get Kenny," Snyder says. "We would have wanted him because of the publicity he would have brought us for being from UCLA." On the other hand, Snyder frankly admits that the Rams would not have signed Washington if the team had remained in Cleveland. "We were looking for names," Snyder says. "I doubt we would have been interested in Washington if we had stayed in Cleveland." It's also important to note that, while Reeves' mission was securing the Coliseum for the Rams, as opposed to breaking the NFL's color line, he did have a battle on his hands before he actually signed Washington.

"All hell broke loose [among NFL owners when word got around that Reeves intended to sign Washington]," Snyder recalls. "There was objection to it—you can bet your butt on that. Quite a bit of objection. But despite the objections, Reeves did it."

"Reeves had the league over a barrel," Washington said. "The Coliseum people warned the Rams that if they practiced discrimination, they couldn't use the stadium. When those NFL people began thinking about all those seats and the money they could make filling 'em, they decided my kind wasn't so bad after all."

When Washington actually signed on March 21, 1946, that made him the first black athlete to sign with a major league professional team in modern-day sports history. Robinson also was signed in 1946, but by the minor league Montreal Royals. He didn't join the major league Dodgers until 1947. Almost immediately after signing with the Dodgers, Robinson phoned Washington. "I asked Jackie if he was afraid," Washington recalled. "He said, 'About as afraid as you were when you became the first last year.' We both laughed."

Above: *Henry McDonald joined the Rochester Jeffersons in 1911, one of four blacks to play in the pre-NFL years.* Above right: *The noted singer, Paul Robeson, was an end in the NFL in 1920, 1921, and 1922.* Right: *Gideon (Charlie) Smith played in Canton for one game in 1915.* Far right: *Rube Marshall, an end from Minnesota, was one of 14 blacks to play in the NFL in the 1920-1933 period.*

There wasn't too much laughter for Kenny Washington during his NFL career, however. He already was 28 when he joined the Rams, and both his knees were in terrible shape, the result of injuries first sustained in college and the additional damage he suffered playing in semipro. And opposing players soon discovered his weakness. "When he first began to play, they'd tee off on him," Snyder says. "They'd drop knees on him." On one road trip, Washington scored three touchdowns against an eastern team, but was seriously injured on one play when he was hit by a swarm of players after the referee had blown the whistle. As he trudged off the field, he turned to teammate Jim Hardy and said, "It's hell to be a Negro." Hardy could never get that moment out of his mind. "I'll never forget the hurt in his eyes," Hardy said in revealing the incident. "But his statement wasn't one of self-pity by any means. It was simply a social comment. He was alone, and there wasn't any way to comfort him."

Socially, the Rams tried to ease the pressure on Washington by providing him with a black teammate, signing Woodrow Wilson Strode, who today is a motion picture actor of considerable note. Strode, a receiver at UCLA during the Washington years, signed with the Rams on May 7, 1946, becoming the second black in modern-day NFL history. Snyder admits there was considerable apprehension about reaction to the signings from the players on the Rams, but insists "there was not one incident." For that, he gives much of the credit

Left: *End Woody Strode, as a 31-year-old rookie, was one of two blacks to sign with the 1946 L.A. Rams. He and Kenny Washington were the first blacks to play in the NFL since 1933.*

Above: *A popular exhibit at the Hall of Fame is The Black Man in Pro Football display, which traces infrequent hiring of blacks in the pre-NFL and early-NFL years followed by a 13-year hiatus until signing black players became commonplace in pro football, starting with the 1946 season.*

Below: *Kenny Washington had played semi-pro football for seven years following his graduation from UCLA before he signed with the Rams on March 21, 1946. He was the first black to sign a pro football contract in the post-World War II era.*

to quarterback Bob Waterfield, with whom Washington had maintained a friendship for several years. "Three weeks before camp opened, Waterfield and Kenny worked out together by themselves," said Snyder. "That broke the ice. Soon [the players] were all playing cards together. But you had to love Kenny—he was a great, great fellow."

Life on the road, however, was different, or as Snyder puts it, "There was trouble in some hotels." Often, Washington would not stay with the team, even when he would have been permitted to live in the same hotel. Asked why, he once told Snyder he was uncomfortable in an all-white environment. "How would you feel if you were the only white in a room of blacks?" he asked. So, the Rams would ask the home team to find a place for Washington to stay, and they usually would locate a black family to take him in. Tex Schramm, currently the Dallas Cowboys' general manager who was the public relations director for the Rams at the time, never felt that Washington resented being apart from his teammates. "He'd always laugh about it," says Schramm, "because that meant he didn't have curfew. I never sensed any type of resentment on his part. But black people didn't show resentment in those days."

Washington played only two seasons with the Rams before his knees finally gave out, but he proved in that short period that he could play with the best of the era. He gained 859 yards in his 2 seasons, rushing for a team record average of 6.14 yards a carry. "If Kenny could have endured it," says Snyder, "he would have played longer. His knees were so bad when we got him, I don't know how he even walked. We used to drain them every week. He was knock-kneed, a funny runner. But he had great takeoff . . . acceleration . . . and was a great open-field runner. He also had the strongest arm I've ever seen. If he hadn't missed those six years [when he couldn't play in the NFL], he would have been a superstar, one of the premier backs of all time. While I was with the Rams, we had three Heisman Trophy winners—Les Horvath, Tom Harmon, and Glenn Davis. He was better than all three. There's no comparison."

If he hadn't chosen to sign with the Rams, Washington might have joined Robinson in baseball's major leagues. As soon as Robinson signed with the Montreal Royals, major league scouts began to recruit Washington. But Washington already had signed with the Rams for the 1946 season and felt there were compelling reasons for him to set a precedent in the NFL while Robinson cracked baseball's color line. "I feel it was just as important for a colored player to break into pro football as it was in baseball," he said. But, when

he was through with football, he did give baseball a whirl, trying out in 1950 with the New York Giants under Leo Durocher. "I could hit the ball a long way," Washington said, "but Durocher told me that all those years of football tightened me up. I was thirty-two and that's no time to be trying to start a baseball career."

A baseball career might have brought Washington the acclaim he never has been accorded, the status that Robinson wrote he must have longed for as he grew older. Robinson, of course, had it, primarily because baseball was a far more popular sport than pro football at the time both color lines were broken. It also is important to remember that Washington, because of injuries, was nearing the end of his career when he joined the Rams, while Robinson was at his peak when he joined the Dodgers. That, naturally, left Robinson onstage much longer, making *him* the symbol for black youths struggling to knock down racial barriers. Ironically, both athletes died young, little more than a year apart, Washington at age 52, Robinson at age 53. Washington died on June 24, 1971, of polyarteritis (inflammation of the body's arteries) and heart and respiratory problems. His death occasioned no more than several paragraphs in many newspapers. Robinson died on October 24, 1972, of diabetes-caused heart trouble. His death precipitated headline coverage throughout the country.

While Washington never seems to be treated by sports fans and/or sports historians with the same reverence as Robinson, Bob Snyder is among those who feel Washington may have been instrumental in helping to break baseball's color line as well as actually breaking the NFL's. "I have no proof of this," Snyder acknowledges, "but it's always been my feeling that Washington's signing finally tipped Rickey over to do what he did with Robinson—that Washington's signing took the pressure off."

There are also those who believe that Rickey might initially have been influenced in his desire to break baseball's color line by having played football some 40 years earlier on the same team with Charles W. Follis, a halfback honored in the Hall of Fame's display as the first black ever to be paid for playing. Rickey and Follis were teammates with the Shelby (Ohio) Athletic Club in 1902 and 1903, and Rickey was impressed enough to say, "Follis . . . he is a wonder."

Nicknamed the Black Cyclone, Follis was a Virginian by birth, but spent most of his short life of just 31 years in Ohio. Equally skilled at football and baseball (he played three years of professional baseball with the Cuban Giants), Follis began his football career in 1899 when he helped Wooster High School organize a varsity program. He was

Left: Fred (Duke) Slater, a tackle from Iowa, was an all-NFL caliber star from 1922 to 1931. Above right: Harold Bradley, a guard from Iowa, played one year in 1928. Bottom right: Charles Follis became the first black to play professional football when he signed with the Shelby Blues in 1904.

Top: *Joe Lillard, seen here in action against Red Grange (#77), played with the Chicago Cardinals in 1933. His contract was not renewed, and no other blacks played in the NFL for the next 13 years.* Left: *Bill Willis, who had starred at Ohio State under Paul Brown, signed with his old coach's new Cleveland Browns team on August 6, 1946. He quickly became a superstar as a defensive middle guard.* Center: *John Shelbourne played one year with the 1922 Hammond Pros.* Right: *Charles "Doc" Baker became the second black to sign a pro contract when he joined the Akron Indians in 1907. Baker played with the Akron team until 1911.*

the team's first captain and right halfback. After high school, Follis played for the Wooster Athletic Association, where he was spotted by Frank Schiffer, the manager of the Shelby Athletic Club. Schiffer lured Follis to Shelby by securing him a job at Seltzer's hardware store, selling bolts of cloth and kegs of nails. He made no waves in the white community and became something of a curiosity for the people in the town, particularly when the Shelby *Globe* began to publicize his exploits and dubbed him "Follis the Speedy."

Follis played for Shelby in 1902 and 1903 without a salary, but the next season Schiffer apparently felt it necessary to legally bind Follis to his team and signed him to a contract on September 15, 1904. The signing was reported in the *Globe*: "The Shelby Athletic Association has secured the services of Charles Follis for this season. The contract has been signed up, and football enthusiasts will be pleased to know that Follis will be on the local team again this year. Follis plays halfback and there is no finer in the state."

Follis led Shelby to a 9-1 record that season. The more Follis succeeded, however, the more bitter his opponents became. Words. Knuckles. Knees. Follis was the target of them all. In a game against Toledo in 1905, the Toledo captain, Jack Tattersoll, became so incensed at the abuse aimed at Follis, that he stopped the game and told the fans, "Don't call Follis a nigger. He is a gentleman and a clean player, and please don't call him that." By 1906, however, ridicule and injuries had taken so large a toll that Follis was forced to quit.

The Hall of Fame history of the black pioneers records only three players besides Follis who were paid for their services in the years prior to the formation of the NFL. The year after Follis left Shelby, the Akron Indians signed a halfback named Charles "Doc" Baker. Baker also played in 1908, 1909, and 1911. The third pro was another halfback, Henry McDonald, who signed with the Rochester Jeffersons in 1911 and played through the 1917 season. The last member of the pre-NFL quartet also was the first lineman, tackle Gideon "Charles" Smith. A star with the Michigan Aggies, Smith was signed by the Canton Bulldogs to play in one of their two annual battles against Massillon, November 28, 1915. It was Smith's only pro game—and he recovered a controversial fumble that preserved a 6-0 victory for Canton.

Of the first four trailblazers, McDonald left the most vivid record of what it was like to play in the early days of the sport. Born in Haiti in 1890, McDonald came to the United States five years later when his natural parents consented to his adoption by an American coconut-banana importer. "He was my father's boss," McDonald explained, "and he just took a liking to me. My natural parents realized it was a great opportunity for me to go to America. I didn't see my mother again for over fifty-five years."

McDonald grew up in Canandaigua and Rochester in New York State, became a schoolboy star in football and baseball, then joined the Jeffersons in 1911. He weighed only 145 pounds, but created quite a stir with his speed and was nicknamed Motorcycle. "Most of the guys were bigger than me," he said, "but I was too quick for them to catch. I could run a hundred yards in ten point two seconds. The world record was ten flat in those days." The Jeffs' owner, Leo Lyons, reveled in McDonald's footwork. "You can't hit or hurt what you can't see," he said. "If you blinked your eyes, McDonald was on his way."

The financial rewards, however, were extremely limited. "I played pro ball for nearly fifteen years, and in all that time I never once took home more than fifteen dollars for one day of football," McDonald said. "And I had to play two games to get that much." He accomplished that by playing a morning game in Rochester for the Jeffs, then hopping a trolley to Canandaigua and playing for the town team in the afternoon. But he gloried in it, particularly because of his role as a running back—for the players who ran with the ball, not the passers, were the stars of that era. "Our football was soft and shaped like a watermelon," he explained. "We threw a couple of passes every game, but they were usually a last resort. The ball was made to be carried, not thrown all over the field." And when the spectators passed the hat to pay the players, McDonald emphasized, it was the running backs who got the most money, followed by the linemen, and then the passers. If the nature of the game was different from what it is today, so were the spectators. "The city folks took trolleys to Cobbs Hill and then walked to Twelve Corners [site of Sheehan's Field]," McDonald remembered. "I can still see those yellow straw hats and pretty flowered bonnets bouncing up and down as the people hiked to the field."

Only once was the idyllic setting shattered by a racial incident. That occurred in 1917, when the Jeffs traveled to Canton to play Jim Thorpe's Bulldogs. At one point in the game, Canton's Greasy Neale shoved McDonald out of bounds, cocked his fists, and said, "Black is black and white is white, and where I come from they don't mix." "But," said McDonald, "Jim Thorpe prevented a real donnybrook. He jumped between us and said, 'We're here to play football.' I never had any trouble after that. Thorpe's word was law on the field." And his ability, according to McDonald, sent waves of fear through those who had to tangle with him when he ran with the ball. "Thorpe hurt you just thinking about trying to stop him," McDonald said. "You were bruised before you ran into him. He scared you with his stare and he rattled your back teeth with his tactics. He was like a runaway horse. You called every collision a gift from God when you were able to rise, breathe regularly, and move on your own power."

The Hall of Fame's display proceeds from the 4 pre-NFL blacks to trace the history of the 13 who played from the time the NFL was formed in 1920 through 1933, when, suddenly and inexplicably, for the next 12 seasons the league signed no black players. Halfback Fritz Pollard and end Paul Robeson of the Akron Pros and tackle Fred "Duke" Slater of the Chicago Cardinals, whose jersey is the only piece of equipment from any of the early blacks on display at the Hall, played as well as any players competing at the time. Pollard and Robeson made unofficial all-league teams in 1921. But Slater, who played his college ball at Iowa, may have been the best of all—he played longer (ten years) and with more success (all-NFL in 1926, 1928, and 1929) than any other early-day black player. A clipping from a 1926 Philadelphia newspaper quoted Red Grange as singling out Slater "as the greatest tackle of all time."

Robeson is one of the most unusual players represented in the Hall of Fame. The son of a runaway slave, Robeson gained worldwide fame as a singer and actor and worldwide notoriety for his political beliefs. He played in the NFL with Hammond in 1920, Akron in 1921, and Milwaukee in 1922, but he was best remembered as a football player for his collegiate exploits at Rutgers. A 6-foot 3-inch, 217-pound end, Robeson was the first black ever to attend Rutgers. He also seemed to conquer it, winning Phi Beta Kappa honors as well as 15 varsity letters in 4 sports. In 1917 and 1918, Walter Camp, the father of all-America teams, named Robeson to a spot on his mythical 11. When he did, he paid this written tribute to Robeson: "There never had been a more serviceable end in football, both on offense and defense. The game of college football will never know a greater end."

While little is known about Robeson's professional football career, that is not the case with Pollard. Like McDonald, a slight running back—5-feet 8 inches, 155 pounds—Pollard was placed in an all-time "Dream Backfield" by Grantland Rice, the dean of American sportswriters at the time. The other members of Rice's mythical backfield were Jim Thorpe, Red Grange, and Ernie Nevers. But while Pollard undoubtedly was one of the best

would sing. Sometimes I would sing, too. I had a pretty good voice then. We even formed an act and performed together."

There is some question when Pollard first began coaching, primarily because there is considerable debate about just what the role of a coach was in the early years of the sport. There is no doubt that Pollard was the coach of the Milwaukee Badgers in 1922, the Hammond Pros in 1923 and 1924, and the Akron Pros in 1925 and 1926. Pollard, however, insists he first coached with Akron in 1920 and 1921. The 1920 season wound up in a dispute over which of three teams actually won the league championship—the first in NFL history—and most record books do not list a champion for that season. But Pollard claims Akron, with a 10-0 record, was the champion. "I remember that real well," he said. "We were given a little gold football [as a trophy for winning]. I found out they didn't want to give the title to my team because I was black."

Relying on an excellent sense of humor, Pollard always tried to fence with those who questioned him about what it was like to be a black player in those days. Invariably, however, he would level with the interviewer. Here's the way it went in one conversation:

All the time I played, which was through 1926, there were always a few colored players. I don't think we were targets or anything. There weren't any real bad situations. About the worst thing that would happen was sometimes when we played an away game the local fans would start to sing "Bye, Bye, Blackbird." But I guess other players were subjected to taunts like that regardless of color. Other times they would have me wait until right before the kickoff to come out on the field. That way I'd just run out and the game would start right away and there wouldn't be any time to raise a ruckus. Once in a while they'd throw stones at me in some of the towns. Now that I think about it, maybe there was a little more prejudice than I first recalled.

Akron was a factory town and they had some prejudiced people there. I had to get dressed for the game in [owner] Frank Neid's cigar factory, and they'd send a car over for me before the game. The fans booed me and called me all kinds of names because they had a lot of southerners up there working. You couldn't eat in the restaurants or stay in the hotels. Hammond and Milwaukee were bad then, too, but never as bad as Akron was. Sometimes it would get a little rough [on the field], but I never tried to mix it up with the other team. I'd just grin if they called me names and jump up and try to run through 'em again. One habit I did develop was rolling over on my back as soon as I hit the ground. That way I could get my feet up and in a position to deal with anyone who might think about piling on.

backs in the NFL, it was as a coach that he established his singular place in history. For Fritz Pollard was the first black head coach in the NFL and—with the exception of Willie Wood of the Philadelphia Bell of the World Football League—the only one ever in American professional football. Pollard, however, never considered himself unique because of that. In an interview conducted in 1977 when he was 83, Pollard commented on his coaching career: "It was no big thing then. I was just another coach and happened to be a colored man."

Born in 1894, Pollard was named Frederick Douglass after the famous abolitionist, but it wasn't long before he was being called Fritz. It was as Fritz Pollard that he went off to college at Brown, and his freshman season led the team into the first modern Rose Bowl ever played, January 1, 1916, against Washington State. He was even better the following season when in successive games he produced 307 of Brown's 431 total yards against Yale, then amassed 254 of 461 total yards against Harvard. Pollard put together those amazing figures, it should be emphasized, at a time when Harvard and Yale annually fielded teams ranked among the best in the country. Pollard began his pro career in 1919 with the Akron Pros and later helped recruit Robeson. "We were good friends," Pollard said. "I used to play the piano for Paul and he

Not much is known about many of the other blacks who played before the curtain came down

Three days after Bill Willis (top) *signed with the Cleveland Browns, fullback Marion Motley* (left) *was added to the roster. Both Willis and Motley, who became roommates on road trips, are now members of the Pro Football Hall of Fame.*

following the 1933 season, but Pollard offers us a picture of one—Robert "Rube" Marshall, who played for the Rock Island Independents in 1919 and 1920. "He was quite a man," Pollard recalled. "He was over forty years old when he played. He'd been an all-America at Minnesota in 1905 and 1906 and was still playing when the NFL was formed. He was a great one for making his own pads. He would make shin guards by rolling up magazines and taping them to his legs. He'd do the same thing to make forearm pads, only use small magazines. I remember one time he used the corrugated metal from a washboard to fashion rib protectors." Pollard, however, was at a loss to gauge the ability of Marshall, and that's the case with six others who played at the same time—Jay "Inky" Williams, Edward "Sol" Butler, John Shelbourne, Harold Bradley, James Turner and Richard Hudson.

Somewhat more is known about the last two blacks who played in that era—Joe Lillard, a runner and passer who came out of Oregon State, joined the Chicago Cardinals for 1932 and 1933 and was said to have excellent ability, and Raymond Kemp, a Duquesne tackle who played for the 1933 Pittsburgh Pirates. Kemp later became athletic director and football and track coach at Tennessee State, where one of his pupils was Ralph Boston, the Olympic long-jump champion in 1960. In an interview conducted at the Hall of Fame in 1980, Kemp was asked directly why there were no black players in the NFL between 1933 and 1945. He left no doubt about his opinion. "It was my understanding that there was a gentlemen's agreement in the league that there would be no more blacks," he said. Was it possible that black players with sufficient ability didn't surface during that period? "I would have to assume," he replied, "that because of the numerous black athletes appearing on the sports scene, some of them would have qualified to play professional football. George Preston Marshall [owner of the Washington Redskins] made a public declaration he wouldn't have a black on his team."

Public declarations are one thing. Gentlemen's agreements made behind closed doors are another if, indeed, they ever were concluded. No one can verify that such an agreement did exist. Tex Schramm, meanwhile, doesn't believe a gentlemen's agreement was in force. "I don't think there was anything that was a gentlemen's agreement," he says. "You just didn't do it [sign blacks]—it wasn't the thing that was done."

Schramm, however, can't tell us why, beginning in 1934, there were suddenly no black players in the NFL. But maybe that's something that never will be known. What is known is that Kenny Washington was the first black in the NFL since 1933; Woody Strode was the second, and it was just months later in August that Paul Brown of the Cleveland Browns provided the other two trailblazers of 1946 when he signed Ohio State guard Bill Willis and Nevada fullback Marion Motley to AAFC contracts. Willis' first contract, on display at the Hall, called for him to be paid $4,000 a year plus $100 for signing. The bonus provision in the standard AAFC contract form was written in long hand, initialed by Brown, and signed by Willis.

While there is no question that Washington and Strode were the first two blacks to break the post-1945 color line, there also is no question that Brown's signing of Willis and Motley had far more lasting significance. Washington and Strode were soon gone; Willis and Motley not only played for a number of years—Willis for eight and Motley for nine—but played with far greater distinction. Both are Hall of Famers. And, according to his autobiography, Brown's decision to sign Willis and Motley was made before Rickey signed Jackie Robinson. "I had made up my mind before Rickey's action that I wanted both Willis and Motley to play for us," Brown wrote. "I never considered football players black or white, nor did I keep or cut a player just because of his color. . . . I didn't care about a man's color or his ancestry; I just wanted to win football games with the best people possible." By signing Willis and Motley, Brown precluded the possibility of a color line forming in the new AAFC. Nevertheless, he did get some heat for his decision. "Some people in our league resented this action and tossed a few intemperate barbs at me," he wrote, "but I felt those were better answered by the players themselves when they played against those teams."

It wasn't always easy to find answers, because Willis and Motley felt they had to maintain restraint in the face of overt antagonism. According to Motley in the book *The Game That Was:*

Paul warned Willis and me. He said, "Now you know that you're going to be in many scrapes. People are going to be calling you names. They're going to be nasty. But you're going to stick it out." It was rough all right. If Willis and I had been anywhere near being hotheads, it would have been another ten years till black men got accepted in pro ball. We'd have set 'em back ten years. I still got many a cleat mark on the backs of my hands from when I would be getting up from a play and a guy would just walk over and step on my hand. I couldn't do anything about it. I'd want to kill those guys, but Paul had warned us. The referees would stand right there and see those men stepping on us, and they would turn their backs. The opposing players called us nigger and all kind of names like that. This went on for about two or three years, until they found out that Willis and

220

SPEED-BURNING OLLIE MATSON

He Exuded Olympic Style Brilliance

I were ballplayers. Then they stopped. They found out that while they were calling us names, I was running by 'em and Willis was knocking the (bleep) out of them. So they stopped calling us names and started trying to catch up with us.

Obviously, that had to be difficult. Both Willis and Motley were outstanding. One of the Browns' smallest linemen at 6 feet 2 inches and 210 pounds, Willis was exceptionally quick and in a class by himself at the defensive middle guard position. "He became the real pioneer of what is now the middle linebacker," Brown says. "Sometimes we'd put him up as the center of a five-man line but quite often, to take advantage of his speed and agility, we'd drop him back and allow him to go to the play. He had no peers through much of his professional career." That is reflected by the fact that in seven of his eight seasons, from 1946 to 1953, he was named all-league, three times in the AAFC and four in the NFL.

Motley, a 6-foot 1-inch, 238-pounder, became the prototype fullback of the era while providing the blocking protection many credit with helping make Otto Graham such an effective passer. Much of his rushing yardage was made on the Browns' famous draw play in which Graham dropped back as if he were going to pass, then handed off to Motley up the middle. "It came about accidentally in one game," Brown says. "Otto got such a hard pass rush he handed the ball to Motley in desperation. The defense had overrun Motley in their desire to get to the quarterback, and Motley swept right through them for a big gain. We looked at the play again and decided it couldn't help but work. In a short time, it became Motley's most dangerous weapon."

Motley was the AAFC's top career rusher with 3,024 yards in four seasons, including his rookie year when he averaged an astonishing 8.2 yards a carry. In 1950, when the Browns moved into the NFL, Motley won the league's rushing title with 810 yards, thus ending Steve Van Buren's three-year domination. He finished his career with 4,720 yards, a 5.7 average, and 39 touchdowns.

The final section of the Hall's tribute to black players lists a number of "firsts," including the first black player on each NFL and AAFC team. That list shows that it wasn't until 1962—16 years after Kenny Washington broke the modern-day color line—that every team finally had at least one black player on its roster. The last team to integrate was Washington, with running backs Ron Hatcher and Bobby Mitchell. Some other firsts of more than passing interest:

- First black drafted by an NFL team—halfback George Taliaferro (Indiana), selected by the Chicago Bears in the thirteenth round of the 1949 draft. Taliaferro, however, signed with the AAFC's Los Angeles Dons.
- First black draftee to play in the NFL—halfback Wally Triplett (Penn State), picked by the Detroit Lions in round 19 of the 1949 draft.
- First "name" star from a predominantly black college—fullback Tank Younger (Grambling), Los Angeles Rams, 1949.
- First black quarterback in the NFL—Willie Thrower (Michigan State), Chicago Bears, 1953.
- First black official—field judge Burl Toler (San Francisco), 1965.
- First black in the Hall of Fame—defensive back Emlen Tunnell, New York Giants and Green Bay Packers, elected in 1967.

Speed-burning Ollie Matson, fresh from an outstanding performance with the U.S. Olympic team, joined the Chicago Cardinals in 1952. Seven years later, he was traded to the Rams for nine players.

THE PRO FOOTBALL ADVENTURE
...a kaleidoscope of happenings
SUPER BOWL I
OFFICIAL SIGNALS
•GAME MANAGEMENT SIGNALS
(Non-Penalty Situations)
•PENALTY SIGNALS

Chapter 11

Record Makers and Breakers

The Pro Football Adventure Room is home to the lifetime statistical leader boards; capsulized films of the first four Super Bowls; displays on officiating, stadiums, and the evolution of the uniform; plus a section containing a representative sample of trophies awarded to players for various feats. There is something to interest almost everyone, in particular those who have followed the last of the four American Football Leagues that have existed throughout pro football's history—the modern-day AFL of Joe Namath and Len Dawson, of Lance Alworth and Jim Otto. The AFL display contains the most unique memorabilia in the room—score sheets of the first regular-season AFL game ever played, the vertical-striped sock salvaged from the Great Sock Barbecue, Bob Dee's helmet, a reproduction of the New York Jets' scouting report on Namath, and Otto's jersey.

The first AFL game took place on September 9, 1960, at Boston University, where Gene Mingo's 76-yard punt return gave the Denver Broncos a 13-10 victory over the Boston Patriots. While the Broncos won the opener, they didn't win many after that. And they became the laughing stock of the league because of their light gold and "barnyard brown" uniforms, complete with ridicule-provoking brown and white vertical-striped socks. The Broncos, beset by limited financial resources, had charged General Manager Dean Griffing with the task of outfitting the players, and Griffing had purchased the uniforms from the defunct Copper Bowl, which had been played in Tucson, Arizona.

Griffing, who was so money conscious he would plunge into a crowd of fans to try and salvage a football kicked into the stands, always felt differently about the vertical striped socks than most critics. "I thought they might make the players look bigger and taller," he explained at one time. Instead, they only made the players feel smaller. "I don't know where they got 'em," says Eldon Danenhauer, a tackle on those early Denver teams. "The players hated them. Besides their looks, you couldn't get them on. They were not made of stretch material."

When Jack Faulkner took over as coach in 1962, he decided to recast the team's image and began by changing the team's colors from gold and brown to the orange, blue, and white the Broncos wear today. He also decided the socks had to go. So Faulkner initiated plans for the Great Sock Barbecue, a spectacle that was witnessed by some five thousand fans attending the unique ceremony at the team's practice site. There, just before the season opened, the players trotted around the field holding up their socks. And then, as the crowd applauded, the socks were heaped onto a huge bonfire. One of the socks was salvaged by team photographer Dick Burnell and is now in the Hall of Fame.

Bob Dee had quit professional football—he played defensive end for the Washington Redskins—before the AFL was formed. There wasn't enough financial reward in playing, he said, and he was opening his own business. As soon as he heard about the AFL, however, the 6-foot 4-inch, 250-pound product of Holy Cross began to yearn to return to the sport. And he did, signing with the Boston Patriots—even though it eventually would cost him a large amount of money. "The same year I started with the Patriots," he explained, "my boiler cleaning business was showing a profit of

The Pro football Adventure Room houses almost 20 major displays that cover a variety of pro football subjects. Many displays in this room are changed annually to keep up-to-date with the ever-changing pro football scene.

over forty thousand dollars. That's a lot more than I was getting for playing football. My second year with the Patriots, I lost most of the money because I didn't pay the attention to the business that I should have."

Dee made history when he scored the first touchdown in AFL history, recovering a Buffalo fumble in the end zone in a preseason game at War Memorial Stadium, July 30, 1960. On display at the Hall is the helmet he wore in 107 of the 114 consecutive games he played for the Patriots. The helmet obviously was ready for the discard heap long before Dee gave it up, but he was reluctant to part with it. "I have an odd-shaped head," he explained, "and I can't find another helmet that feels comfortable on me."

At the time Dee retired after the 1967 season, he and Otto were the only two players to have started and finished every game their team had played since the inception of the league. Otto went on to play with the Oakland Raiders through the 1975 season, extending his starting streak to 210 regular-season games, 73 preseason contests, 12 All-Star clashes, and 13-play-offs, including Super Bowl II. And, as soon as he became eligible for the Hall of Fame, he was elected—not bad for a guy who was totally ignored by the NFL when he graduated from the University of Miami. Otto obviously was overlooked because he weighed just 205 pounds, by NFL standards far too small to play center or linebacker. It was only natural that he try the AFL—the NFL was certain Otto couldn't make it and their prognosis for the AFL was just about the same. For that reason, Otto became something of a symbol in the new league, especially after he discarded the number 50 jersey he had been assigned during his first AFL season and assumed the distinctive number 00 he wore the remainder of his career.

Centers are the most anonymous players on a football field, but the 00 jersey and the Double O nickname that went with it made Otto as visible as any of the other stars who made the league a success. He did not, however, do it as a 205-pounder. He came to the Raiders' camp at 210, built himself to 230 pounds by the end of the season, and, at the height of his career carried 255 to 260 pounds on his 6-foot 2-inch frame.

Like the Broncos, the Raiders had some extremely embarrassing early situations—and Otto still remembers them clearly. "We had some very low moments," he says. "I remember wishing I was a lot of other places. I never got bitter, though. I never asked to be traded. Oakland gave me my chance to play pro football, so I felt I owed them a certain amount of loyalty. But embarrassing things just kept happening. One time we were practicing in another town, and it was on a Little League ball field. When the Little Leaguers came, their coaches kicked us off. That tells you how much respect we got. Very often we'd have buses supposed to pick us up at an airport or a hotel that would never show and we'd have to thumb it. Once the buses took the players to one stadium and the coaches rented a car and drove to another. What made that so bad was that neither one of us went to the right place."

Through the embarrassing moments and the early on-the-field disappointments, Otto never lost his poise and became a team leader. "He loved to win," said long-time teammate George Blanda. "He led by example and he set the tempo. He gave the Raiders an image of hard discipline, hard work, and hard-nosed football." But, then, Otto had loved the sport from the moment he became aware of it as a boy in Wausau, Wisconsin, Green Bay Packer country. "In, that atmosphere I couldn't but dream," Otto says. And when that dream was fulfilled, he never seemed to want to let it go by coming out of a game, even if it was lopsided. "I just like to play football," Otto said. "There are a lot of people in this country who would love to play football but aren't physically able to. I am, so I don't want to come out of a game."

As an enshrinee, Otto received the ultimate honor pro football can bestow on a player. But Otto also is honored in an AFL display saluting the 19 players who were active in the league during the entire decade from its inception in 1960 to its amalgamation into the NFL following the 1969 season. Included with Otto and Blanda are running back Billy Cannon (Houston-Oakland), wide receiver Gino Cappelletti (Boston), linebacker Larry Grantham (New York), guard Wayne Hawkins (Oakland), defensive tackle Jim Hunt (Boston), linebacker Harry Jacobs (Boston), running back Paul Lowe (Los Angeles-San Diego-Kansas City), quarterback Jacky Lee (Houston-Denver-Kansas City), running back Bill Mathis (New York), linebacker Paul Maguire (San Diego-Buffalo), wide receiver Don Maynard (New York), tackle Ron Mix (Los Angeles-San Diego), quarterback Babe Parilli (Oakland-Boston-New York), safety Johnny Robinson (Dallas-Kansas City), defensive tackle Paul Rochester (Dallas-Kansas City-New York), tackle Ernie Wright (Los Angeles-San Diego-Cincinnati), and Jack Kemp.

Kemp, today a United States congressman from New York and close ally of President Ronald Reagan, played for the Chargers in both Los Angeles and San Diego from 1960 to 1962, and then with the Buffalo Bills until the AFL curtain went

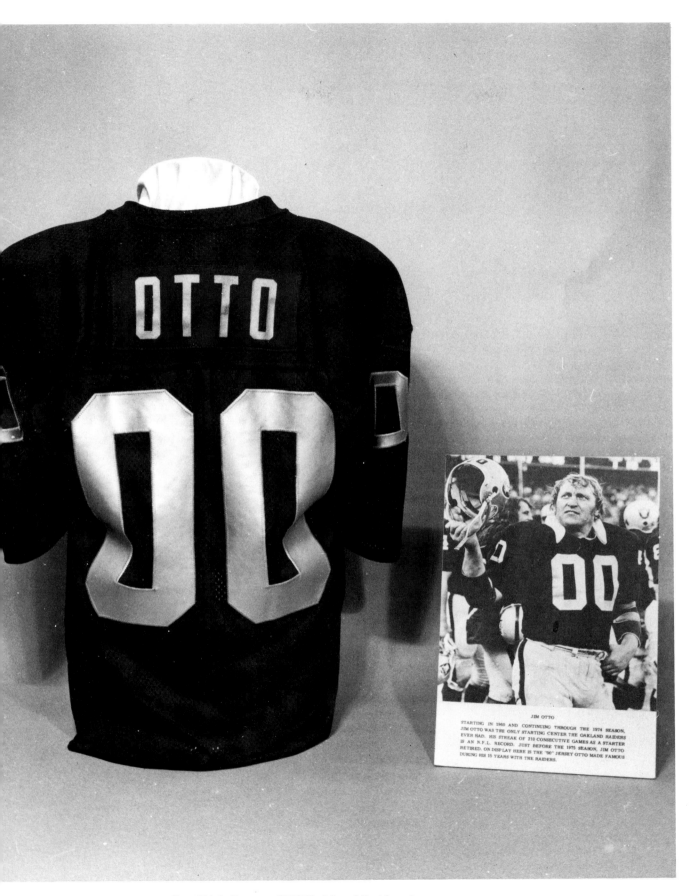

Jim Otto's famous "00" Oakland Raiders jersey was presented to the Hall immediately after his retirement following the 1974 season. He was the only all-league center the AFL ever had.

THE FIRST TOUCHDOWN

BOB DEE, BOSTON PATRIOTS' DEFENSIVE END, SCORED THE AFL'S FIRST TOUCHDOWN IN A PRE-SEASON GAME IN BUFFALO ON JULY 30, 1960. DEE WORE THIS HELMET FOR 107 CONSECUTIVE GAMES BEFORE DISCARDING IT JUST BEFORE HIS RETIREMENT IN 1967.

Bob Dee, Boston Patriots end, scored the AFL's first touchdown in a pre-season game in 1960. The helmet he wore for all but the last few games of his career is a part of the AFL display.

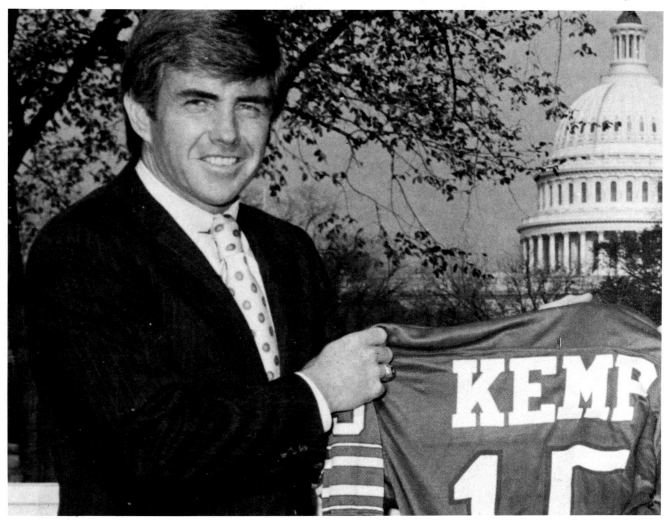

down. He, like Otto, succeeded in the AFL after the NFL had rejected him. "I never really got a chance to play until I signed with the Chargers," Kemp says. "Detroit, Pittsburgh, and New York [with whom he played in the NFL] all had name quarterbacks when I was with them." Kemp made a name for himself in the AFL—he called signals in half of the league's ten championship games, quarterbacked the Bills to two championships, and earned the league's Most Valuable Player award in 1965. He also had the unique distinction of being the only quarterback to have been a starter through all ten years of the league's existence.

The most famous quarterback in the AFL's history, however, was Joe Namath, the charismatic Alabama star signed by Jets' owner Sonny Werblin for a reported $427,000 at a time when player contracts in the $100,000 neighborhood were vir-

tually nonexistent. But Werblin knew what he was paying for—in his scouting report Namath was rated outstanding or above average in every category in which the Jets rated players at the time. He was given outstanding marks for quickness, agility, reaction time, coordination, intelligence, aggressiveness, and pride. He was rated above average in strength, size potential, durability, speed for position, and character. The report also noted:

> An outstanding passer with big, strong hands and an exceptionally fast delivery. Sets up and stays "in the pocket" well, but is quick and can "scramble" when he senses a heavy rush. Fires the short pass quicker than anyone since Sammy Baugh, and throws the "bomb" with great accuracy. Is smart, a good leader, and the squad has great confidence in him. He is a complete and outstanding player and will be everyone's number-one draft choice.

228

Opposite: *Joe Namath, who signed with the New York Jets in 1965 for an estimated $400,000, did much to bring respectability to the new league. A scouting report on Namath that appears in the AFL section of the Pro Football Adventure Room clearly indicated that he had the potential to be a superstar. Below : In 1972, the Miami Dolphins won 17 straight games, including Super Bowl VII, the only team ever to enjoy a perfect NFL season. This colorful display covers the season week by week with a different hero emerging every game.*

The history of the American Football League is traced through the 1970 merger with the NFL with a separate panel each year being devoted to each season's American Football Conference champions and news-makers.

The history of the National Football League from 1920 until 1970 is traced in capsule form with a separate panel each year devoted to the latest National football Conference headliners.

Joe Namath was all that Werblin and the Jets anticipated. He not only attracted fans to the ball park, he proved he was an exceptional quarterback when he led the Jets to a stunning 16-7 victory over the heavily favored Baltimore Colts in Super Bowl III. Namath did not pass for a touchdown in that game, but he did complete 17 of 28 passes for 208 yards, and his play-calling often caught the Colts off-balance. The victory was the first for an AFL team in the Super Bowl and brought the league instant parity with the older NFL in the eyes of fans throughout the country. For that reason alone, Namath has secured a singular place in pro football history. By pushing a button at the Super Bowl display in the Adventure Room, the visitor to the Hall of Fame can watch film footage of Namath as he dissected the Colts' defense. The Hall's Super Bowl display zeroes in on the first four Super Bowls—the AFL versus NFL Super Bowls—in which Vince Lombardi's Green Bay legions won the first two games for the NFL, then the Jets and Kansas City Chiefs evened things up for the AFL. Also on display in the room is a replica of every winning team's Super Bowl ring, designed by the team and worn by every member.

Included among the rings is the one fashioned for the 1972 Miami Dolphins, with its 17 diamonds—one for each of the Dolphins' victories during their undefeated season. It is a unique ring commemorating a unique season—the only one in the entire history of the NFL in which a team won every one of its regular-season and postseason games. The Hall pays tribute to that amazing accomplishment directed by Coach Don Shula in a display called the Anatomy of a Perfect Season. The display follows through on the theme of the ring and the season, using 17 pictures to single out one important play or player in every one of the Dolphins' 17 wins culminating in the 14-7 victory over the Washington Redskins in Super Bowl VII. Here the Hall salutes a number of the players who made the achievement possible—Larry Csonka and Jim Kiick, Larry Little and Manny Fernandez, Bob Griese and Earl Morrall.

Dolphins' owner Joe Robbie labeled the accomplishment "the greatest single achievement in the history of sports." Whether it was or not remains for historians to determine. However, it has to be pointed out that Robbie wasn't talking just about winning the Super Bowl, but winning it in the short span of time that had elapsed from the birth of the team to the Dolphins' defeat of the Redskins—a world title and undefeated season just 7 years, 4 months, and 26 days after the franchise was granted. There is little doubt that Shula was the person most responsible for taking a team that

The early-day Denver Broncos became the laughing stock of the AFL because of the vertically-striped socks they wore with their second-hand uniforms. When Jack Faulkner took over the Broncos, in 1962, he staged a public sock-burning ceremony. Only a few socks "survived" including this one on display at the Hall.

The Collection of Trophies displayed in the Pro Football Adventure Room includes a sampling of some of the more unusual trophies from among the many that are given each year.

The Justice Byron "Whizzer" White Award honors the former Colorado all-America and pro football star and is given annually by the NFL Players Association to an NFL player who demonstrates unusually outstanding service to his community.

had a 3-10-1 record the year before he arrived on the scene in 1970 and turning it into an instant contender. But, while Shula's role is always remembered, what is often forgotten is that when quarterback Bob Griese was injured, the Dolphins put together their undefeated season with Earl Morrall, the backup quarterback, doing most of the signal calling. Griese had gone down with a broken ankle in the fifth game of the season, but Morrall took the Dolphins through the remainder of the regular season and through the first half of the AFC championship game against Pittsburgh before giving way to a recovered Griese.

It was during the regular season, as the streak built, that Shula revealed the philosophy driving the Dolphins toward their unmatched achievement. Asked whether the Dolphins wouldn't be better off losing one of the "meaningless" games prior to the postseason in order to ease the pressure of the winning streak, Shula shot back, "I just can't buy that attitude. I don't think there's anything you ever gain by losing. I go along with Jack Nicklaus—he said once, 'You know what breeds winning? *Winning* breeds winning.' "

When it came to winning, Shula never let anything stand in his way, not even the decision he had to make when Morrall was unable to move the club against the Steelers in the AFC title game. With the Dolphins trailing at halftime, Shula relieved Morrall and replaced him with Griese. Griese proceeded to pull the Dolphins from behind for a 21-17 victory, then got the job done against Washington in the Super Bowl. For some strange reason, in recent years the 1972 Dolphins never seem to be seriously considered when the subject of the best Super Bowl teams is discussed, their singular achievement perhaps somewhat obscured by the fact the Pittsburgh Steelers won four Super Bowls during the 1970's. The Hall, however, honors the "perfect" Dolphins.

If the Dolphins of 1972 appear to be somewhat overlooked because of the time that has elapsed since their achievement, it's nothing compared with the backseat receivers seem to have taken throughout the history of the sport. Most of the accolades traditionally are saved for the quarterbacks and running backs or the hardest-hitting defenders. But that may be changing with the sudden focus on receivers brought about by the new rules that have opened up the passing game. The Hall of Fame, however, always has treated passers, running backs, and receivers equally in its displays on the top 20 lifetime statistical leaders. The all-time leaders as 1984 unfolded were Joe Montana in passing (he first became eligible for the leadership title in 1983), Jim Brown in rushing,

George Blanda in scoring and—the most unheralded of all—Charley Taylor in receiving. Taylor caught a record 649 passes for 9,110 yards and 79 touchdowns in 13 seasons with the Washington Redskins, but probably is not as well known to the average fan as the other lifetime leaders, or even some of the other receivers lower on the list.

Taylor always felt he was overlooked because he lived in Reston, Virginia, rather than near a major media center. "Sure, things would be a lot different if I lived in New York or Los Angeles, but I'd be a fool to be upset about it," he says. "Sure, a lot of things would have happened to me, but, hey, that's life. I'm very happy the way things have turned out." He should be. Besides catching more passes than anyone else in history, Taylor tied the NFL record for most seasons with 50 or more receptions (7); led the league twice in pass catching; joined the 1,000-yard club in 1966, when it was a feat far more difficult to achieve than in today's air-dominated atmosphere; and was fully recognized for all his accomplishments by being selected to the Pro Bowl eight times and to the Pro Football Hall of Fame in 1984. And, he achieved all that after beginning his career as a running back good enough to gain 775 yards his rookie season.

A somewhat stormy relationship between Otto Graham, who took over the Redskins' reins in Taylor's third season in 1966 and Taylor, first began when the two met for the College All-Star game two years earlier. "Otto used to predict certain things about players," Taylor explains. "At the All-Star Game he said things like I was lazy, that I wouldn't make it in the pros." Graham's first decision involving Taylor was to play him at cornerback for the All-Stars. (He had played the position occasionally) at Arizona State.) However, under Coach Bill Mc-Peak in Washington, he started his pro career as a running back. When Graham arrived on the scene, he decided to move Taylor to split end. By that time, however, Taylor had established himself as a ground gainer of considerable ability and was reluctant to change.

"I had my mind set on being a great running back," Taylor says. "I wasn't pleased when he told me what they were going to do. But then we had a meeting, and it was just a matter of me deciding to do it because he wasn't going to change his mind. I also knew nothing about running patterns or being a receiver. But I had great help from [teammate] Bobby Mitchell and an assistant coach, Ray Renfro. I spent a lot of time with them after practice, but it took me all of that year [1966] and part of the next to really feel comfortable at it."

Graham obviously made the right move the second time around because the combination of

Charley Taylor is remembered in the Hall with his Redskins jersey in the exhibition rotunda and by his top position among the all-time receiving leaders in the popular Top Twenty display, which ranks the career statistical leaders in the receiving, passing, rushing, and scoring categories.

Taylor catching and Sonny Jurgensen passing gave the Redskins one of the most potent offenses in the league. "It seemed like that was the offense, me to Charley and Charley being long gone," Jurgensen recalls. "He was a natural. Just get it in the area, and Charley would catch it." He caught enough to wind up first on the Hall's leader board, squeezing ahead of Don Maynard (633 in 15 seasons) and Raymond Berry (631 in 13 seasons). Taylor also accumulated his total in 13 seasons, but it must be remembered that 2 were spent primarily as a running back, or he might have pushed close to the 700 mark.

If the Charley Taylors have been overshadowed by quarterbacks and running backs, what about off-the-field contributors such as Fred Gehrke and on-the-field contributors such as Harold Carmichael? There are few awards in sports that honor unlikely heroes, but two are on display in the trophy section of the Adventure Room. There, along with the NEA Jim Thorpe Trophy, the Washington Touchdown Club Timmie Award, the Maxwell Club-Bert Bell Trophy, and the Pro Football Writers Schick Trophy (all of which are awarded annually to the NFL's MVP or Player of the Year), are a pair of trophies given to those who might otherwise be overlooked—the Pioneer Award and the Gino Cappelletti Award. The Pioneer Award is a Hall of Fame-sponsored honor given periodically to an individual who has made a significant innovative off-the-field contribution to professional football. The Gino Cappelletti Award is an annual presentation of the 1776 Quarterback Club of New England to an "athlete whose entry into professional football was without fanfare."

The Pioneer Award was established to honor the memory of the late Dan Reeves, long-time owner of the Los Angeles Rams credited with a number of far-reaching decisions that affected modern-day football. The most noteworthy involved his daring move of the Rams from Cleveland to Los Angeles following the 1945 season, despite bitter opposition from NFL owners fearful because it marked the first time an established major league sports franchise had been located on the West Coast. Reeves' vision of the West Coast as the next frontier for sports development proved totally accurate, and his decision made the NFL truly national in scope while at the same time stimulating a vast western franchise boom in every professional sport. Reeves also opened the NFL to blacks when he signed Kenny Washington; was the force behind the development of the Rams' scouting system, which became the standard for all teams; and helped put together the television policy that today assured the NFL's success.

The Pioneer Award is given by the Pro Football Hall of Fame on a periodical basis to recognize those individuals whose innovative off-the-field activities have contributed to the betterment of pro football. Fred Gehrke and Arch Ward, the only two winners to date, are honored in this display in the Collection of Trophies area.

THE
CAPPELLETTI
AWARD
PRESENTED
ANNUALLY BY
THE 1776
QUARTERBACK
CLUB OF
NEW ENGLAND

HAROLD JACKSON
1981   PATRIOTS

ERROL MANN
1970   LIONS

WILLIE WOOD
1971 PACKERS

RANDY VATAHA
1972   PATRIOTS

RAY MAY
1973 COLTS

MANNY FERNANDEZ
1974   DOLPHINS

ERNIE McMILLAN
1975 CARDINALS

MICK TINGELHOFF
1976   VIKINGS

RAY HAMILTON
1977 PATRIOTS

BILLY JOHNSON
1978   OILERS

GARO YEPREMIAM
1979   DOLPHINS

HAROLD CARMICHAEL
1980   EAGLES

The 1776 Quarterback Club of New England presents this award annually to honor an NFL player who reached stardom after starting his pro career as a free agent or a low-round draft choice. It is named after Gino Cappelletti, who rose to become a Patriots star and the leading scorer in AFL history.

Just two men have been singled out to receive the Pioneer Award—Arch Ward, developer of the Chicago All-Star Game, and Fred Gehrke, a talented halfback with Reeves' Rams. In 1948, Gehrke painted the first insignia design on a helmet, starting a trend that didn't end until every NFL team except the Cleveland Browns had its own. "Dan was always trying to professionalize our uniforms, improve 'em," Gehrke recalls. "We were changing all the time, adding a border to the numbers, stripes, something. Dan got me thinking about it. The first thing that needed improving was that plain, brown leather helmet [worn at the time]." Gehrke, who had majored in art at the University of Utah, took that leather helmet, painted it blue, and then superimposed a reddish-gold ram's horns on the blue background. Coach Bob Snyder was ecstatic when he saw the sample, leading to any number of sleepless nights for Gehrke while he sat up in his garage painting the new design on 75 helmets—and then repairing them whenever they were battered in action. In 1949, the Riddell plastic helmet was introduced by the Rams, and Gehrke's design was baked into the helmet beneath the surface of transparent plastic. It's been that way ever since, and now is universal throughout the league.

Gino Cappelletti's entry into pro football certainly was without fanfare—both times. Hardly anyone noticed the first time when, as a quarterback out of Minnesota in the mid-1950's, he joined the Detroit Lions. Two weeks later he was gone. No one noticed the second time around when he joined the Boston Patriots in 1960 straight from a tour of duty with the Sarnia Imperials of the Ontario Rugby League and the Minneapolis municipal touch football league. Cappelletti actually had given up any hope of playing professional football by the time the AFL was formed and was tending bar for his brother, Guido, in Minneapolis for $80 a week. "The only football I played was in the city touch league a couple of times a week" Cappelletti recalls. "We wore jerseys with Mac and Capps across it—the name of my brother's place—and baseball caps." The lure of playing eventually brought Cappelletti to the Patriots' camp with the clothes on his back and no more than change in his pockets. "I kept going by hustling up card games in camp," Cappelletti recalls. "One time I went flat broke and [teammate] Bob Dee loaned me some money to keep going."

Cappelletti began his AFL career as a defensive back, but, as he explains, "I was so good on defense that they told me I'd have to make the team next year as a pass receiver or not at all." He did make it as a pass receiver and that, combined with his exceptional placekicking ability, made him one of the AFL's earliest stars. He had the distinction of scoring the first regular-season points in AFL history when he kicked a 38-yard field goal as the Patriots lost their opener to the Denver Broncos. And he admits he was more than just a bit nervous at the time. "When they snapped the ball back, I kinda froze because I so much wanted to make it," Cappelletti remembers. "I knew it would mean a lot to me because the way things were in those days if I didn't make it they might try someone else next time." The Patriots didn't try anyone else for 11 seasons as Cappelletti went on to become the league's first 1,000-point producer. Today he stands number 7 among the top 20 lifetime scorers with 1,130 points, an average that makes him the only player among the leaders to exceed the 100-points-a-season plateau. In all, he scored 42 touchdowns, kicked 350 conversions, and 176 field goals.

Cappelletti always gave much of the credit for his success to his father, a little old wine maker from Keewatin, Minnesota, he insisted turned him into the perfectionist he had to be to finally succeed. "Pa took great pride in his wine," Cappelletti says, "and I was his human press. Fall is wine-making time as well as football season, and I can remember playing football in front of the house and seeing the grape truck coming and wanting to hide before my father called me. I had special rubber stomping boots—and he made sure every grape was crushed. I hated it because it deprived me of playing football. But if I'm a perfectionist, it's Pa who made me that way."

It takes a player with a perfectionist philosophy to succeed when he isn't at first recognized. And that's why the 1776 Quarterback Club initiated the award that now carries Cappelletti's name—to applaud free agents and low-round draft choices who succeed in the NFL.

There has been no more deserving recipient of the Cappelletti Award than another receiver, Harold Carmichael, the 1980 winner who came out of Southern University in 1971 such a long shot that no one selected him until the Philadelphia Eagles risked a seventh-round draft choice. Why did he last that long? Simply because few scouts believed a wide receiver with a 6-foot 8-inch, 220-pound frame could withstand the pounding he'd have to take in the NFL. Carmichael not only has been able to withstand the pounding, he withstood the derision he had to endure during the period when he was cited as one of the reasons why the Eagles were a lackluster team.

"I felt I was made the scapegoat for problems that were widespread [on the team]," Carmichael says. "I guess I made an easy target—with my size, playing wide receiver. Good or bad, I stuck out. I felt I was portrayed [in the media] unfairly, inaccurately. People assumed they knew what was going on inside my head . . . but they didn't. They said I didn't care, I didn't play hard. That's ridiculous."

The record books show how ridiculous—Carmichael has averaged 45 receptions a year and set an NFL record by latching onto at least one pass in 127 consecutive games.

That record brings us to the story revolving around the world's largest trophy, which sits on the first floor of the Hall and rises high into the second floor Adventure Room—a 22-foot 10-inch trophy commemorating Carmichael's streak. The story begins with the Action Trophy Manufacturing Company of Philadelphia, which, noting that the *Guiness Book of World Records* listed the world's tallest trophy at 15 feet, decided to outdo it. So, the people at Action built a challenger, then took it to a trophy convention in Dayton, Ohio, where it was properly measured and certified at 23 feet 9 inches.

The people at Action now had a world champion—and nothing to do with it. But they sensed opportunity knocking when Carmichael's streak reached 105 games, just one short of the NFL record. They dialed the Eagles, and it was agreed that giving the tall receiver the tall trophy would add a nice touch to his stellar performance. The record-setting day came on November 4, 1979, when, on the fifth play of the game against the Cleveland Browns, Carmichael gained five yards on a pass from Ron Jaworski. Play stopped at that point for several moments while formal ceremonies took place. But the big moment was reserved for halftime.

During halftime, the trophy was brought out. It took 11 workmen to stand it upright and, when they did, no one had any doubt that a fitting award had been found for Carmichael. It towered over him. "I couldn't believe that trophy," Carmichael said with sincerity. And, when he was asked after the game if he had a room in his home big enough to house the trophy, he replied with equal sincerity, "Most of my rooms are barely big enough for me." That said, Carmichael dressed and left for home, while the trophy remained in the bowels of Veterans Stadium.

No one gave it much thought as Carmichael continued to add to his record, until the Hall of Fame decided it could provide a spot for the trophy by fitting it into a space formed by the stairs between the first and second floors of the Adventure Room. Officials called the Eagles. The Eagles called back. There was one small problem: When no suitable place had been found to store the trophy, it had been dismantled. Worse—it was damaged.

The Hall still wanted the trophy. The Eagles still wanted the Hall to have the trophy. And Action Trophy still wanted the trophy displayed. It was agreed among the three organizations that a new trophy would be built to the specifications of the first; it would be shipped to the Hall of Fame and become the world's largest "perpetual" trophy to be awarded "to the wide receivers in the NFL who have broken the record for most catches in consecutive games in league play." Two names were inscribed on the trophy—Danny Abramowicz, for establishing the record at 105, and Harold Carmichael, for breaking it.

However, there had been two noteworthy changes by the time the trophy was erected at the Hall of Fame. Carmichael's streak had been extended to 127 before it ended, and the new trophy when measured, stood at 22 feet 10 inches. Carmichael had added 21 games to his streak; 11 inches had been subtracted from the trophy. But one thing is certain—no visitor can miss it.

*The tallest trophy in the world—22-feet, 10-inches—was
donated to the Hall by the Action Trophy Co. of Philadelphia
to commemorate the streak of 127 straight games in which
Harold Carmichael of the Eagles caught at least one pass.*

Chapter 12

"The Pro Football Quiz"

One of the most popular exhibits at the Hall of Fame is the Pro Football Quiz, the Hall's response to the trivia-quiz craze. In the Hall's version, the visitor tries to match an exceptional feat accomplished on the football field with the Hall of Famer who did it. Like to try the quiz? Here's the way it looks at the Hall of Fame:

Feat Accomplished
1. He caught 18 passes in one game
2. He did not play college football
3. He dropkicked four field goals in one game
4. He returned eight punts for touchdowns
5. He intercepted four passes in one game
6. His two touchdown passes won the 1933 NFL title game
7. He played in five College All-Star Games
8. He scored 40 points in one game

Player
1. Charley Trippi
2. Sammy Baugh
3. Tom Fears
4. Bronko Nagurski
5. Ernie Nevers
6. Joe Perry
7. Jack Christiansen
8. Paddy Driscoll

1. (3) Tom Fears

Fears, a product of UCLA, was drafted by the Los Angeles Rams in 1948 primarily as a defensive specialist. But it wasn't long before Coach Clark Shaughnessy decided that Fears' sure hands would be more productive catching passes thrown by his own quarterback. Fears went on to lead the NFL with 51 receptions his rookie season, then broke Don Hutson's record with 77 catches in 1949, the year the Rams employed the first 3-end offense ever used on a regular basis in pro football. Shaughnessy was the man who devised the formation, revolutionary at the time but now used universally.

The formation took shape when halfback Elroy "Crazylegs" Hirsch joined Fears as a wide receiver, flanked 8 to 10 yards outside tight end Bob Shaw. A year later, with the formation working effectively and both Bob Waterfield and Norm Van Brocklin hitting him with passes, Fears raised the NFL record to 84 receptions. It also was during that record-setting 1950 season that Fears put together his 18-catch day, against the Green Bay Packers, December 3, 1950. No one ever has caught more, and the record remains one of the oldest in the books.

2. (6) Joe Perry

Perry was spotted by John Woudenberg, a tackle for the San Francisco 49ers, when the fullback was piling up rushing yardage for the Alameda, California, Naval Training Station after having played at Compton Junior College. Woudenberg told owner Tony Morabito and Coach Buck Shaw, "Just point him in the right direction and watch him go." Perry, however, was not an unknown commodity and also was being chased by a number of colleges. But the 49ers' offer was too good to turn down, right, Joe? "It wasn't as good as some of the offers I had received from fourteen or so colleges that had contacted me," Perry remembers. Nevertheless, Perry decided to skip college and began to play pro ball in 1948. It wasn't long before he was leading the league in rushing with 1,018 yards in 1953 and 1,049 yards in 1954. That made him the first ground gainer in NFL history to put together successive 1,000-yard seasons. Before his career ended in 1963, he had amassed 9,723 yards, a total that leaves him fifth on the all-time list behind Jimmy Brown, Franco Harris, O. J. Simpson, and Walter Payton.

243

3. (8)Paddy Driscoll

Driscoll, whose given name was John, played his college ball at Northwestern, then joined the Hammond Pros one year before the official formation of the NFL. In 1920, he played for both the Decatur Staleys and the Chicago Cardinals, remaining with the Cardinals through the 1925 season when he joined the Bears (nee Staleys) for his final three years. The 5-foot 11-inch, 170-pounder was a triple threat as a rusher, passer, and kicker and also was a more-than-capable defender. He is, however, best known for three kicking feats. Against Buffalo in 1922, he dropkicked a 50-yard field goal that is tied for the longest in NFL history by that method. On November 23, 1925, he produced the achievement for which he is included in the Pro Football Quiz, dropkicking field goals of 23, 18, 50, and 35 yards against Columbus in what at the time was a record-setting performance. But Driscoll probably is best remembered for punting the ball 23 times in an attempt to keep the ball away from Red Grange in the Galloping Ghost's pro debut. Driscoll succeeded so well the game wound up 0-0.

4. (7) Jack Christiansen

Christiansen was an outstanding cornerback for the Detroit Lions, playing on three NFL championship teams and gaining all-NFL honors six successive seasons, from 1952 through 1957. During his career, he totaled 46 interceptions. But his name is in the record books because of his unique ability to return punts for touchdowns. The Colorado State University player entered his name for the first time his rookie season in 1951, when he returned four punts for touchdowns, a feat matched only once in the more than thirty years since then (Rick Upchurch of the Denver Broncos scored on four in 1976). Christiansen returned two punts for touchdowns against Los Angeles, on October 14, then repeated with two more against Green Bay, on November 22. Against the Packers he produced 175 yards returning—the fourth-best total of all time. Christiansen's quick four-touchdown start propelled him to his career total of eight, which still remains the all-time record

5. (2) Sammy Baugh

This represents the toughest match up on the quiz board, baffling more visitors than any other. Baugh became the first player in NFL history ever to intercept four passes in one game when he accomplished the feat against the Detroit Lions, on November 14, 1943. Although 13 others have managed to match the record, no one ever has been able to surpass it. Baugh also led the league with a total of 11 interceptions that season. What makes this match up difficult for most visitors is that almost all recognize Baugh as a great passer, and many even know that he was an outstanding punter. Few, however, seem to be aware that Baugh also excelled as a safety during the first half of his career with the Washington Redskins. Baugh also won the passing and punting championships in 1943, giving him three titles. He and Bill Dudley of the Pittsburgh Steelers are the only triple-crown winners in NFL history. Dudley won the rushing, punt return, and interception titles in 1946.

6. (4) Bronko Nagurski

Nagurski was best known as a bull-like fullback for the Chicago Bears, but for years he employed a pet play that worked so effectively it constantly baffled opponents. It also led to a major rules change. Nagurski would fake a rush, step back five yards (all passes had to be made from five yards behind the line of scrimmage at the time), and then throw a pass. When Nagurski did that and hit Red Grange for the winning touchdown on a disputed play in the 1932 championship game—the Portsmouth team questioned whether he was five yards back—the rules were simplified to permit a pass anywhere behind the line of scrimmage. That also served to make Nagurski's pet play even more effective. After the change, he could race toward the line of scrimmage as if he were going to smash into it, then just rear up and lob a pass downfield. He did that twice for touchdowns in the 1933 championship game, leading the Bears to a 23-21 victory over the New York Giants.

7. (1) Charley Trippi

Trippi's accomplishment is so unusual because four of his All-Star Game appearances came as a collegian. Manpower shortages during World War II forced the waiving of the rule that prohibited anyone but college seniors from playing in the game. So, the elusive runner from the University of Georgia was an All-Star in 1943, 1944, 1945, and 1947 as a collegian and then again in 1948 as a member of the NFL-champion Cardinals. Trippi was the first of the big-money players on the NFL scene, signing a four-year contract for $100,000. He proceeded to earn every bit of it as a member of the Cardinals' Dream Backfield that also included Paul Christman, Pat Harder, and Elmer Angsman. After appearing in All-Star Game No. 5 prior to the 1948 season, Trippi went into the regular season and led the Cardinals to an 11-1 record while underscoring his tremendous versatility by finishing second in the league in rushing, fifth in punt returns, sixth in scoring, seventh in kickoff returns, and tenth in punting.

8. (5) Ernie Nevers

Nevers produced his 40-point total on November 28, 1929, when he scored 6 touchdowns and kicked 4 conversions while leading the Chicago Cardinals to a 40-6 Thanksgiving Day win over the Chicago Bears. A week earlier, he had scored all 19 of the Cardinals' points in a shutout against Dayton, an unmatched accumulation of all 59 of his team's points in 2 games. The 40-point outburst by Nevers remains the oldest record in the NFL *Record Manual.* Two players have made a run at the mark by scoring six touchdowns—Dub Jones of the Cleveland Browns in 1951 and Gale Sayers of the Chicago Bears in 1965—but no one has been able to match it. Earlier Nevers had gained significant stature as the iron-horse fullback of the Duluth Eskimos who missed only 26 of the 1,740 minutes the Eskimos played during a marathon 1926 season.

Credits

Action murals make up an integral part of each enshrinee's niche at the Pro Football Hall of Fame. Copies of those murals are included with each biography in chapter 7 of this book. The murals have been created by 10 different artists, who are named below, along with a list of the murals they have produced.

GARY THOMAS—Alworth, Battles, Baugh, Bednarik, Bert Bell, Berry, Bidwell, Blanda, J. Brown, R. Brown, Butkus, Carr, Chamberlin, Conzelman, Davis, Driscoll, Dudley, Edwards, Fears, Flaherty, Ford, Fortmann, Gregg, Groza, Guyan, Healey, Herber, Hewitt, Hinkle, Huff, Kiesling, Lambeau, Lane, Lary, Lavelli, Layne, Lilly, Lombardi, Luckman, Lyman, Marchetti, Matson, McAfee, McCormack, Michalske, Millner, Mitchell, Motley, Nitschke, Olsen, Otto, Owen, J. Parker, Perry, Pihos, Ray, Reeves, Robustelli, Rooney, Starr, Stautner, Strong, Stydahar, C. Taylor, Thorpe, Trafton, Trippi, Tunnell, Turner, Van Buren, Warfield, Waterfield, Willis, Wojciechowicz

MURRAY OLDERMAN—Connor, Donovan, Ewbank, George, Gifford, Henry, Hunt, McElhenny, McNally, Mix, Nagurski, Neale, Sayers, Schmidt, J. Taylor, Tittle

DOUG WEIST—Adderley, Badgro, Bobby Bell, Canadeo, Christiansen, Kinard, Musso, Nomellini, A. Parker, Van Brocklin, Weinmeister, Wilson

ROBERT RIGER—Clark, Hubbard, Hutson, Leemans, Mara, Marshall

BARBARA RIEGER—Atkins, W. Brown, Gillman, Jones, Ringo

LOU DARVAS—P. Brown, Graham, Hein,

JIM BAMA—Grange, Nevers

DAVE BOSS—Halas, Hirsch

TOM SEGARS—Moore, Unitas

NEAL HAMILTON—Jurgensen

"Canton, Ohio, is thousands of miles from Lucca, Italy, where I was born. But Canton, Ohio, and the Hall of Fame are proof of what opportunity and sportsmanship in America really are."

Leo Nomellini, Class of 1969

"We walk through the Hall of Fame and the history of professional football just seems to come alive."

Ron Mix, Class of 1979

"Every man is free to rise as far as he is able or willing, but it is only the degree to which he thinks or believes that determines the degree to which he will rise."

David (Deacon) Jones, Class of 1980

"When the grand master, the architect of this universe blows the whistle some day in the future and assembles this great gang out on the field up above, I don't know if I'll be in that starting lineup, but I'll be proud to be sitting on the bench."

Ken Strong, Class of 1967

"I feel like I'm even with all the red dogs and all the safety blitzes now."

Bobby Layne, Class of 1967